FALLING
INTO THE
LESBI
WORLD

FALLING INTO THE LESBI WORLD

Desire and Difference in Indonesia

Evelyn Blackwood

University of Hawai'i Press
Honolulu

15 14 13 12 11 10   6 5 4 3 2 1

Library of Congress Cataloging-in-Publication Data
Blackwood, Evelyn.
   Falling into the lesbi world : desire and difference in Indonesia / Evelyn
Blackwood.
      p.   cm.
   Includes bibliographical references and index.
   ISBN 978-0-8248-3442-5 (alk. paper)—ISBN 978-0-8248-3487-6 (pbk. : alk.
paper)
   1. Transgender people—Indonesia—Padang.   2. Gender identity—
Indonesia—Padang.   3. Sex role—Indonesia—Padang.   4. Lesbians—
Indonesia—Padang.   5. Queer theory.   I. Title.
   HQ77.95.I5B53 2010
   306.76'8095981—dc22

                                                                2009051472

University of Hawai'i Press books are printed on acid-free
paper and meet the guidelines for permanence and durability
of the Council on Library Resources.

Designed by Publishers' Design and Production Services, Inc.

Printed by Sheridan Books, Inc.

In honor of Esther Newton,
Clark Taylor, and Sue-Ellen Jacobs, who
made books like this one possible

Contents

Acknowledgments

Ever since I began to study anthropology it has been my fervent desire to do a project such as this one. During my dissertation research in West Sumatra, I realized I had a site for the project, and then with the support of a Fulbright grant, I was able to return to Indonesia to conduct the fieldwork.

I owe a huge debt of gratitude to the many people who made the field project possible. I was extremely fortunate to have Sri Setyawati work with me as my research associate both in 2001 and 2004. I am ever grateful for her daily support, generous spirit, open-mindedness, unflagging enthusiasm and energy for this project, her skill in interviewing and willingness to stay up late hours to finish work, all while teaching at the University of Andalas and raising two small children. I could not have accomplished this fieldwork without her. Thanks also to Max, Sri's husband, who took time off work to accompany us on trips and became my driver on several occasions. I am most grateful for the privilege of living with Sri and her family during my second field trip in 2004 and spending time with Puti Evelyn, my goddaughter.

Many thanks to Dr. Pamoedjo Rahardjo and the staff at the American-Indonesian Exchange Foundation (AMINEF) in Jakarta. I especially want to thank Nelly Paliama at AMINEF for her willingness to support this project in an uncertain political climate in Indonesia, and for being my rock steady during several nerve-wracking weeks following September 11, 2001. Thanks also to David Adams, Patricia Garon, and the Fulbright Scholar Program and CIES staff, and to Greta Morris and Mitch Cohn at the American Embassy in Jakarta, who all provided excellent support and helped to make my 2001 trip very comfortable and successful. Douglas Ramage provided a memorable Thanksgiving dinner during that trip for the Fulbright scholars.

My sincere thanks go to Dr. Abdul Aziz Saleh, the Department of Anthropology, FISIP, University of Andalas, and the Indonesian Institute of Sciences (LIPI), for supporting my project and providing assistance during my stay. Thanks also to Damsar and Herwandi at FISIP and Anas Nafis for stimulating intellectual conversations and help with my research. I am also grateful to the staff at Hotel Bumi Minang, who made my stay in Padang in 2001 very comfortable and secure, and to Armando de la Cruz for his tips on living in Padang.

Several people were very helpful in Padang, including Ing and Sinardi Susilo, who helped me make contact with some of the individuals who participated in my research. Mamay, renowned Padang hairdresser and friend, provided the initial contacts with lesbi in Padang. My thanks to Jennifer Fraser, who was in West Sumatra conducting her own research in 2004, for great conversations, for "participating" in my project, and providing invaluable information on the Minangkabau art scene. Jeni became a great source of field data through her interactions with the research participants, and yes, you are in the book.

My greatest debt of gratitude goes to the tombois and femmes who enthusiastically joined in this project and offered their friendship and good will. I am grateful to have had the chance to share in their lives. I am also grateful to Farah for providing feedback on some of the material and offering her own insights. I thank the members of Sector 15 of Koalisi Perempuan Indonesia and members of Swara Srikandi, especially Wina and Mila, for sharing their knowledge about lesbi lives in Indonesia. Their work is critical to the well-being of lesbians in Indonesia.

Many people have encouraged me along the way and enabled me to carry out this research. As always, my deep gratitude goes to Saskia Wieringa, who has been my great friend, colleague, inspiration and friendly critic. My esteemed friend Jeff Dickemann has offered constant encouragement over the years and generously provided copious notes and comments on several chapters. Many thanks to Megan Sinnott, whose comments on various drafts and versions were extremely insightful and helpful, and to my valued colleagues Ellen Lewin, Deborah Elliston, Bill Leap, Martin Manalansan, Don Kulick, Mary Gray, Cymene Howe, Michael Peletz, and Dédé Oetomo for their support, comments and encouragement over the years. Ben Orlove provided helpful comments on how to frame the book. In addition I am very grateful to my editor, Pam Kelley, at the University of Hawai'i Press for her unwavering support and encouragement.

Support for this project has been provided by a Fulbright Grant for Senior Scholars, the American Psychological Foundation Wayne F. Placek Investigator Development Award, and the 2008 Martin Duberman Fellowship given by the Center for Lesbian and Gay Studies at City University of New York. I was also the recipient of several small grants from Purdue University, including the Center for Humanistic Studies fellowship, which provided me with a needed semester off to write. I am very thankful to my wonderful colleagues at Purdue, including Ellen Gruenbaum and Mimi Van Ausdall, for reading chapters and pointing out things that needed to be explained; also Berenice Carroll, Val

Moghadam, and other Women's Studies colleagues whose encouragement and collegial manner have enriched my work. Carolyn Perrucci and Viktor Gecas extended essential departmental assistance during the early phases of this project. In addition I appreciate the assistance of the staff in the Department of Anthropology at Purdue, including Pam Leap, and the Women's Studies Program, especially Julie Knoeller.

I want to thank both my parents for the sacrifices they made so that I and my siblings could go to college. In her lifetime my mother, Katherine Thomas, could never quite appreciate my work on sexuality, but she gave me the determination to pursue my dreams. My father, John Thomas, provided support in his own quiet way. I am above all thankful to Diana Hardy, my life partner, who in so many ways makes this all possible. Thanks for all the love, support, patience, and laughter.

Parts of this book were developed from "Transnational Sexualities in One Place: Indonesian Readings," *Gender & Society* 19 (2):221–242, 2005, and "Gender Transgression in Colonial and Post-colonial Indonesia," *Journal of Asian Studies* 64 (4):849–879, 2005. Parts of chapter 6 were developed from "Transidentities and Contingent Masculinities: Being Tombois in Everyday Practice," *Feminist Studies* 35 (3): 454–480, 2009. Parts of chapter 7 were developed from "Transnational Discourse and Circuits of Queer Knowledge in Indonesia," *GLQ: A Journal of Lesbian and Gay Studies* 14 (4):481–507, 2008.

CHAPTER ONE

Gender, Sexuality, and Queer Desires

To the extent that gender is an assignment, it is an assignment which is never quite carried out according to expectation.

—JUDITH BUTLER

M Y RESEARCH ASSOCIATE AND I dropped by the small apartment of a *lesbi* couple in Padang one afternoon. We had been chatting with them for a few minutes when suddenly Robi, the *tomboi* partner, said to h/er girlfriend Noni, "Sis, go make some tea for them!"[1] Noni jumped up, mumbling apologies, and went into the kitchen to prepare tea for us. This exchange caught my attention because there was nothing keeping Robi from making the tea h/erself; we were all just sitting and talking.[2] H/er insistence that h/er girlfriend fulfill the duty of tea-making therefore pointed eloquently and simply to the norms of masculinity that s/he maintains and the difference that defines this couple's relationship.

This book seeks to understand how Robi, Noni, and the other lesbi I interviewed learn about and produce gender, how it becomes the cement of their relationship, and how ideologically defined categories of normative gender, of man and woman, are only starting blocks for the production of gendered and sexual selves. In the process of making sense of their lives, I explore the discourses that circulate in their lives, the practices they engage in, their social relations with kin and community, and their linguistic strategies, to contextualize the rich and complex subjectivities they express. I do not provide any simple answers regarding how they identify. In fact I refuse to situate them neatly in the social categories of men, women, lesbians, transgender, or masculine females. Rather in each chapter I offer a different perspective on the multiple and apparently contradictory ways in which they position themselves.

The subjects of this book are Indonesian lesbi who live primarily in the regional metropolis of Padang on the coast of West Sumatra. "Lesbi" is an Indone-

1

sian term derived from the English word "lesbian," but as is discussed more fully later, it does not have precisely the same meaning as its cognate. "Lesbi" as well as "lesbian" have been used in Indonesia in two ways since the 1980s. Both popularly and among lesbi individuals the terms refer either to two women involved in a romantic relationship or to a couple in which one partner is masculine and the other feminine. The different perceptions of lesbi identity speak to some of the problems in using universal signifiers. The lesbi I interviewed in Padang position themselves under the term "lesbi," but they prefer to use gender-marked terms for themselves. These terms include the Indonesian word "tomboi" (derived from the English word "tomboy") or the slang terms *cowok* and *cewek*, meaning guy, for the masculine partner, and girl, for the feminine partner. While recognizing that any choices are fraught with difficulties, I follow their preference for gender-marked terms by using "tomboi" for the masculine partners and "girlfriend" or "femme" for the feminine partners. None of these terms signify a fixed identity, however, and will in fact be frequently revisited throughout the book as I examine the ways individuals claim, contest, rework, and blur the terms by which they define themselves.

Although I use terms, such as "tomboi" and "lesbi," that are familiar across much of Indonesia, I am not making any claims that the lesbi I interviewed are necessarily representative of others in West Sumatra or Indonesia. As demonstrated in *Women's Sexualities and Masculinities in a Globalizing Asia* (Saskia Wieringa, Blackwood, and Bhaiya 2007), butch lesbians, masculine females, and transgendered individuals throughout Southeast Asia and Asia more broadly express a range of masculinities informed by particular sociocultural and historical specificities as well as by global media and lesbian, gay, bisexual, and transgender (LGBT) movements and discourses. Several excellent studies in Southeast and East Asia document the nuances and complexities of masculinities among such female-bodied individuals, who identify variously as hunters, *tom*s, tombois, TBs, and butches. The English-derived terms speak to the influence of global LGBT signifiers, but these masculinities are far from identical.

In South Sulawesi, Indonesia, three terms are used to refer to masculine females who desire women: "hunter," meaning one who pursues a goal; *calalai*, meaning literally "false man" in the Bugis language of the area; and tomboi (Davies 2007a). Sharon Davies (2007a, 2007b) classifies these masculine females as a distinct gender because, according to those she interviewed, they are female-bodied, but they do not identify as women, nor do they aspire to be men. Megan Sinnott (2004, 2007) argues that *tom*s in Thailand are transgendered females who strategically appropriate and manipulate cultural stereotypes of Thai masculinity and emergent sexualities to create a hybrid form of masculinity. Older butches whom Saskia Wieringa (1999, 2007) studied in Jakarta, Indonesia, refer to themselves as men and see themselves as possessing a male soul in a female body. The versions of masculinity represented in these studies point to the complexities of each situation; they highlight the asymmetrical reception of global and national discourses, which produces not homogeneous national or international queer identities but a plethora of dynamic subjectivities that exceed any simple categorization.[3]

Through stories of lesbi in Padang I analyze the sexual and gendered practices in which tombois and their partners engage. I offer an in-depth focus on a small number of lesbi to ask by what processes and in what moments tombois and their girlfriends take up particular subject positions in childhood and adulthood. For tombois, I explore how female-bodied individuals come to identify in childhood as boys, how they deal with their emerging desires in adolescence, and how as adults they consolidate, negotiate, and manipulate their trans-identities in relation to family, community, and lovers. My analysis of childhood narratives provides insight into the cultural processes of gender acquisition for tombois. It demonstrates how children's practical knowledge of gender enables them to take up a particular culturally defined gender position, even one not marked for them. As adults, tombois lay claim to the social category "man," by which I mean the ideologically dominant conception of manhood that circulates through much of Indonesia. In speaking of themselves as men, tombois state that they not only dress and act like men, they physically embody masculinity as well. Yet their self-positioning as men is not uncomplicated. Despite articulating a sense of self that they consider to be nearly the same as other men's, tombois enact different versions of masculinity and femininity as they move through space, from the familiarity of domestic spaces inhabited by kin and neighbors to the anonymity and vulnerability of public spaces. Because of the complexity of tomboi subjectivities, this book reveals gender to be contingent and relational rather than bounded and consistent.

This book also presents compelling stories of the femmes, or girlfriends, who are romantically involved with tombois. Girlfriends identify themselves as normative women and face the same ideological constraints as other women living in this region of Indonesia. Moving between tomboi and men partners, they situate their desires as attraction to men. Together tombois and their girlfriends negotiate what it means to be partners in a gender-binary world. Rather than offering explicit resistance, both tombois and girlfriends enact the gender binary in ways that tend to maintain the differences and inequalities between men and women. By drawing on hegemonic ideologies of gender difference to make sense of their lives, both tombois and their girlfriends reproduce state and Islamic gender discourses, even though their lack of perfect fit with those discourses positions them somewhat on the margins of social space. Ultimately their self-positionings challenge normative gender because they do not inhabit their subject positions exactly as they are represented in the dominant ideology. Thus tombois' and girlfriends' enactment of normative categories of gender offers insights into nondominant subjectivities and their relationship to hegemonic discourses.

Through the study of tombois I address in particular the broader question of transgender identities as represented in the literature by U.S. and European transgender scholars. Because tombois' gender expression exceeds or transgresses normative gender categories, they may be included in the category of transgender people, if "transgender" is defined broadly, following Susan Stryker, as "an umbrella term that refers to all identities or practices that cross over, cut across, move between, or otherwise queer socially constructed sex/gender binaries" (1994, 251, fn 2).[4] However, the word "transgender," which began to circulate as an adopted term in lesbi and *gay* activist communities in Indonesia only in the late 1990s, is not a term that tombois I interviewed use for themselves.[5] In an effort to demonstrate the complexities of transgendered selves, I use "transgender" in this book in a provisional manner to speak to both Indonesian and U.S. practices, while acknowledging that I am navigating widely different terrains. Further, I explore Gloria Anzaldúa's (1987) concept of mestiza consciousness and Judith Halberstam's (1998) concept of female masculinity to think about the relation between transgender identities and normative constructions of gender.

While providing rich, in-depth, and provocative stories and analyses of the particular experiences and meanings of tomboi and femme selves, I examine their gendered selves in light of national and transnational processes that flow through Padang and West Sumatra. I analyze this particular locale from a theoretical approach to transnational sexualities that takes into account the importance of global movements of queer identities and discourses. I explore the ways nationally and globally circulating queer discourses are received and reinterpreted by both tombois and femmes, making them part of and yet different from the global gay models of sexuality. Thus one of the central questions addressed in this book is how national and transnational discourses are reflected, reproduced, and altered in the narratives and practices of tombois and their girlfriends.

This book focuses on a specific locality in Indonesia and the discourses that circulate in that location. My emphasis on locality is not meant to suggest that forms of sexuality are produced in specific locations.[6] Rather, attention to a specific locality enables me to ascertain the particular circuits of queer knowledge these lesbi access and hence the micro processes by which gendered and sexual

MAP 1.1. Map of Indonesia. Courtesy of the University of Texas Libraries, The University of Texas at Austin.

subjectivities are produced. Where much of the theorizing about queer globalization has focused on Internet-savvy, educated activists in major urban centers, I focus on the lives and experiences of working- and lower-middle-class individuals in a regional city to tell the story of a different sort of "queer." Yet by following the circuits of queer knowledge that travel back and forth through the lesbi, gay, and *waria* communities and networks in Padang, I demonstrate that Padang's tombois and femmes are part of the global gay ecumene.[7]

Finally, this book explores the consequences of asymmetrical flows of queer knowledge by examining interactions between lesbian activists in Jakarta and tombois in Padang. The friction produced as identitarian positions bump up against each other within and across lesbi communities in Indonesia demonstrates the unpredictability of encounters with global queer knowledge. For those in Padang, the circulation of queer knowledge, as reflected in their linguistic practices, helps to create an imagined space of "like-minded," but not necessarily identical, lesbi individuals across and beyond Indonesia. For lesbi activists in Jakarta, access to international LGBT networks solidifies for them a lesbian identity category of women-loving-women. Tombois' and girlfriends' complex positionings challenge those activist identity categories.

Lesbi Lives: Tombois and Femmes

Conducting anthropological research on lesbi in Indonesia presents a number of challenges related to lesbi visibility and mobility as well as to cultural assumptions about female-bodied individuals.[8] I have already discussed some of the definitional issues, but here I reflect on the methodological challenges that I faced. During dissertation fieldwork on a rural agricultural community in West Sumatra in 1989–1990, I was fortunate to meet several lesbi from the small towns near my research site. Some had lived in the same town most of their lives, while others had migrated between Jakarta and their home towns in search of jobs.[9] When I returned to Indonesia in 2001 to conduct research on lesbians, I was told by lesbians in Jakarta that there were no lesbians in West Sumatra. Relying on a popular view that the region is devoutly Islamic, they assumed that the supposed conservatism of the region would make it impossible for lesbians to live there. Their impression of West Sumatra was, needless to say, erroneous, and yet it points to the level of invisibility and secrecy most lesbi maintain not only in West Sumatra but elsewhere in Indonesia. Consequently it was impossible for me to simply inquire where the lesbi were in Padang. Instead I worked with my research associate Sri, a Minangkabau woman and university professor, to contact a waria individual who had been interviewed by one of Sri's students. Like other waria, who dress and act in a manner like "women" and usually take men as lovers, s/he was fairly visible as a hairdresser and performer.[10] S/he agreed to ask h/er tomboi friends if they would talk to me, but it took nearly three weeks before I was able to meet h/er closest tomboi friend.

From that point it became easier to contact other lesbi. Despite my difference as an educated, middle-class white woman from the United States, our commonality as lesbians, however they or I imagined that commonality to be, seemed to allay their fears about my intentions. In contrast some of the tombois were at first reluctant to talk to my research associate, despite their shared Muslim faith, because they felt that she would not respect them. Most importantly, my interest in them and their stories provided a certain validation for their relationships and reinforced their connection to a larger LGBT community in a way that was not possible in their daily lives. In effect I was the material realization of a global queer connection that they perceived from afar—as well as the source of assorted gay pride "rainbow" paraphernalia that I gave as gifts.

Because tombois and their girlfriends are very careful about keeping their relationships secret, I conducted my research with extreme care to avoid exposing them. Most interviews were carried out in my hotel room in 2001 and in the house of my research associate in 2004 in order to provide the privacy that interviewees needed to talk freely about their life stories and relationships. When we went on excursions together or met in public places, their behavior was very guarded. They used code words in their conversations to keep bystanders unawares. I learned quickly that uttering the word "lesbi" in public was sure to make them cringe and look around nervously. Both "lesbi" and "lesbian" are used in the Indonesian print media and are well-known to the general public, hence they avoided these terms in their own conversations. Physical contact between a lesbi couple was very minimal in public places, limited to a hand laid casually on a partner's leg or to simply sitting in close proximity. Beyond the caution needed to maintain their privacy, I had to rely on the individuals I met to introduce me to other lesbi. Without these personal connections, I found it impossible to make contacts. Even then some individuals felt that participating in an extended way in my research project was simply too risky; they were fearful of their families' reactions, should they find out they were lesbi.

Despite these limitations, and with the assistance of my research associate Sri during my field visits in 2001 and 2004, I met twenty-eight individuals who were either tombois (thirteen) or women involved with tombois (fifteen). Most of these individuals lived in Padang, or had lived there at some time in the past few years, although three were from other towns in the province. The bulk of my analysis is based on the sixteen individuals with whom I worked most closely, and whom I formally interviewed, including eight tombois and eight femmes. I also obtained demographic data for an additional six individuals.[11] Of the sixteen, I spent time with them in the spaces that they inhabited, including their work spaces as well as their social spaces. I collected detailed life histories and asked questions that addressed how they understood themselves and their world. Questions focused on their self-identity, their knowledge of and access to local, national, and global discourses on gender, sexuality, women and womanhood, and their sense of relationship to other lesbi, gay, and waria across Indonesia and beyond. In addition I draw on conversations with several lesbi whom I met in 1990, mentioned earlier, as well as meetings and informal discussions in 2001 and 2004 with members and leaders of activist lesbi organizations in Jakarta. This ethnographic approach has the advantage of revealing the narratives as well as the practices that produce gendered and sexual selves. As Anna Tsing points out in *Friction*, global connections can be understood only in the "sticky materiality of practical encounters" (2005, 1), that is, the everyday actions and practices that are the stuff of ethnographic research. Though my time with them could never make me an insider, given our very different histories and life experiences, it offered insight into the everyday meanings of their lives.

My own process of learning what lesbi meant to tombois and femmes in West Sumatra began in 1990 with my relationship with Dayan, my tomboi lover. Despite my anthropological training and efforts to be aware of ethnocentric biases, I assumed before I met Dayan that individuals who used the label "lesbi," which I thought was just a shortened form of the word "lesbian," would have identities and desires in line with my own understanding of lesbians. I came out in the early 1970s in San Francisco, California, at a time when a lesbian bar culture and an activist lesbian feminist movement were flourishing. The lesbians I knew identified as "women-loving-women" and were generally androgynous in their appearance and fairly egalitarian in their relationships. The terms "butch" and "femme," which referred to masculine and feminine roles, had circulated in lesbian communities in San Francisco and elsewhere in the United States prior to the 1970s, but by 1970 they were not seen as self-defining or necessary in the way they had been for an earlier generation in the United States.[12]

Many of my early insights about lesbi came as a result of my relationship with Dayan. I did not expect lesbi to identify as men, nor did I expect to be considered a femme, but these expectations soon unraveled as Dayan's masculine behavior and attitudes toward me made our differences apparent (see Blackwood 1995a). My failure to cook for Dayan or organize Dayan's birthday party led to tensions in our relationship, as did my comment to Dayan that s/he was "pretty," a descriptive term for a woman, but not for a man. These tensions slowly forced me to recognize that I was misreading Dayan's gender identity. Gloria Wekker (1998) notes similarly that the most intense moments of learning as an ethnographer came, for her, when her notion of equal lesbian partners was confronted with the age-based power of older *mati* women in Suriname. Part of the incentive for conducting this study, then, was my desire to explore the complexities of the lesbi world in Indonesia and come to a better understanding of tomboi trans-identities within their particular historical and social contexts.

Geography of Desire: The Regional Metropolis of Padang

The city of Padang, the primary location for this study, sits on the coast of West Sumatra in Indonesia. It is a sprawling metropolis with a population of over 700,000 people, according to the 2000 census figures (Badan Pusat Statistik 2000). It has been a major trading port in Southeast Asia for hundreds of years.[13]

Located near the equator, this tropical city is currently the provincial capital of West Sumatra and a province of the state of Indonesia. Most of its inhabitants identify as Minangkabau, an ethnic group that is both Islamic and matrilineal (see Blackwood 2000). Mosques and prayer houses (*surau*) can be found throughout the city of Padang. The evening call to prayer carried over ubiquitous loudspeakers finds young and old, women and men, putting on prayer shawls and heading to the nearest mosque.

Padang is well connected to Indonesian and global circuits. Two large shopping malls in the city boast an agglomeration of fashionable clothing and cosmetic shops, hair salons, fast-food restaurants, and electronics stores. Via a quick one-hour trip, daily flights from the small airport in Padang take passengers to Singapore for shopping forays and business meetings. Flights also depart hourly for major cities throughout Indonesia. The port in nearby Teluk Bayur handles both inter-island and export shipping for a range of commodities, the bulk of which is cement, palm oil, coal, and rubber. Ships travel to destinations predominantly in Asia, but also to Europe, Africa, and elsewhere.[14] Large and small buses depart from Padang's central bus terminal to points throughout Sumatra and Java. Minangkabau themselves have been migrants and transnationals well before the term became fashionable in academia. Circular migration (*merantau*), the practice of migrating to (and returning from) locations both within and outside of Indonesia, including Medan, Jakarta, Kuala Lumpur and Hong Kong, is a valued part of adulthood for both Minangkabau men and women (see also Naim 1971).

Although Padang is metropolitan and globally connected, it occupies what I call an intermediate position as a metropolis. I base this assessment on its size relative to other cities in Indonesia and its status as a provincial capital and active trade center and port (see Rutz 1987). Jakarta is the largest city in Indonesia, with a population of well over 8 million, whereas Padang's 700,000 places it as the twelfth largest in Indonesia (World Gazetteer 2006).[15] Padang's position as a regional metropolis makes it an intriguing place to study global sexualities because, though it is not a global metropolis, neither can it be considered a "nonmetropolitan" area. In queer studies the metropolitan locations of Europe and North America come to stand for the primary sites of gay culture and identity, while spaces and peoples outside these centers are bracketed together as nonmetropolitan (see Phillips et al. 2000). For instance, Alan Sinfield (2000, 21) posits a model of gay cities, such as Rio de Janeiro and Delhi, that interact with "traditional local, non-metropolitan models," thereby setting up a distinction between metropolitan sexualities and sexualities beyond the metropolis. In addition to obscuring the differences within and across nation-states, the term "nonmetropolitan" keeps the gaze on the putative metropolitan "centers" of gay sexuality, making those centers the standard for other queer sexualities.

Picking up on the distinction between metropolitan and nonmetropolitan, Halberstam discusses the possibility of shared characteristics among nonmetropolitan or "local sexual economies" (2005, 38). In Halberstam's (2005) study of Brandon Teena, she offers U.S. small town and rural populations as nonmetropolitan spaces. Although Sinfield rightly notes that "metropolitan gay and lesbian concepts should be regarded ... not as denoting the ultimate achievement of human sexuality, but as something we have been producing ... in determinate economic and social conditions (2000, 22)," it is not clear what constitutes "nonmetropolitan" spaces. Such spaces seem to be problematically associated with broadly defined "other" cultural spaces that are "different" than global queer metropolitan spaces and therefore stand in contrast to them.

Because in this kind of mapping Padang falls silently into the vast space of nonmetropolitan, I identify Padang as a regional metropolis to contest its supposed location on the margins of queer space "outside" metropolitan areas. Identifying Padang as metropolitan forces recognition of different scales of queer space beyond the binary of metropolitan and nonmetropolitan. It also shifts the focus away from gay metropolitan "centers," and their model of queer subjectivity, toward the possibility of multiple queer models and subjects—crosscut by class, ethnicity, gender, and nation—in the global gay ecumene. By looking at Padang as a regional metropolis, new sets of questions become salient. Are there differences in global gay processes between large and intermediate metropolises? How can these differences be accounted for without resorting to oversimplified notions of local versus metropolitan or global? What is the relation of either of these spaces to localized queer practices and subjectivities? I suggest that a regional metropolis is neither a "local version" of the gay metropolis, nor part of a common "metropolitan" gay culture, but a locus in the circuit of global queer knowledge situated within particular sociocultural, regional, and historical contexts.

Ethnicity and Indonesian Citizenship

As a regional metropolis, to what extent does Padang's ethnic composition and identity produce localized practices that affect the contours of lesbi lives? The largest cities of Indonesia have very diverse populations that use the national language of Indonesian as the common language. However, Padang, like other provincial capitals, is dominated by its largest ethnic group, the Minangkabau.[16] The language of daily use in Padang, as in all of West Sumatra, is Minangkabau, a Malay language with some similarities to Indonesian. Most people except the very elderly are also fluent in Indonesian, which is taught in the public schools. In addition, as the home of the Minangkabau, West Sumatra and Padang are identified by other Indonesians as the land of *adat matriarchaat* (literally, matriarchal customs), which refers to their practices of matrilineal descent and inheritance.[17] Minangkabau language use and the practice of matrilineal kinship encourage a sense of ethnic identity among the inhabitants of West Sumatra.

While identifying as Minangkabau, those living in Padang are less invested in the matrilineal practices of highland villages, which are considered the heartland of the Minangkabau region. Despite their ethnic identity, Padang residents, particularly those without land or nearby kin, are more typical of residents in regional metropolises throughout Indonesia. Rita Kipp (1993) describes kinship in urban Indonesia as a bilateral system that blurs the intricacies of clan affiliation and weakens distinctive elements of *adat* (customary practices, laws, and ideals). She suggests that wealth differences and interethnic marriages are part of the reason for a homogenization of cultural practices in metropolitan areas. State policies have also worked to disconnect ethnic identity from everyday life by refiguring *adat* as culture (*kebudayaan*). Ethnic identity, in the form of dress, songs, dances, and handicrafts, were recognized by Suharto's New Order state as expressions of "culture," which were literally paraded about to celebrate Indonesia's Independence Day or placed in museums for the edification of children and tourists.[18] An example of this change from *adat* to culture is found among the Batak people of North Sumatra. Spurred on by urban migration and state-sponsored "*adat* festivals," they have come to view wedding speeches as much an expression of Batak "art" as of *adat* (Rodgers 1979). Through state policies *adat* has come to be seen as something people *possess* rather than something that they *practice*, making it distinct from and in many cases irrelevant to everyday life in urban areas.

The processes of *adat* homogenization are apparent in Padang as well. Comparable to residents of other regional metropolises, many of Padang's residents have migrated to Padang from villages and provinces throughout West Sumatra. Married couples in Padang tend to be "mixed," that is, comprised of individuals from different towns and villages in West Sumatra or (to a much lesser degree) other islands. Since each Minangkabau village has its own version of *adat*, metaphorically referred to in the saying "different pond, different fish" (*lain lubuk, lain ikan*), couples from different villages have to contend with and negotiate conflicting versions of *adat* at home as well as across communities in Padang. Further, residents born or schooled in Padang come to know Minangkabau *adat* at a very elementary level of knowledge, usually through lessons learned at school or from parents and grandparents. The result is that Minangkabau *adat* in Padang has been formalized into a generic set of customs or codified rules that can be practiced by its diverse inhabitants without conflict (see Sanday 2002). The customary authority of the mother and her brother in kin affairs is acknowledged in Padang but not carefully observed by most families because they do not maintain ties with or are too distant from the extended networks of kin in which such relationships flourish. Consequently, the practice of *adat* in Padang tends to have less salience in people's daily lives than it does for those in highland villages.

For the lesbi in Padang who identify as Minangkabau, most confess to knowing little about *adat*, although they claim it as the source of their understanding about what it means to be a Minangkabau woman or man. Based on my interviewees' responses, Minangkabau *adat* in Padang consists of a mix of kinship and wedding practices that are most clearly associated with the tendency for families to live with maternal kin, the passage of land and/or houses from mothers to daughters, the wearing of appropriate costumes at weddings, and the observance of rules about whom one is allowed to marry. It is also associated with the authority of the *ninik-mamak*, a term that Padang people understand to refer to the mother's brothers (*mamak*), rather than the authority of the mother. In Padang mother's brothers are said to be concerned with the status and social propriety of their matrilineal kin, while kinswomen are said to be concerned primarily with the management of household affairs and wedding ceremonies.

Adat in Padang, then, is a mix of village and urban practices, crosscut by migrant influences and national processes. As I discuss in the next chapter, this version of *adat* consists of kinship, gender, and sexual norms that are infused and partially constituted by state and Islamic discourses about properly gendered Indonesian citizens. Consequently, the importance of *adat* and Minangkabau ethnic identity to those living in Padang is muted by the diversity and history of the city in which they live. Lesbi in Padang hold an ethnic identity as Minangkabau that reflects as much about contemporary discourses and practices circulating in Indonesia as it does about a specifically Minangkabau identity.

Social Context of Lesbi Lives

Surrounding the business district of Padang are sprawling residential neighborhoods that reflect the differences in wealth among its residents. The lesbi individuals whom I met come from a range of socioeconomic backgrounds, from quite poor to ordinary or average households, with two tipping toward well-to-do.[19] Of the twenty-two from whom I was able to obtain demographic data, about two-thirds (fifteen) come from roughly the same class location, an intermediate strata, to use Kenneth Young's (1990) term, while about one-third (seven) were from the lower strata. People in West Sumatra typically refer to three classes of people, rich, ordinary folk, and poor folk (*kaya*, *biasa*, and *miskin*), designations that are associated primarily with levels of income.

These folk designations are usually referred to as upper, middle, and lower classes by Indonesian scholars and journalists. However, class designations for Indonesia have been the subject of on-going debate.[20] Terms such as "middle class" or "lower class" fit imprecisely with Indonesian social groupings, leaving some scholars to rely on them merely as handy reference points rather than empirical categories. As Richard Robison (1990) points out, the term "middle class" is used to cover such a wide spectrum of Indonesian society as to render it fairly useless. Furthermore, the language of class ignores the relevance of clan rank and affiliation to social status (see Blackwood 2000). Clan rank is closely attended to in rural areas of Indonesia, for it provides the structure of village and ceremonial life. In Minangkabau villages the rank of an individual's clan (*suku*), whether high-, middle-, or low-ranking, signifies their place within the community.[21] These clan rankings are less salient among multiethnic urban populations.

Political analysts seem to agree that an Indonesian middle class is not homogeneous; it is comprised of people with education, some wealth, and some power, which in Indonesia includes civil servants, professionals, white-collar workers and employers (Dick 1985), or an "urban technocrat/administrative/managerial class" (Robison 1982, 131). Young (1990) makes a useful intervention in this debate by pointing out that even rural communities have an intermediate strata of entrepreneurs, village elites, low-level state functionaries, merchants, shopkeepers, and independent farming households, but these disparate groups possess no coherent political outlook. Robison's own modification incorporates Young's analysis more generally into a "populist lower middle-class" of "clerks, teachers and lower-level civil servants which ... intersects with the petty bourgeoisie and, in the countryside, with the smaller landowning families" (Robison 1996, 88). His take on a "lower middle class" is useful to describe many of the individuals and their families in this study but at the same time demonstrates the difficulties of identifying a singular "middle" class. Although scholars have been unable to agree on what constitutes these classes, the terms have become common usage in the academic literature on Indonesia. As Kipp (1993) points out, class is very much a factor in Indonesian society. Class differences exist, but what constitutes a particular class continues to be fairly amorphous.

Designating arbitrary categories of class is at best problematic and thus one task I wish to avoid. Therefore, for my purposes in this study, class signifies primarily differences in income, education, and ownership of property, a characterization that falls in line with people's views in West Sumatra and elsewhere in Indonesia. It is not meant to signal the existence of real or definitive social categories along the lines of Western political analysis. Within Padang, the "middle class" (*kelas menengah*) can be said to include families whose members work as small business owners, lower-level state-employed civil servants (which includes teachers and nurses), salaried professionals, and small landowners (in line with Robison's "lower middle-class"), while those in the lower class (which shades imperceptibly from the middle class) work as petty market traders, food sellers (selling food from home, in the market, or from *kaki lima*, wheeled carts), and wage laborers (for instance, maids, construction workers, factory workers, and laborers on fishing trawlers). The status of the "middle class" in Padang speaks to its intermediate status as an urban area because its social classes do not have the same levels of wealth and power as those in the middle and upper classes in Jakarta.

Family income and occupations are relevant to understanding tombois and their girlfriends in Padang because, like most unmarried Indonesians, they live with their natal families or close relatives and in some cases work for the family business. For lesbi whom I met in Padang that belong to the intermediate stratum or "middle class," their natal families have modest incomes and limited property, including some land and/or houses and a little surplus for leisure activities or family ceremonies. In this group, fathers' occupations include civil service jobs—in the military, state bureaucracy, and education, including public school teaching and administration—as well as self-employment, such as petty shop owners; mothers' occupations include primarily teaching or managing the family business with their husbands. When I asked my interviewees about their mothers' occupations, many told me their mothers were housewives, meaning they do not work outside the house, although in some cases these women own rice fields that they supervise. Families in this stratum are typically extended rather than nuclear families; other family members, including married siblings and their families, live in the same household or nearby and contribute to the family income or work in the family business. For the lesbi in Padang whose families come from the lower stratum or working class, parents and other siblings work as wage laborers, such as clerks and factory workers, or in petty trade operating small stalls in the market; additionally some of their kinswomen provide income through the sale of cooked food.

Though most of the lesbi I met lived with their natal families, other arrangements were possible. Tombois, unlike their girlfriends, do not actually sleep at home every night but may stay with friends or at their girlfriends' houses. In 2001 two couples lived together; one couple occupied a room together at the tomboi's family house, while the other couple rented their own house, but had additional kin living with them. Most tombois and girlfriends work to support themselves and provide money to their natal families, although four are without work and are supported by their families. All rely on their families for access to jobs, extra cash, and education. Whether they are living at home or not, their lifestyles reflect their family's class location. As I discuss later in the book, this class location is an important factor in the particular readings that tombois and their girlfriends make of gendered and sexual discourses in West Sumatra.

In terms of religious orientation all but one of the tombois and girlfriends are Muslim; the one non-Muslim is Christian. Those who identify as Muslim are not devout practitioners. Women in West Sumatra must cover their heads when they observe *salat*, the ritual prayers performed five times daily. Tombois are reluctant to ignore this religious dictate in public, so they tend not to observe religious practices or do so only in private, where the requirement can be ignored. In addition they do not feel comfortable praying with men on the men's side of the mosque, although one tomboi said s/he did so once on a dare, and no one took notice. Both tombois and femmes told me that according to Islam homosexuality is a sin, but they find their own accommodations between their religious beliefs and their desires.[22] Islam, like *adat*, is part of the world in which they live, its holy days shaping their calendar, but the practice of piety is not important to them.

Similar to their socioeconomic backgrounds, the education levels of the twenty-two tombois and girlfriends I profiled are quite varied, but their age range is less so. Six had completed some or all of middle school (Sekolah Menengah Pertama, SMP); thirteen had completed a high school education (Sekolah Menengah Atas, SMA); three had or were currently completing an undergraduate college degree (*stratum satu*, S1). In 2004 their ages ranged from late teens to forty years of age; the average age was twenty-eight.[23] The bias in age toward individuals in their twenties and early thirties is due to several factors. Because I used friendship networks to make new contacts, most of the individuals I eventually met were of a similar age cohort. In addition, older individuals were less accessible. Married women involved with tombois had an established family life or professional reputation to protect and were unwilling in general even to meet me. Older tombois were hesitant to discuss their lives with me for fear of exposing their girlfriends and themselves to unwanted scrutiny from neighbors and kin.

Only five of these lesbi were or had been married, four girlfriends and one tomboi. Marriage in Indonesia is seen as the marker of adulthood, something all parents want for their children. In a country where women of twenty-four to twenty-five years of age are said to be getting past the proper age for marriage, the high percentage of nonmarrieds in this group speaks to the determination of tombois to remain unmarried and the willingness of femmes to delay marriage, a point I discuss more fully later in the book. The three women married at the time had husbands living with them, including a newly married woman who was living in her tomboi partner's house with her new husband.[24]

Although not all of the twenty-two lesbi I profiled were born and raised in Padang, twenty of them identified as ethnically Minangkabau, and all spoke the Minangkabau language. The translocality of the group is evident in their family histories. Some of their families had come to Padang from locales in West Sumatra and beyond over the past twenty-five years.[25] Those who migrated to Padang from other towns and highland areas in West Sumatra maintained ties with their home village and ancestral kin group. Marriage, death, and, above all, the holy month of Ramadan, were occasions to visit kin and renew ties. However, since migration is often prompted by poverty and/or the hope of bettering one's chances for success, many of these families probably came from the lower ranks of village households, with little or no claim to land, and thus feel little "pull" to return home or follow village practices. Other families had lived in Padang for several generations and owned land and houses there. The family of one Minangkabau lesbi lived in Jakarta from the time she was born and only returned to Padang after she was an adult. Three lesbi were offspring of marriages between Minangkabau women and non-Minangkabau men. These three identified as Minangkabau due to the matrilineal orientation of Minangkabau people. In sum these individuals reflected the diversity of class and educational levels found in a regional metropolis. They shared an urban sensibility that drew on ethnic as well as national and religious discourses in creating the contours of their lives.

Global Gays and Transnational Sexualities

Equally important to understanding lesbi in Padang is their access to and reception of international lesbian and gay discourse. The topic of globalized queer identities has received considerable attention since the early 1990s from both feminist and queer theorists. Ken Plummer (1992) pointed out that same-sex experiences are increasingly fashioned through the interconnectedness of the world. He suggested that queer identity "moves in fits and starts along diverse paths to disparate becomings" (1992, 16), an astute recognition of the diversity and difference that marks the lives of people in same-sex relations. As a way to bridge global and local processes, he argued that lesbian and gay studies should pay close attention to the "international connectedness yet local uniqueness" of diverse practices (1992, 18). In contrast Dennis Altman (1996) initially spoke confidently about the "apparent globalization of postmodern, gay identities," claiming that new "globalized" queer identities would replace older indigenous identities, resulting in a homogeneous global gay identity. In his later work (2001), he was more attentive to cultural specificities among same-sex communities, but at the same time suggested that globalization will "lead to a gradual convergence of sexual behavior across different societies" (2001, 38). Many scholars have rightly criticized Altman's view of global gay identity for its reductionist view of globalization, its progressive narrative from "traditional" to "modern," and its assumption that others would strive to emulate the Western gay model (see, for example, Binnie 2004; Rofel 1999).

Indeed, the term "local-global" sets up an imaginary hierarchy of relations that index traditional to local and modern to global. In relation to sexualities the term suggests the difference between traditional (and oppressed) sexualities and a Western-defined liberated gayness (Manalansan 1997). Feminist theorists Inderpal Grewal and Caren Kaplan (1994) move beyond the limited and simplistic dichotomy of "local-global" by using the term "transnational." This term points to the lines that crosscut binaries of local/global and traditional/modern; it suggests that the "global" and "local" thoroughly infiltrate each other. Carrying this definition to the discussion of sexualities, they define "transnational sexualities" as the way particular genders and sexualities are shaped by a large number of processes implicated in globalization, including capitalism, diasporic movements, political economies of state, and the disjunctive flow of meanings produced across these sites (Grewal and Kaplan 2001). From a queer theory perspective, Elizabeth Povinelli and George Chauncey encourage reconsideration of "the self-evident nature of the national, the local, and the intimate" in light of the relevance of transnational processes in the production of localized sexual subjectivities (1999, 442). They identify transnational as that which moves beyond and that which circulates in specific spaces through "speech, cyberspace, film, television, telephonic media" (1999, 445).[26]

Various theories are offered within queer globalization studies to situate the "local" in relation to the global world. Mark Johnson, Peter Jackson, and Gilbert Herdt (2000) offer the concept of "critical regionalities" as a way to address specific historical circumstances and imagined sexual communities. They argue that this concept "provides one means through which we can move beyond the essentialized field of the 'local' and the unspecified and unsituated field of the 'global'" (2000, 373). Gayatri Gopinath's theory of queer regions similarly situates the key economy of meaning between local and national/transnational. Drawing on work on black sexuality in the American South, she argues that regions, such as

Kerala in India, are always crosscut by global processes but in ways that differ from those in other regions or other national frames. Regional analyses then become a way of "destabilizing dominant national narratives, and of foregrounding 'other' narratives that tell an entirely different story of gender, sexuality, and nationalist subjectivity" (Gopinath 2007, 343).

Thomas Boellstorff's (1999, 2005b) efforts to locate Indonesian gay and lesbi subjectivities at the translocal scale provide another way to surmount the "local" with its sense of fixity and self-containment. Importantly, Boellstorff's "translocal" is not predicated on the movement of people, as most gay and lesbi Indonesians "live in the towns and even households where they grew up" (1999, 481). Yet his concept is emphatically not localized. According to Boellstorff, lesbi and gay meanings are not learned at the local level but are produced through "archipelagic" or national and transnational processes, creating a translocal gay community in which "someone thousands of miles away might be 'closer' than someone next door who is not *gay* or *lesbi*" (2005b, 34, italics in original). By defining translocal as disconnected from locality, however, he offers only a national scale for alternative subjectivities, overlooking the specificities of locales, places, and even regions in the circulation and production of gender and sexual subjectivities. His point is well taken that lesbi and gay subjectivities are not the product of traditional or fixed local identities, but, as I demonstrate in this book, differences in sexual subjectivities across Indonesia underscore the importance of attending to regional scales and particular locales in the circulation and reception of queer knowledge.

The concept of "locality" I use here draws on Arjun Appadurai's (1996) notion of "ethnoscapes," a term that points to the disjunctive flow of meanings across cultural spaces. Particular global, regional, and historical flows of meaning create specific discourses, knowledges, and ways of understanding, which in turn constitute particular locations. As Ulf Hannerz suggests, locales are enduring settings with certain routines, long-term relationships, and shared understandings, comprising a unique combination of influences that are neither territorial nor privileged sites of cultural process, but a place "where various people's habitats of meaning intersect" (1996, 28). Attention to locale can also include and take into account inequities in global processes and inequalities of place that condition the reception of these meanings (Grewal and Kaplan 2001; Tsing 2004).

If we follow Tsing's appealing metaphor of friction, which she defines as the effect of global encounters across difference, such encounters can occur at any place and are, as she argues, "congeries of local/global interaction" (2005, 3). Her analysis then tacks back to the messy intersections where cultures and subjectivities are produced at a point that is never purely local nor purely global. Although "transnational" is often used to refer to movement, even diasporas, and imaginaries beyond national borders, I argue that transnational sexualities can be found in one locality as well as in the queer diasporas inhabited by migrant subjects. I use the term "transnational" to signify the way individuals in place (nonmigrants) are implicated and participate in processes that extend globally. To study sexuality transnationally, then, requires a mapping out of the different scales of meanings and practices, discourses, and economies, both historically and today, in particular locales as well as across nations and regions.

Other effects of a globalizing queer studies are the tendency to essentialize and universalize human experiences by assuming the relevance of Western categories to the lives of people elsewhere (see also Plummer 1992; Jolly and Manderson 1997).[27] Paola Bacchetta (2002) argues that the Western neocolonial version of queer discourse tends toward an "effacement" of sexualities that do not have the appearance of modern same-sex identity emblematic of the lesbian and gay liberation movement of Europe and North America. The traditional/ modern dichotomy of Western thought perpetuates the assumption that individuals who do not reflect "modern" sexual identities are backward and in need of education to become fully liberated modern queers (Grewal and Kaplan 2001). Western queer discourse to a certain extent relies on this dichotomy to create a developmental teleology that situates other sexualities as premodern, that is, not yet lesbian or gay, while placing Western sexualities at the pinnacle of modern, autonomous sexuality (see also Manalansan 1997; Cruz-Malavé and Manalansan 2002; Gopinath 2002).[28] Similarly, as Bacchetta (2002) notes, the "from-Stonewall-diffusion-fantasy" situates the origin and foundation of the modern queer movement at a particularly American moment in time. In this universalizing turn, Western queer discourses bypass the historicity and specificity of gendered and sexual subjects within and outside the "West," relegating their stories to the margins of queer movements.

The effacement of ethnic, postcolonial, and non-Western sexualities is particularly disabling for lesbian and transgendered subjects, who are less visible in national and global gay (men's) movements and narrowly defined in global lesbian-feminist organizing (Bacchetta 2002; King 2002). When gay men's practices, spaces, desires, and subcultures are the focus of transnational sexualities, they achieve iconicity as the standard by which all queer sexualities are measured.[29] If lesbians are not already subsumed under the term "gay" through the flawed pairing of "gay-and-lesbian," they are simply measured against gay men, their supposed counterparts, and found to be less visible or less public, while the processes that produce these gendered subjectivities are overlooked.[30] In contrast my study not only shifts the focus away from putative gay metropolitan centers but away from a model of gay subjectivity based on Western white gay men's global practices. Of particular interest in this study are the normative domestic and public spaces that serve as sites of queer female subjectivity.[31]

Drawing on a queer feminist approach, this book differs from global queer studies by theorizing the processes of gendering in the production of globalized queer subjectivities. In Indonesia the consequences of gender discourses are apparent in the differences in lesbi and gay communities and practices—in styles of dating, in sexual expressions, in freedom of movement, and in sociopsychological issues related to self-esteem and identity. Open, public expression of sexual desire is more acceptable, even encouraged for men than for women. Men's search for sexual adventure is more widely tolerated and institutionalized, while women's efforts to gain access to birth control or to be sexually active before marriage are roundly rejected (Bennett 2005). Expectations of marriage and motherhood leave little room for other models or goals for women, whereas the same expectations of marriage and fatherhood for men prove less restrictive to their sexual expression.[32]

Although many representations of femininity circulate in Indonesia (Sears 1996), the dominant state ideology offers no options to females other than heterosexual marriage and motherhood. This expectation remains hegemonic at the same time that the discourses of modernity—the importance of education, careers, and middle-class status for women—create a space for them to develop careers and postpone marriage (Blackwood 1995b). Nevertheless, as Gopinath suggests, the dominance of heterosexual and patriarchal configurations leads to the "illegibility and unrepresentability of a non-heteronormative female subject" (2005, 16). At the same time images of gender transgressive males, such as hijra in India or waria in Indonesia, are fairly commonplace.[33] Focusing on queer diasporic texts, Gopinath's project excavates intimate desires between women that evade the label lesbian, thus expanding the domain of queer female subjectivities. While her work and others challenge assumptions about heteronormatively oriented women, I explore the way gender discourses produce female subjects (tombois) who become legible by exceeding or transgressing normative gender.

By applying a transnational queer feminist approach to global queer studies, I seek in this book to make visible gender-transgressive or masculine females as queer subjects of the global gay ecumene. The global translation of Western sexual cartography has resulted in the misrecognition and erasure of female subjects such as tombois, who enact a culturally contextualized masculinity, as well as other transgendered females whose subjectivities and desires are expressed through gender transgression and partnering with normatively feminine women.

20

Despite these erasures, masculine females, who express a range of queer masculinities, are imaginable and intelligible both historically and currently in many contexts globally.[34]

My work unsettles the categories of lesbian and transgender by refusing to situate female/queer masculinities in either camp, preferring to stay right along the border, which is not the space of a continuum but the space of collaboration and multiple allegiances. Anzaldúa's work, and those who have followed her, point to the synergy of multiple allegiances and multiple subjectivities through which ambiguities of ethnic and sexual identities or, in this case, of femininity and masculinity, are strategically maintained. In fact Anzaldúa's metaphor of borderlands, and subsequent theorizing by queers of color from a multiracial, multiethnic perspective, play an important part in understanding the subjectivities that tombois express, a point I develop in chapter 6.[35] This subjectivity, which I call contingent masculinity, is conditioned by circumstances, a process rather than an entity, a masculinity that acknowledges the culturally inscribed femaleness of tomboi bodies and the material effects of that embodiment.

Gendering Queer Subjectivities

In writing a book about gendered and sexual subjectivities, I develop an approach to tomboi and femme selves that relies on a particular framing of self, subjectivity, and gender. I use the language of subjects and subjectivity, rather than identity, in order to address the processes by which tomboi and femme selves are produced and negotiated over time. Although Stuart Hall (1996) argues that identities are never unified but are fragmented and multiply constructed, the prevailing notion that a lesbian or gay "identity" meant one had a stable or unchanging sense of self, evidenced in the LGBT movement in the 1980s and 1990s in the United States, became problematic as the boundaries of those identities began to blur (Jagose 1997). The works of Michel Foucault, Judith Butler, and others are central to rethinking the processes by which queer subjects are constituted, offering new insights as well as new difficulties in imagining everyday lives and their material consequences. While, as has already been noted, any term has its problems, I use "subject positions" to refer to culturally constructed and ideologically dominant social categories within which individuals are slotted. I use "subjectivity" in place of "identity" because it offers a more dynamic perspective on processes of selfhood. Sherry Ortner's definition of subjectivity is useful for this analysis. It is "the ensemble of modes of perception, affect, thought, desire, and fear that animate acting subjects" (Ortner 2006, 107). In addition I think of

21

subjectivity as the sense of self, that is, the way individuals perceive themselves in relation to the subject positions they occupy. More importantly, subjectivity points to a dynamic and transformative process of self-positioning as subjects take up, engage and rework socially constituted subject positions.[36]

In order to address how subjects take up particular gendered positions, I begin with a conceptual framing of self as agentive. The concept of agency is a contentious issue in poststructuralist theory, which asks whether subjects actively recognize and chose their subject position(s). Many feminists find useful the poststructuralist contention that individual actions are constructed within a social reality but raise concerns over the apparent inability of the subject to act with intentionality (Alcoff 1994). In an attempt to resolve this debate within poststructuralist theory, Nicholas Dirks, Geoff Eley, and Sherry Ortner find that "subjects," however defined, "can no longer be seen as only the effect of subjection" (1994, 18). They argue that actors always carry around or have access to enough disparate knowledge so as to be in a critical position (Dirks et al. 1994), allowing room for the possibility of transformative action. I take the stance that individual subjects are historically and culturally constructed with particular kinds of knowledge and understanding and can act within that knowledge to take up particular subject positions; their agentive ability is not, however, that of the autonomous, rational Self acting from an innate consciousness.[37] Rather subjects experience and embody a range of discourses and practices that make sense to them, yet set the conditions for what is thinkable or imaginable.

One strategy I use to think about the relation between self and subjectivities is to focus on the bodily aspects of subjectivity, or body knowledge. This approach follows on social theorist Henrietta Moore's statement that the "multiple nature of subjectivity is experienced physically" (1994, 81). To slightly paraphrase Moore, to move in different spaces is to know in your body what differences involve. Theorists such as Anzaldúa (1987) and bell hooks (1990) speak of the physical feelings evoked as one moves across communities or borders, feelings that signify one's difference in a racially oppressive context. These feelings of difference are equally telling for tombois in contexts in which their transgressive gender practices create friction.

Body knowledge refers to physical sensations experienced in interactions with others that are perceived or interpreted as feelings of, for instance, safety, comfort, and pleasure or discomfort, unease, and anxiety. Tombois told me how certain interactions feel right, or awkward, or uncomfortable; they rely on these embodied feelings as markers and signposts of their masculinity. In relying on their bodies to confirm their masculinity, tombois substantiate "a theory in the flesh," which is the term E. Patrick Johnson uses to describe knowledge that is rooted in the body (2005, 135). Johnson envisions this knowledge as the basis for "quare" studies, a version of queer studies that "moves beyond simply theorizing subjectivity and agency as discursively mediated to theorizing how that mediation may propel material bodies into action" (2005, 135). This move to attend to bodies, whether racialized or transgendered, offers a more nuanced approach to the processes by which subjects mediate and manage multiple discourses and subject positions.

Another useful strategy I employ to understand the ways subjects experience and express their subject positions is to look at what I call practical enactment. Moore suggests that "the enactment of subject positions based on gender provides the conditions for the experience of gender" (1994, 56). She highlights here the importance of enactment in giving meaning to and constructing a particular experience of gender, a process that creates the feelings of rightness and belonging to a particular gendered subject position—for that moment and in that context but not necessarily always. This notion of enactment offers the possibility of strategic agency that does not necessarily require conscious thought because, as Moore suggests, "actions themselves can be a type of critical reflection that does not necessarily have to involve conscious, discursive strategizing" (1994, 77). Thus individuals can take up particular gender positions through a practical enactment of those positions and not necessarily through conscious choice. Moore's thinking here draws on Pierre Bourdieu's (1990) understanding of the relation between practice and structure, or "habitus" in Bourdieu's terminology. Bourdieu states that practical sense is made of the world through the constant reinforcement given to particular practices. Here emphasizing the homogeneity of a particular habitus, Bourdieu is intent on demonstrating the intelligibility of ordinary everyday practices and the sense of reality that they create. For him, particular practices, constantly reinforced, create a practical sense of the world.

Because practical enactments and manipulations of gender knowledge have social consequences, however, I want to strengthen Bourdieu's concept of "practical sense" by accounting for the power of normative social categories. Such categories have a certain power or efficacy that is gained when one adheres to the proper models, in this case, the models of man or woman as culturally defined. Bourdieu calls this efficacy the "sense of reality" found in mastery of a common code or dispositions (1990, 60). The force of these discursively produced social categories, if understood in Bourdieu's sense of habitus, lies in the way people understand the world; it is "what causes practices and works to be immediately intelligible and foreseeable, and hence taken for granted" (1990, 58). In this sense the power of normativity lies in its ability to "naturalize" particular social categories or subject positions and make them invisible because they are taken for granted. This perception of normativity is somewhat different from Foucault's, in which the power of normativity resides in its material and social effects. Bourdieu moves us some distance toward understanding normalizing processes, but Foucault provides a sharper edge to make sense of processes and technologies of normalization *and* stigmatization in the proliferation of sexualities and, for my purposes in this book, gendered subjectivities.

Normative social categories may generate a practical sense of reality, but their material and social effects are critical to their power. Normative gender sets the conditions for the subject positions that people take up, yet in order to account for the appearance of non-normative genders I draw on Foucault's notion of power as productive. The social rewards, or in Foucault's terms, the pleasures associated with normativity, include family and community approval, social access and status, a self consistent with others, a future, a family, sentiments of cultural belonging, and a certain ability to act and make decisions that are valued and recognized by others. These pleasures move one toward the subject position culturally assigned to one's body, race, or class. Challenges to normative categories risk social disapproval and loss of material or social benefits, but at the same time they provide other social or material rewards. Those who take up alternative or subordinate subject positions may see themselves, and may even be seen by others, as brave, individualist, scandalous, provocative, or desirable, depending on the particular dispositions available. Even if negatively construed, the intelligibility of such positions and the space created for them imbues them with a certain meaning and power that offers other ways to social status, family, and cultural belonging. Thus non-normative subject positions are enabled by the same processes that produce normative ones, but within certain limits and dependent on certain conditions.

Lesbi, Tomboi, Female Masculinity, Transgender, Queer: Meanings and Contexts

The history of colonization by the West, including its social scientists, has been the history of imposing categories and meanings on others. The terms I have chosen to use in this book reflect my desire to avoid conflating Western and Indonesian meanings while at the same time making connections across their differences.[38] Any English classificatory term for "gender" or "sexuality" that I use in this book can be contested because their meanings are not fixed and their use in translation to represent other meanings and practices may be ill fitting at best. In fact, my own preferences have changed over the time I have been writ-

24

ing about Indonesian tombois and their girlfriends, in part due to the growing popularity of certain terms in the American English lexicon, such as "queer," and in part to my own developing ideas about the meanings of gender, transgender, and globalization. Here I lay out the reasons for the choices I have made and then elaborate on these terms throughout the book.

The terms "lesbi" and "lesbian" are Indonesian words used in Indonesian print media and by lesbi, gay, and waria individuals and activists. The terms have circulated in Indonesia since the early 1980s and tend to be used interchangeably. The meaning of lesbi fluctuates depending on who is using the term. I have seen it used in print media to refer to a woman involved with another woman, a woman who is attracted to a tomboi, or a female who acts like a man. With the emergence of the lesbian activist movement in Jakarta in the 1990s, efforts were made to restrict the definition of the term "lesbi" to a woman who loves another woman, which was in accord with the lesbian feminist and international lesbian activist definition of "lesbian," a process that I discuss more fully in chapter 7. In this book I use "lesbi" instead of "lesbian" for two reasons. First, despite the fact that "lesbi" is a cognate of the English term "lesbian," it does not share the same meanings and resonances as its English counterpart. The English word "lesbian" calls up Eurocentric notions of a sexual orientation directed toward other women and an identity that is a core aspect of one's self. Katie King, who argues against using a global term, points out that in global lesbian feminist writing, "lesbian" has come to be defined as "lifelong, stable after 'coming out,' autonomous of heterosexuality, sex-centered, politically feminist, not situational, and exclusive of marriage" (2002, 42). In contrast, the term "lesbi" is used in Padang as an umbrella term to refer to both tombois and their partners, thus signaling a gender-based practice marked by difference.

Second, using the term "lesbi" serves as a reminder of the differences between Indonesian lesbi and Euro-American lesbians, who are themselves quite various. Gopinath rightly warns against a tendency to hold the category of lesbian as the standard against which other forms of female desires are measured. She encourages descriptions that "exceed fixed framings of sexuality" (1998, 119), to which must be added gender. And yet at the same time North American, Australian, and European LGBT terminologies have been appropriated and complexly intertwined with localized meanings (Blackwood and Wieringa 2007). In some cases the terms "lesbian" and "gay" are used by members of national activist organizations, as is the case in Indonesia, because these are internationally known terms that can be used as identifiers across multilingual and ethnically diverse countries. Consequently, the word "lesbian" has a place in the Indonesian lexicon despite its foreign origin.

I use the term "lesbi" as an inclusive term for both tombois and femmes. The term is used and acknowledged among lesbi in Padang, although, as I noted earlier, they prefer to use the gender-marked terms *cowok* (guy) for tombois and *cewek* (girl) for women involved with tombois (see further Blackwood 1998). The lesbi I interviewed usually used the terms *cowok* and *cewek* without any modifier when they were talking amongst themselves or to me. However, if I was not sure whether they were talking about ordinary men and women or tombois and femmes, they would clarify by saying *cewek lesbi*, girls who are lesbi, or *cowok lesbi*, guys who are lesbi.[39]

Because I think it is important to mark the gender differences between masculine and feminine partners in a lesbi relationship, and because this is the practice among Padang lesbi, I use the gendered terms "tomboi" for a masculine partner and "girlfriend" or "femme" for a feminine partner. My choice of the English cognate "tomboi" and the English word "femme," rather than *cowok* and *cewek*, as is commonly used in Padang, stems from a desire to use words that are recognizable to English speakers (and more easily pronounceable). Saskia Wieringa (1999, 2007) prefers to use "butch" for masculine-identified lesbi, which would seem to be the obvious choice when paired with "femme," but I am afraid the term "butch," which is so closely identified in the United States with a type of lesbian, would foreclose readers' ability to imagine tombois as transgender.

My preference for using tomboi as well as lesbi differs from other scholars writing on lesbi in Indonesia, some of whom have chosen to use lesbi only, including Dédé Oetomo and B. J. D. Gayatri, or lesbi primarily, with brief references to tomboi (Boellstorff). Davies uses terms particular to South Sulawesi (hunter, *calalai*). Gayatri notes that tomboi "is indeed generally used, especially in Jakarta" (1994, 8), but avoids using it herself because of the implication of masculine behavior that she feels is inappropriate for lesbi *women*. The term was apparently available in the 1980s in Indonesia but became more commonly used in the 1990s for a masculine lesbi. Although tombois can be included under the label lesbi, a tomboi is not always the same as a lesbi. The term "tomboi," which refers to gender behavior, does not necessarily connote sexuality, while the term "lesbi" does. Boellstorff (2005b) notes that the term "tomboi" first appears in a 1991 Indonesian dictionary, where it is defined as a young girl with boyish behaviors. Thus young girls who act boyishly by wearing pants and being physically active in sports may be called tombois, as one twenty-four-year old tomboi's statement indicates: "All my sisters [and I] are tombois, but I'm the only lesbi."

As should be clear by now, even though tombois may be included under the umbrella category of lesbi, they are not "women" as that construct is normatively defined in Indonesia. I address various aspects of tomboi gender subjectivity throughout the book. At this point let me say that tombois identify as men and therefore do not consider themselves women. They interact with others in everyday life as men; however, they enact feminine behaviors in certain contexts and are addressed by female terms by their relatives and neighbors.

In the conundrum of sex and gender there are no easy solutions for the translation problem that tombois' gender subjectivity poses. No English pronoun adequately conveys the Indonesian usage, in which the third person pronoun (*dia*) is gender neutral. Saskia Wieringa (2007) uses "s/he" and "hir" to refer to Jakarta butches, while other writers have chosen to use the English pronoun that seems to most closely resemble their subjects' gender identity.[40] For instance, Boellstorff (2005b) refers to tombois as "he" based on their statements to him that they see themselves as having men's souls, although he includes them in the category of lesbi *women*. Sinnott (2004) uses "she" for *tom*s in Thailand, which is based on her assessment that *tom*s are transgendered females who do not "pass" as men, and who claim a hybrid masculinity that both appropriates and rejects aspects of Thai masculinity.[41] While not negating these other choices, to my mind "he" or "she" act as glosses that foreclose the complexity of multiple subjectivities that tombois (or *tom*s) enact. These English pronouns also have the potential to reinsert transgressively gendered individuals into binary genders.

My own choices reflect a rethinking over time. In the very first article I wrote on tombois, a reflexive piece about my relationship with Dayan that sought to challenge the distance inscribed in ethnographic fieldwork between "us" and "them" (Blackwood 1995a), I used "she" when referring to Dayan. At that time, given my own self-positioning as a lesbian, I was more comfortable thinking of Dayan as female despite h/er comments that s/he felt like a man. I assumed that because s/he used the word "lesbi" for h/erself, s/he was somewhere between butch and transgender. By the time I wrote "*Tombois*" in 1998, however, I had become convinced that female pronouns were inappropriate for tombois because they consider themselves to be men. Consequently, in that journal article I switched to the gender-neutral third-person pronouns "s/he" and "hir," which were gaining currency in the U.S. transgender movement, as a way to disrupt the binary genders of the English language. I continue to use s/he but have changed hir to h/er in part for consistency in the form of the two words (I use the same pronouns for male-bodied women). More importantly, pronouns such as "ze" and "hir" mentioned by David Valentine (2007) seem to me to signal a "third gender" slot for transgendered individuals that I want to avoid because they have the potential to reinforce the normality of binary genders. By using the pronoun constructions "s/he" and "h/er," I want to leave open the meanings of tomboi (and waria) subjectivity. Note that the pronouns s/he and h/er are different from the construction "she/he," which has a somewhat derogatory connotation in U.S. English of someone who is both woman and man, suggesting a confused blending of genders.[42]

Tombois' girlfriends do not trouble gender pronoun usage because they identify as normative women, making "she" the appropriate third-person pronoun in English. Girlfriends, however, are not simply normative women, but women who are involved with tombois. Lesbi in Padang sometimes distinguish between ordinary women (*cewek biasa*) and women who are lesbi (*lesbi cewek*). Because the women I interviewed generally identify as lesbi only when they are in relationships with tombois, I refer to them as "girlfriends," which is a translation of the Indonesian word *pacar*, a gender-neutral term for girlfriend or boyfriend, used by both tombois and girlfriends. But since "girlfriend" indexes these women only in relation to their partners, I also use the term "femme." As I discuss further in chapter 7, both "butch" and "femme" were part of the Indonesian lesbi vocabulary probably as early as the 1980s and were derived from the U.S. English terms used in lesbian communities historically (see Nestle 1992b; Kennedy and Davis 1993). The terms appeared in print in at least one Indonesian women's magazine sometime in 1981–1983 (Puteri 1984; the original date of publication is not given). By using "femme," I am not suggesting that girlfriends have the same feelings or desires as femmes in the United States, who, according to Joan Nestle (1992a), see themselves differently from normative women. And of course "femme," as used in the United States, is itself not static but has changed over time and incorporates a range of differing subjectivities.[43] Further, as I demonstrate in this book, the Indonesian terms are contested among lesbi as well, either directly or indirectly through localized processes of meaning construction. Thus my translation of Indonesian terms with words such as femme or girlfriend must be taken as provisional glosses rather than fixed signifiers.

I am equally cautious when applying the term "transgender" to tomboi subjectivities because the complexity of their practices makes untenable a simple equation of tomboi with transgender. As a term used in the United States, "transgender" has shifted in meaning since the 1990s from a more general category to a specific identity. In discussing the U.S. transgender movement Riki Wilchins (1997) warns against the likelihood of "transgender" becoming an identity with a capital "T."[44] Ten years later David Valentine's (2007) discussion of transgender studies identifies some of the processes at work in the institutionalization of the term. My own caution, then, stems not from any desire to reinstitute the border wars between categories of butch and FTM (Female to Male), as it has been debated among transgender and lesbian writers in the United States, Canada, and Europe, but to leave open the possible meanings of "transgender."[45] As I discuss in chapter 7, "transgender" is used by lesbian activist groups in Jakarta to distinguish *between* lesbi women and masculine-identified tombois; this usage, however, conflicts with tombois' understanding of themselves as lesbi.

Ultimately I am not interested in seeking new or better ways of imagining transgender, to borrow David Valentine's phrase, but to complicate masculinity and femininity by addressing the possibility of multiple and contingent selves. By situating tombois' masculinity as contingent, I offer a concept of trans-identities and gendered subjectivities that takes into account the social relations and cultural frameworks within which people live and make sense of their self-understandings. In this vein I understand "gender" as a process of meaning assignment to particular bodies that is always in negotiation and always being produced in relation to particular social, political, and historical contexts. Or, as Wilchins (1997) aptly puts it, gender is a fiction that does not exist prior to the political system that created it.

Another term that may avoid the potential fixity of "transgender" in a global world is Halberstam's (1998) concept of female masculinities. Halberstam employs the term as a way to separate masculinity from men, thereby usefully undermining the naturalness of men's performance of masculinity. In creating a new taxonomy, she offers a way to see subjectivities beyond the binaries of Western gender categories. By not fixing a position called "transsexual" or "transgender" or "butch lesbian," she offers a way to think about female masculinities that can incorporate differing versions of masculinities, such as those found in Southeast Asia and elsewhere, although for transmen in the United States who see their bodies as male, the term is less apt (see Noble 2006). In using "masculine females," I make no claims to the coherence of such a category, nor do I place all masculine females within a single identity framework (see also Rubin 1992). I do not mean to suggest that these individuals are "men" or even that they constitute a "third gender," as such assignments tend to overlook the particular histories, practices, and experiences of culturally and globally situated individuals.

I also find it useful to use the term "queer" in this book. The term has become popular in academic and activist circles primarily in the United States and Australia (less so in Europe), where it is used to disrupt identity politics. Because it emerges from and defines a particular Western discourse, it is problematic as a global signifier for groups and movements oriented around sexualities. But at the same time, because it is proliferating in the discourse of U.S. and Australian academics and activists, as well as in international conferences and Web sites, I find it difficult to make an artificial distinction between (Western) discourses

29

that use the term "queer" and (other) discourses on sexualities that might not use the term. In a transnational world there are no borders or neat boundaries that contain particular words. Nor, as Ruth Vanita (2002) points out, are words or meanings ever fixed; all terms are approximations and never fit well across or even within borders. Transnational sexualities are by definition porous sites.

My use of "queer" stems from my understanding of the complexity of sexual discourses and knowledges that circulate and proliferate globally under such signifiers as lesbian, gay, LGBT, same-sex sexuality, bisexuality, and transgender, as well as words in national languages adopted from or in reference to those terms. The use of "queer" may reify or reproduce a Western way of understanding a current profusion of non-normative gender and sexual subjectivities in the United States, but I think the value, and also the problem, in using "queer" lies in its nonspecificity. As I use it, "queer" refers to a range of transgressive possibilities that encompass and surpass "LGBT," thus creating a more inclusive global gay ecumene (see also Rofel 1999), even as it erases specificities across those same spaces.

Although "queer" is not used in Indonesia at this time, it is available to Indonesians via the Internet and at the queer international conferences they attend.[46] Part of the purpose of this book is to examine the processes by which labels are established, appropriated, and claimed. I use "queer," then, when I discuss multiple forms of gender and sexual subjectivities, discourses, or knowledges. Terms such as "queer knowledge" and "queer discourses," in relation to Indonesia in this book, refer to discourses that are inflected by and participate in the globalized discourses of sexualities. I do not use "queer," however, in reference to specific subjectivities in Indonesia but instead use Indonesian words, such as lesbi or tomboi.

This discussion of terminologies is meant to provide some preliminary guidelines to the subjectivities represented in this book. It is my intent to analyze the complexities and reworkings of these subjectivities without limiting them to rigid definitions or expectations about what "modern" selves must be like. Whether tomboi, girlfriend, masculine female, lesbi, transgendered, femme, or woman is used, none of these labels are meant to suggest fixity, consistency, or unidimensionality. Each one reflects part of the complex and contradictory practices in which tombois and their partners engage.

This book offers the experiences and words of tombois and femmes as a way to understand the global connections and localized practices that constitute their subjectivities. Even though tombois and their girlfriends in Padang do not fit the model of Western sexual identity, they are a product of national and transnational processes in much the same way as those in the West. By examining tomboi and femme selves in the context of global queer movements, this book demonstrates the multiplicity of sexual and gender subjectivities in Indonesia and the importance of recognizing and validating these subjectivities in global queer space.

Shifting Discourses of Gender and Desire

The paradox of [The History of Sexuality] *volume 1, however, is that while sexuality inscribes desire in discourse, Foucault's discussion of the discourses and technologies of sex says little about what sorts of desires are produced ... and what people do with them.*

—Ann Stoler

Contemporary Indonesian discourses create an image of innate gender difference in which modern women are oriented to domestic and wifely tasks, while men are encouraged to be heads of households and active leaders in the public domain. These discourses, which offer no state-sanctioned place for tombois or their girlfriends, set the norms for two distinct, socially defined categories of gender, woman and man. In this chapter I set the context for the particular gender subjectivities that tombois and their girlfriends express by examining the shifts in gender discourses historically from precolonial times to the present, focusing on the period of the New Order, the regime of General Suharto, which extended from 1966 to 1998. In this time period I look particularly at the discourses produced in state policies, clerical pronouncements, and media reports, as well as their effects on literature and performing arts. The ensuing chapters present how tombois and girlfriends have responded to, negotiated with, and reconstituted these dominant discourses.

Contemporary Indonesian gender discourses coalesce around a binary in which men and women are believed to have different and contrastive bodies and natures. This gender binary and its associated ideologies have important implications for the production of gender transgression, more broadly, and for the particular ways that tombois and their girlfriends interact, which is, as presented in chapter 1, simply expressed through Robi's expectation that Noni should make the tea. I ask, first, how normative gender is variably framed and institutionalized in Indonesia and West Sumatra and, second, what desires are figured as appropriate to Indonesian women and men. Given the changing political situation in Indonesia in the late 1990s and early 2000s, at the end of the chapter I discuss what, if any, shifts have occurred in the normative constructions of gender and sexuality during this period.

While this chapter documents the pervasiveness of a binary gender discourse in New Order Indonesia, I do not mean to suggest it is seamless and unchanging or rigidly adhered to. As Foucault's analysis of power and knowledge suggests, such discourses inevitably produce their alternatives.[1] I explore the historical shifts in meaning as state discourses replaced, but failed to subsume, older, cosmologically oriented gender discourses that validate movement between genders, either temporarily or permanently. These alternative discourses made gender transgression imaginable, while New Order state discourses produced the forms of transgression taken up by tombois and femmes. By using the phrase "gender transgression," I am referring to a range of cultural practices that *go beyond* normative gender. Although a "transgression" is usually thought of and used to mean a violation or breaking of a law, command, or moral code, it also possesses a more neutral meaning, that of going or passing beyond (a limit, boundary, etc.) (*Oxford English Dictionary* 1989, 2nd ed.). Both meanings are relevant to the discussion here.

My attention in this chapter to the gender and sexual discourses circulating in Indonesia follows Foucault's insight concerning the importance of discursive practices in the construction of sexual subjects. One of the questions prompted by Foucault's work is what sorts of desires are incited or imagined by what discourses. Ann Stoler notes that in Foucault's *History of Sexuality* "desire follows from and is generated out of the law, out of the power-laden discourses of sexuality where it is animated and addressed" (1997, 27). Desire, for Foucault and the many studies that follow his theoretical approach, is closely associated with sexuality and the discourses and technologies of sex. Foucault argued that the deployment of homosexuality and heterosexuality through scientific and medical discourses created the possibility of those subject positions. Stoler pushes for recognition of the wider matrices of this discourse by insisting that "sexual desires were structured by desires and discourses that were never about sex alone" (1997:43). In her work gender, racial, and class hierarchies in the colonial discourse on sexuality are key elements producing particular colonial images of European and native men and women. Stoler demonstrates that desire is not just about sexed bodies; it is also about the particular forms of gender, class, and race that those bodies express. Similarly, as George Chauncey documents in *Gay New York* (1994), forms of male homosexuality and masculinity changed with the increasing emphasis on middle-class masculinity in 1930s United States, substantiating the importance of attending analytically to class and gender issues in relation to sexuality.

To the extent that Foucault focused attention on discourses of sexual desire, the gendering of those desires was overlooked, as Stoler and others have pointed out.[2] In his analysis the categories of "woman" and "man" remained unproblematized, their gendered desires unexamined. Butler's (1990) rethinking of gender successfully inserts gender (back) into sexuality studies. Butler writes, "Gender ought not to be conceived merely as the cultural inscription of meaning on a pre-given sex (a juridical conception); gender must also designate the very apparatus of production whereby the sexes themselves are established" (1990, 11). In line with these Foucaultian critics, I seek in this book to broaden desire's object to include forms of masculinity and femininity and thus to examine how gendered desires are produced in and through particular dominant and alternative discourses and gender regimes.

Foucault and the Deployment of Sexuality

Foucault's *History of Sexuality* delineated a transition from what he called the deployment of alliance, in which social relations were governed by marriage and kinship practices, to a deployment of sexuality, which turned the focus on the use individuals made of their sexuality. In Foucault's history, an architecture of sexuality created through medicine, psychiatry, and criminal justice developed and incited a proliferation of sexualities through, among other things, the cataloguing of sexual disorders. According to Foucault, a discursive explosion in the eighteenth and nineteenth centuries created peripheral sexualities. However, sexuality as it was deployed in this period, like race and class, rested upon powerful assumptions about what it meant to be a woman or a man, assumptions that Foucault only hinted at (see also Dirks, Ely and Ortner 1994). Nevertheless, his theory can be used to explain the creation of "modern" genders, if, as I argue, it is not just sexuality that is produced in this discursive explosion but sexualities defined by the gender of the subject.

Foucault (1978) pointed to the emergence of "population" as a new economic and political problem in the eighteenth century, which at its heart was about sex and sexual conduct. From birth rates to questions of legitimacy and frequency of sexual relations, he asserted, the state became obsessed with the question of sex. Yet looking more closely at Foucault's assertions, for instance in the case of "children's sex," it was not a gender-neutral sexuality that was being trained and disciplined, but an explicitly masculine sexuality, the "sex of the schoolboy" (1978, 28–29). At the same time a different but equally obsessive discourse, whose details Foucault did not attend to except for the "hysterical woman," was deployed to catalog and delimit women's and girls' sexualities.[3] The deployment of sexuality that Foucault theorized was equally a deployment of gender, a deployment that produced the modern dichotomies of man/woman, each with their own forms and perversions of sexuality. Foucault hinted at this dichotomy when he mentioned that sexuality was deployed in "the family cell" through "the husband-wife axis" (1978, 108), but he did not follow through on this analysis.

Foucault's work has been critical to the development of queer studies in the United States, but as Stoler (1995) and others argue, his history of sexuality in Western Europe cannot be as easily extrapolated to other contexts and histories.[4] In reading colonial discourses, Stoler (1995) points out that the deployment of sexuality is recognizable in some colonial contexts but questionable in others. In fact, as I argue more fully elsewhere, in colonial Indonesia the deployment that occurred was one of gender as much as sexuality (see Blackwood 2005a). Operating through the mechanisms of both Christian and Islamic religious conversion and reformation, this deployment produced "women" and "men" who were said to act and dress like the other "sex" in *violation* of their gender.

The deployment of gender in colonial Indonesia resulted in a striking transformation in which certain gendered practices that had been coded and understood as legitimate and powerful ("ritual transvestism") were recoded as illegitimate, destructive, and unnatural ("acting like men").[5] Across Indochina, transvestite ritual practitioners who combined masculine and feminine attributes had been revered in precolonial times. From small inland groups to coastal kingdoms came reports of healers, sacred intermediaries, ritual specialists, or members of a priestly class, who were said to occupy gender-ambiguous positions or switch genders in the performance of their duties. Mark Johnson notes that "various forms of gender-crossing and cross-dressing were associated with sacred personages, ritual healers and … accomplished singers and dancers who performed at various celebrations and rites of passage as embodiments of, and mediatory figures for, ancestral unity and potency" (1997, 12). These individuals did not exist on the margins of society, but were entrusted with the care of royal regalia, in the case of the *bissu* of South Sulawesi, and with the spiritual well-being of the community, in the case of other ritual specialists.[6] By taking on attributes or dress associated with the other gender, ritual practitioners embodied a gendered cosmology that enabled them to transcend or transgress human difference to achieve a sacred oneness or unity of opposites. They moved beyond the realm of ordinary folk, beyond the limits of behavior and practice ascribed to male and female bodies in those cultural contexts, to become either temporarily or consistently transgressively gendered.

Due to the spread of Christianity and Islam across this region, however, these practitioners slowly disappeared as Islamicist and Christian scholars and teachers declared that "man" and "woman" were objects of God's creation and were therefore bound to the form that God gave them.[7] During this period the mythologies of sacred gender were replaced by a mythology of innate gender divested of its magical power and reduced to human form. Islamic discourse articulated a strikingly different division between men and women than was given in the old cosmologies. The sacred gender binary of the older religions, in which even the universe and the gods embodied dual genders, was reconfigured within Islamic beliefs in a way that made gender a fixed, unchangeable, and god-given attribute of humans. Confined to limited, mortal, and eternally sex-dichotomized bodies, men and women would no longer be able to legitimately bridge masculine and feminine elements. Under this new ideological regime, individuals could understand themselves only as either women or men—in line with or in transgression of their "sex." Those who exceeded the normative boundaries of this god-given nature were said to "act like" the other sex, rather than express a fusion of sacred genders. This new view of gender produced alternative gender subject positions, such as *calabai* and *calalai* in South Sulawesi, *bante* in Central Sulawesi, *banci* in Java, and *bujang gadis* in West Sumatra.[8]

In South Sulawesi in 1948 an anthropologist observed one female "who did not feel at home with her own sex. She wore her hair like a woman, but her sarong like a man" (Chabot 1960, 153). This person worked as a farmer and took produce to market, which Chabot attests were men's work. H/er kin apparently accepted these transgressions without problem. From the Wana of Central Sulawesi during the twentieth century, Atkinson (1990) provides an anecdotal account of three females who "became" men and married. One female, who was reported to dress and work like a man and who had married a woman, preferred to be called "uncle" and would get mad if someone called h/er "aunt" (Atkinson 1990, 90). Atkinson states that the term *bante* was used for both males and females. *Bante* is a close cognate of *banci*, suggesting that the category *banci* circulated throughout island Southeast Asia in the twentieth century.

In West Sumatra in 1939 a local paper published an account of two women who desired to be married. The two, one a widow of eight years and the other a young, unmarried woman (*gadis*), asked the village headman to marry them.[9] According to the report, the headman and villagers all seemed astounded by this request. The young woman's parents had not agreed to the marriage, pointing out that she had always acted like a woman. When the couple next appeared before the headman, the young woman had cut her hair short and stated that she had had relations with her partner as "husband and wife" (Alhamidy 1951). In this story the villagers "see" the couple as two women and are therefore in great confusion as to why they should make such a request. In order to make her case, the young woman cuts her hair and speaks of having heterosexual relations with her partner, thus making sense of her request within the dominant gender binary of masculine-feminine, husband-wife. Unfortunately, the final response to their request is not reported. In these cases, gender transgression is made intelligible, and in some instances acceptable, by "acting like" the other sex/gender, thus reflecting an ideological discourse about proper gender behavior that encapsulates "men" and "women" within ontologically prescribed domains.[10]

This historical transformation differs from the one Foucault outlined for Europe. It points to processes at work in Southeast Asia in which a deployment of gender produces different forms of gender transgression in relation to dominant religious, cultural, and social discourses of particular historical eras. Although the prevalence of these discourses from colonial to postcolonial Indonesia is less well documented, they remain a potent ideology that, in the process of nation-making and nation-building in Indonesia, are reworked into notions of fixed and binary gender to fit "modern" state purposes.[11] This new mythological formulation does not completely replace the older myths, however, which continue to provide powerful stories of transgressive behavior.

Normative Indonesian Discourses in the New Order

Early in my research I asked participants to describe what is expected of Minangkabau women. Reflecting the opinions of girlfriends, Jeni said, "I learned from my grandmother that a Minangkabau woman must be polite, must cover her *aurat* [Islamic term referring to parts of the body that must be covered], and know how to cook because she will eventually marry and have her own house." Nila, another girlfriend, noted that a Minangkabau woman works in the kitchen and should stay mostly in the house and not go out. Tombois' views of womanhood were very similar. Arief declared, "Minang women must be clever at everything, including cooking." Danny, another tomboi, used a crude but witty expression to sum up women's duties, saying, "It is the kitchen (*dapur*) and the bed (*kasur*)," referring to women's duties to cook and meet their husbands' sexual needs.

If subject positions are offered by particular discourses, then one tactic to understand the positions taken by tombois and femmes in Padang is to examine the current discourses circulating in the context of their everyday lives. As modern Indonesian subjects, tombois and their girlfriends are situated within the terms of a dominant gender discourse deployed by the state, by Islamic clerics, and by regional ethnic leaders. By dominant gender discourses I am referring to the discourses that are produced by the state through its education agenda, development policies, and civic programs and through Islamic clerics and their national organizations. These discourses are not identical, but they are surprisingly consistent in their ideological constructions of women and men. I document below the dominant ideology of the New Order period and the transition to a more rigid gender hierarchy that it produced. Then later in this chapter I discuss representations of lesbi in print and visual media, where stories of lesbi couples are given various interpretations, both positive and negative, that provide possibilities for imagining other ways of being.

The Indonesian state was formed in 1945 from a Dutch-created territory that contains some 300 ethnic groups and over 13,000 islands, 6,000 of which are inhabited. The early years of the new state, which was centered physically and ideologically on the island of Java, saw a period of liberal democracy under Sukarno replaced by a more restrictive and authoritarian Guided Democracy (Blackburn 2004). With Suharto's rise to power and the establishment of the New Order government in 1965–1966, the Indonesian state cut off all grassroots political movements and effectively monopolized all political power within the state bureaucracy. At the same time that it began moving away from Sukarno's early accommodation of differing political views, the state began consistently to emphasize development based upon integration into the world capitalist economy. Further, the rulers of the new state built a substantial ideological structure to legitimate their considerable power and authority. The primary means of indoctrination was the Pancasila, the five guiding principles of the Indonesian state, which were developed under Sukarno's leadership (Morfit 1986).[12] All state organizations acknowledged these principles as their sole foundation, a requirement that was expanded in the 1980s to include all social and political organizations (Hefner 1997).

Beginning in 1968, the New Order government established five-year plans to guide the state's economic efforts and to hasten Indonesia's progress as a "developing nation." The state formulated an ideology of modernization aimed at creating an Indonesian citizen in step with the "modern" world. This ideology was not divorced from broader historical and transnational discourses, as both the Netherlands and other Western nations were central in the formation of Indonesian state laws and policies (see Blackwood 1995b; Dwyer 2000). Their "transnational hegemonic 'borrowings' " underscore Grewal and Kaplan's point that "patriarchies collaborate and borrow from each other in order to reinforce specific practices that are oppressive to women" (1994, 24). The state's reliance on Western ways of framing policy led to their embrace of economic rationalism and development programs in line with the agendas of international organizations such as the World Bank.

If for Foucault the deployment of sexuality constituted the modus operandi of sexual knowledge in the Enlightenment West, the primary vehicle for conveying normalizing messages of sexuality in Indonesia during the New Order period, as in the earlier colonial period, was through the deployment of gender. New Order discourses were not directed at sexuality per se but at the creation of properly gendered, reproductive citizens situated within heterosexual nuclear families (see also Blackwood 1995b). The discourses of the New Order period are critical to my analysis in this book because the lesbi I interviewed grew up within the milieu of its educational and development policies. Among my primary interviewees, all except one were born in a twelve-year span between 1969 and 1981 and attended school from the mid-1970s to the mid-1990s.[13] This time period of Suharto's New Order saw the consolidation, through state policies and educational programs, of a rigid gender binary that situated women in the home and men as household heads and workers.

The ideological discourse on "gender" in Indonesia was and is represented linguistically, at least in part, as a sex/gender system, to use Rubin's (1975) phrase, by which she refers to the interconnections between sexed bodies and gender attributes. In the U.S. popular science construction of the terms, "sex" refers to the physical genitalia of males and females and "gender" to the social attributes of men and women. In Indonesian the two are not distinguished linguistically but operate in a single discursive framework in which gender is part of the "nature" of sexed bodies (see also Bennett 2005). One way in which this is evidenced can be found in the Indonesian words for "man" and "woman," which are the same words for "male" and "female." "*Perempuan*" means both female and woman, "*laki-laki*" means both male and man; "*kelaki-lakian*," for example, which has the root "laki," is defined as manliness, mannish. In using these terms, Indonesians express a concordant relationship between bodies and behaviors. When people speak of *kodrat perempuan* or *kodrat laki-laki*, they are referring to the nature or character (*kodrat*) of women and men (Echols and Shadily 1989). *Kodrat perempuan*, then, refers to the intrinsic or essential character of a person with female sexual organs. This relationship means that in the dominant Indonesian sex/gender system, one's gender attributes are seen as naturally and indivisibly part of one's sex. In fact, "gender" was not part of the Indonesian language before the 1990s.

When I use the term "sex/gender," I am referring specifically to the dominant Indonesian construction of an intertwined "sex/gender" system. For my own analysis I differentiate between sexed bodies and gender because, as tombois demonstrate, one's gender can be separate from the sex of one's body.[14] I am not suggesting, however, that any essential meanings exist for sex or gender. My point is that "sex" and "gender" are social constructs that need to be analytically distinguished because, as cultural artifacts, they are assigned different and unequal meanings that have consequences for those inhabiting particular bodies.

The "Nature" of Men and Women

Although the Indonesian state claimed to have emancipated women, giving them greater access to education and some occupations, under Suharto's New Order the state enshrined mother and wife as women's primary role and duty. After the inception of the New Order in 1965, the Indonesian state avidly pursued a policy promoting nuclear families and motherhood. Development policies were oriented to the modern nuclear family ubiquitous in Western economic planning.[15] Using this model, the state outlined separate roles for men and women as husbands and wives, and these then became the basis for a modern Indonesian family limited to one or two children (Sullivan 1994). The new Indonesian woman in this configuration became a wife (*isteri*), who was defined primarily "in terms of her commitment to follow her husband's lead and limit her reproduction capacity to the ideal older son-younger daughter" (Sullivan 1994, 133). State pronouncements articulated a vision of women's nature (*kodrat*) that emphasized women's maternal role and responsibility for their children's health, care, and education. State family-planning programs engaged in the construction of normative families through messages advocating birth control and two-child families (Dwyer 2000). These messages were directed at married individuals, particularly women.[16] State and religious education broadcast this new woman through a variety of media.

The Indonesian state undertook to develop and expand a state-run school system that by the 1970s had elementary schools in villages throughout the archipelago. Junior and senior high schools were less numerous, usually located in towns and cities, so that rural students had to travel and in some cases move to town to attend school. In line with state development goals, primary education was envisioned as a means to create good Indonesian citizens (Parker 1997). In pursuit of this vision the state imposed a national curriculum, using textbooks assigned by state authorities that were designed to emphasize gender difference (Leigh 1994). In a number of subtle and not-so-subtle ways, school texts portrayed men in positions of authority and women in subordinate positions. Martha Logsdon notes that in school texts developed in the late 1970s the word "mother" (*ibu*) was never capitalized but the word "father" (*Bapak*) always was; in second grade texts mother is described as "staying at home," while father "goes to the office" (1985, 248). The misrecognition of women's productive activities, Logsdon (1985) argues, indicates that Indonesian children were being taught that women are reproducers and a source of domestic labor, while fathers are economic providers for the family. Similarly, in her study of elementary education in Bali, Lynette Parker found that teachers' behavior, school curricula, and routines enforced the ideals that "girls have responsibility for virtue, moral education and service, principally within the family, and boys are responsible for economic development" (1997, 502). In effect the national school system was used to inculcate state notions of two distinct and separate sexes, each with their appropriate gender attributes.

My own observations of state-sponsored gender differentiation in West Sumatra accord with Parker's and Logsdon's findings. Preschool and school-age children were mute witnesses to the New Order's architecture and embodiment of sex/gender. Students wore uniforms according to their sex; boys wore shorts or pants, girls wore skirts. These differently marked school uniforms were visible not only in school but in public spaces, as throngs of students walked to and from school every morning and afternoon. The vast civil service of Indonesia, which included teachers, state officers, and health-clinic workers, was also marked according to gender. Civil officials were omnipresent in their gender-differentiated grey uniforms, men in shirts and pants and women in blouses and skirts, thus silently but profusely bespeaking the normality of difference.

The state also employed historical figures as models of its new gender code, thereby linking its practices to what it considered a traditional past. Kartini, an aristocratic Javanese woman born in the late 1800s, is celebrated annually in Indonesia on Kartini Day (Hari Ibu Kartini), a state-sponsored holiday that commemorates her as emblematic mother of the nation. Kartini's published letters to a Dutch friend in the early years of the twentieth century, however, revealed a woman deeply unhappy with her predestined lot in life as wife and mother (Tiwon 1996). Married against her wishes to an older man with three wives, she died shortly after the birth of her first child. Yet during and since the New Order, "Mother" Kartini has been presented as the model of true motherhood. School-age girls participate in a variety of contests that are "generally focused on activities normally done by women, such as cooking, arranging flowers, and dress making" (Pikiran Rakyat 2002). If Kartini is admired by some for her struggles for women's rights, her celebration reminds students only of women's duties as wives and mothers. In the state version of Kartini's story, woman and mother become synonymous, an image that creates "a new kind of prison for women" (Tiwon 1996, 54). By focusing on her (very brief) role as mother, this refiguring of Kartini "stresses the nurturing, self-sacrificing qualities of the woman, the being-for-others rather than the being-as-self" (Tiwon 1996, 55).[17] The emphasis on hyperfemininity and motherhood for women expressed in Kartini Day reinforces restrictive gender boundaries. Through its various policies and programs the Indonesian state continues to convey the message that it is women's nature and national duty to marry heterosexually, to become mothers, and to nurture others first.

Although women in the New Order were generally represented as "housewives" first in Indonesia, Sen (1998) argues that a new "working woman" or career woman (*wanita karier*) replaced the housewife in the 1990s as the paradigmatic female subject. The career woman is a professional woman exemplified by affluent middle-class women who work in white collar jobs as teachers, civil servants, managers, and administrators (see also Brenner 1998, 1999). According to Sen (1998), the Indonesian state now promotes the professional woman as a new development emblematic of Indonesia's modernity. The great majority of these women are civil servants and so directly controlled by state mandates for employees. Consequently, like her housewife sister, this new career woman is bound by notions of proper femininity; she wears to work the markers of her gender in her clothes, makeup, and demeanor. She must be careful to maintain proper feminine deportment so as not to become subject to accusations of sexual impropriety. If she is married, expectations about her duties to care for her household, husband, and children remain the same despite her career interests.

During the New Order, the deployment of gender entailed a consistent and comprehensive discourse about the proper positions of women and men in the Indonesian state. It stabilized a limited heterosexuality for women, which was (and is) properly and permissibly expressed only within marriage and under the control of a husband. This discourse operated primarily outside of any juridico-legal framework through an extensive network of policies, programs, and institutions that encouraged and enforced normative gender meanings. While it would be incorrect to assume that this discourse was everywhere received and replayed in the same manner, or that this was the only message available, its dominance created a broadly accepted model of gender in which women and men were encouraged and in some cases required to think of themselves as distinct and unequal types of people with different attributes, capabilities, and sexual privileges.

Islamicist Interpretations of Women's Duties

For individuals living in West Sumatra gender messages are as ubiquitous as daily prayers, which require dress distinctions and gender segregation in prayer and in the public spaces of mosques. Five times a day women prepare to pray by donning bulky white shawls that cover their heads and bodies to the waist, leaving only their faces visible, while men put small black caps on their heads to kneel and pray in their ordinary clothes. These visible religious practices attest to gender difference. Tombois' descriptions of marriage and domestic tasks reflect these Islamic practices. Andri said, "A woman must pray, wear the *jilbab* and cover her *aurat*." Dedi, a tomboi, said that according to Islam a woman is supposed to marry and be a housewife; in addition she must ask her husband's permission to go out. Jon, the one tomboi who had married (and divorced) a man, stated, "According to the Qur'an, one must have a husband (*harus punya suami*)." Danny mentioned that women's service to their husbands is a prescription of Islam. Whether based on Minangkabau *adat* or Islam, their views of womanhood and marriage are closely aligned in positioning women solely as wives and mothers.

Many threads of Islam exist in Indonesia, each with its own particular school of thought. In addition Islamicist discourses arise from a number of sources in Indonesia, including Islamic political parties; national Islamic organizations, such as Nahdlatul Ulama (NU) and Muhammadiyah; Islamic educational institutions, including *pesantren* (private Islamic boarding schools) and the collegiate level State Institute of Islamic Studies; the religious courts; state-sanctioned religious bodies, such as the Council of Indonesian Religious Scholars (Majelis Ulama Indonesia, MUI), and the Ministry of Religion (Hooker and Lindsey 2003). The diversity of these sources suggests that there is no one "Islamic" view of women in Indonesia. However, certain positions are quite generally agreed on; debates primarily concern technicalities of particular interpretations and their application to everyday life.

Most of the scholarly attention on Islam in Indonesia has been directed at political Islam, with little or no attention being paid to gender or women's issues.[18] Yet according to Pieternella van Doorn-Harder (2006), women in the two largest Islamic organizations in Indonesia, NU and Muhammadiyah, have been quietly examining women's issues for decades by rereading Islamic texts.[19] The 1990s and the post-Suharto era have seen increased discussion of these issues within Islamic women's groups. Efforts by the women of NU in the 1990s to disseminate gender-sensitive interpretations of Islamic teachings resulted in the publication of *Islam and the Advancement of Women* (Munir et al. 1994), a collection of writings by nationally known men leaders of Islamic organizations.

Without ignoring all the complexities of Islamicist discourse, and setting aside for the moment some of the reinterpretations by Islamic women activists (see van Doorn-Harder 2006), I examine below the writings found in *Islam and the Advancement of Women*, as well as certain fatwa (legal opinions on a point of law based on the classical texts of Islam), to gain clarity on the underlying Islamicist principles concerning gender (and their possible interpretations).

As with state discourses, Islamicist doctrine in Indonesia draws strict boundaries between men and women. These discourses represent men and women in dichotomous terms to create a knowledge of gender difference. As an example of this discourse, *Islam and the Advancement of Women* is both an apology for Islamic "tradition" and an effort to elaborate on women's rights within Islam. The interpretations presented in the text are based on an analysis of the Qur'an, *hadith* (the words and actions of the Prophet as written down by his followers), and *fiqh* (Islamic jurisprudence). The writers generally agree with the modernist idea of men's and women's equality, but they find incontrovertible the "fact" that men and women by nature are different. This difference makes women's realm the family and household, whereas men's realm is the nation and religious community (Wahid 1994, Hefner 2000). Their position can be summarized as follows: Men's and women's bodies are different. Men have more strength, and women have the ability to bear children. Therefore each sex is created to fulfill particular functions—men to protect and provide for women, women to raise and educate children. The difference that gender embodies was summed up by K.H. Ali Yafie, chair of the Council of Indonesian Religious Scholars (MUI), "However advanced women are, none of them wears the moustache" (1994, 99).

Given this basic difference, the writers generally agree that men and women have different dispositions and different social and cultural obligations and responsibilities. Men and women each have their own *kodrat* (nature), determined by Allah, as noted in the following: "Women have a different nature, character and tendencies from men" (Shihab 1994, 52); and, "Women need love, protection and people who can support them and make them able to fulfill their natural function" (Wahid 1994, 43). Therefore, as husbands and wives, men's and women's positions are complementary, not the same. "Islam views both men and women as mutuality, biologically and socioculturally in need of each other" (Umar 1994, 72). Nasaruddin Umar and Yafie argue that this situation puts women in a favorable position because they are always taken care of by men; if unmarried, they have their father's support; if married, their husband's. Men's strength and resilience are given as the reason men should be the protectors and leaders of women. Citing the *fiqh* standard that a male witness is equal to two female witnesses, Quraish Shihab works out the following: "Because women are required to give more attention to the family and the child, it is very natural if their testimony/ memory on this is not comparable to men's" (1994, 55). Through such statements the writers maintain the naturalness of differences between men and women.

At the same time the writers envision some progress in women's rights beyond the domestic arena. According to Umar, women have the right to be active in politics, to choose a career, and to attain an education under certain conditions. The matter of careers, however, is a contentious issue among the various writers. Yafie states that further study is needed before any blanket permission can be given for women to work. Masdar Mas'udi (1994) argues that it is men's obligation to provide for their families, therefore women's work should be voluntary or only if the family needs the additional income. Shihab mentions that Islam does not encourage women to work outside the home, but concludes that "women have the right to work as long as they need it" (1994, 60). These writers reason that necessity is the only acceptable reason for women to work, a position that runs counter to the development of *wanita karier* in Indonesia. In contrast to these others, Abdurrahman Wahid points out that it is common for women to work in Indonesia, particularly selling in the market, where men and women can safely intermingle.[20] He warns, however, that intermingling without adequate protection for women could lead to "negative excesses" that might increase the incidence of adultery and threaten the institution of the family (1994, 38). For Wahid, women's right to work must be weighed against its potential to disrupt families.

This text offers a glimpse of Islamicist scholars struggling to situate Muslim women within the contemporary state while declaring that women are mothers and wives first. Although these views are drawn from one text, they reflect a view of gender difference that is widespread in Indonesia. A similar stance taken by Aisyiyah, the women's branch of the reformist Muhammadiyah Muslim organization, proclaimed in 1999 that a woman can be a leader "as long as she does not ignore her main duty 'as housewife'" (van Doorn-Harder 2006, 14). An Islamicist message of gender difference varies in intensity from region to region, but its several strands support a view of women as creatures whose innate being and purpose is to bear children; men are seen as more rational beings whose duty is to protect and care for women. Although the Islamic scholars discussed above are willing to support women's rights to education and careers, these rights are conditioned on the fulfillment of women's duties as mothers and wives. The failure to fulfill one's duty as a woman or man is seen as contrary to one's god-given nature.

While I have been careful to distinguish between state and Islamicist gender discourses, these discourses are by no means insulated from each other. It is not always possible to make unambiguous distinctions, given the intersections of state bureaucracy with religion in institutions such as the Ministry of Religion and the religious court system, or the state-sanctioned Council of Indonesian Religious Scholars (see further Hooker and Lindsey 2003). While the relations between the state and Islamic political parties and organizations are not without contention, their views on gender difference are quite consistent. In many ways these discourses work together to produce a knowledge of gender and sexuality that strictly differentiates women and men.

Popular Representations of Women

Television and magazines carry messages of the pretty, domestic, submissive housewife to all corners of the archipelago. Although foreign films and popular Indonesian magazines sometimes offer contradictory messages that highlight female desire and sex outside of marriage, in Indonesian media "ideals of domesticity, dependence on men, and passivity in heterosexual relationships are relentlessly promoted" (Bennett 2005, 38; see also Brenner 1999). The Sinetron television series, which was originally produced by the state-owned television system TVRI, stereotyped women characters as "dependent, irrational, emotional, and obedient" and "incapable of solving their own problems" (Aripurnami 1996, 253–254). All the Sinetron series revolved around families in which women occupied primarily domestic roles. According to Sita Aripurnami, "The meaning is plain: women must devote most of their energy and activity to cooking, cleaning, and taking care of children, even if they already have other responsibilities outside the home. ... [T]hey must never forget their essential nature as homemakers" (1996, 252). The prominence of this message of women's dependency and domesticity assured that viewers were well aware of the state's expectations of its women citizens.

The film industry in Indonesia, particularly during the New Order years, cooperated with the state agenda in its representations of men and women. The state Board of Film Censorship encouraged filmmakers to show "how Indonesian people put unity, unification, as well as the well-being of the nation and the state above personal and group interests" and discouraged them from making films "in conflict with policies of the government" (Sen 1994, 70). Krishna Sen's extensive research on Indonesian cinema found that while censorship regulations did not stipulate how men and women were to be portrayed, other than banning overtly sexual scenes, films reinforced mainstream gender constructions. Women had very few roles in films except in the genres of romance and teen films. These films typically portrayed families with a working husband and a stay-at-home wife. The ideal woman was portrayed as long-suffering and silent, her sexuality totally contained within her marriage (Sen 1994). Disorderly and rebellious women, such as prostitutes, independent women, and boyish girls, although visible in these films, were reformed and brought back into the ordered spaces of family and marriage by the end of these movies (Sen 1994). In one film about a young girl who acts like a boy, the girl is taught that such behavior is unnatural and so changes her ways. In Indonesian films socially productive roles belong to men and socially reproductive roles to women, thus ensuring that the gender binary remains intact (Sen 1994).

The ideal woman represented in Indonesian films and television series was not, however, the only popular image of women available in Indonesia during and after the New Order.[21] As noted above, other types of women were visible but marked as disreputable. In performance arts, however, a wider variety of women characters were and are portrayed, including characters in Javanese *wayang* (shadow puppet plays) and other theatrical arts. Javanese *wayang*, which is based on the ancient Indian epics, the *Mahabharata* and the *Ramayana*, are populated with both men and women characters who can change their sex.[22] Although *wayang* stories contain few prominent women figures, two well-known women characters are Srikandi and Sumbadra, wives of Arjuna. Srikandi is brave, strong-willed, heroic, and active, while Sumbadra is often portrayed as her opposite, "elegant, gentle, reserved, utterly loyal and obedient to her husband" (Pausacker 1991, 271). Srikandi is a more active character, who masters archery and military skills and becomes a female warrior. Sumbadra, in contrast to Srikandi, is frequently abducted by amorous suitors and has to be rescued by Arjuna.

In some *wayang* stories both Srikandi and Sumbadra change their sex; with the aid of the gods they transform into men and engage in battle (Pausacker 1991). Although as women, both Srikandi and Sumbadra are said to be erotically attracted to and in love with Arjuna, when they are men, "they want to abduct women" (Pausacker 1991, 287). In one story Srikandi changes her sex and becomes a man called Kandihawa in order to marry a woman named Dewi Durniti (Saskia Wieringa 2000; also Gayatri 1993). A shaman helps Kandihawa attain manhood by exchanging genitals with him, so that s/he and Dewi Durniti are able to have a child (Pausacker 1991).

These *wayang* performances are cultural legacies that constitute important models for transgressive female behavior. According to Saskia Wieringa, many of the older butch women she interviewed in Jakarta told her proudly that "they were called Little Srikandhi in their youth" (2007, 79). Gender-switching mythological figures reflect a worldview in which the two sexes have distinct physical and behavioral characteristics, but spiritually potent beings can nevertheless transgress these sex/gender boundaries to achieve supernatural tasks and fulfill erotic desires. This transgression is consistent with a sex/gender binary in which desire is always heterosexual, that is, between a man and a woman. One is able to desire and have sex only with the other sex, thus necessitating a gender switch, yet such stories offer the possibility of becoming a different sex/gender.

During the New Order the Indonesian state's support for the development of regional art institutes had serious implications for the gendered practices expressed in performance arts (Fraser 2007). Billed as a way to promote ethnic artistic expression and tourism, state sponsorship and the additional support of Islamic leaders led to the promotion of particular artistic forms that depended in part on the appropriateness of gender portrayed in the performances. In particular, several forms of theater and dance that crossed gender boundaries were discouraged. As late as the 1960s, gender play, in which male and sometimes female performers played the role of the other sex, was a well-known feature of several forms of Indonesian theater, including Javanese *ludruk* theater (Peacock 1968; Anderson 1990). James Peacock notes that many of the men who played transvestite roles had men admirers and lovers. His classic work on the topic documents a shift in *ludruk* performance style in reaction to state intervention as well as Muslim complaints that "it was a sin for male and female elements to be mixed in public performances" (1968, 19). By the late 1980s the transvestite role in theater performances was shrinking in response to state pressures (Fraser 1998). In Bali the dance-drama form *arja*, which embraces gender fluidity through women's performance of both masculine (coarse) and feminine (refined) styles, lost its popularity, as the state increasingly controlled art education (Kellar 2004). The repressive gender ideology of the New Order era meant that non-normative gender expression in theatrical performances was increasingly stigmatized (Kellar 2004).

Representations of Lesbi in the Media

While state and Islamic discourses in the New Order emphasized gender normativity and women's domesticity, Indonesian popular media since at least the early 1980s have been the primary source of information on non-normative sexualities for the general population and lesbi and gay individuals (Gayatri 1993). As Foucault (1978) pointed out, the deployment of sexual knowledge in the modern era operates through a multiplicity of mechanisms to create a knowledge of sex. Me-

FIGURE 2.1. Jossie and Bonnie at home: The first female couple in Indonesia to call themselves husband and wife. Originally published in *Tempo* in 1981, adapted by Helen Pausacker for publication in *Gays in Indonesia.*

dia attention to an increasingly international gay and lesbian movement brought into common use the terms "lesbi" and "tomboi" and made visible new lesbi and gay subjectivities.

Some of the very earliest stories about lesbi published in Indonesian print media in 1981 described the efforts of two couples to marry. Aty and Nona, who ran away together, were the first case to grab headlines. One was an underage student and the other a well-known singer in Jakarta. Parents of the young woman claimed their daughter had been kidnapped. Only a week later news of another lesbi couple's wedding appeared in the same weekly magazine (Gayatri 1993; Boellstorff 2005b).[23] The news report described the couple, Jossie and Bonnie, as follows: "Jossie, 25 years old, looked handsome in a blueish [sic] white suit with a flowery red tie, and Bonnie, 22 years old, looked prettier than ever in her long red gown" (*Tempo* 1984b, 5). Besides describing them in gendered terms, the report claimed that "their manner as husband and wife seemed excessive." The report mentioned Jossie's feelings of being more male than female, h/er prowess at fighting, h/er 75 percent male hormones (confirmed by an "expert"), and h/er nickname "*banci*," which is the derogatory term usually associated with transgender males. Jossie's description was counterposed with Bonnie's, who was said to be "quite normal" before she met Jossie, meaning that she was feminine and attracted to men. Because the couple wanted to be legally married, Jossie was said to have considered "a sex-change operation," but Bonnie rejected it. In this very early story a new lesbi sexuality is represented in gendered terms as a husband-and-wife couple, one of whom is "normal" and one who desires to be a man physically. This story aligns Jossie's desires for Bonnie with h/er feelings of being a man, positioning lesbi within a gender binary of man and woman and leaving open the possibility of transsexuality as a way to understand Jossie's desires.

Newspaper columnists in some of the mainstream newspapers have played an important role in making visible non-normative sexualities. Some have offered helpful information to reader queries about homosexuality, but other columnists discourage expressions of same-sex sexuality, relying on outdated Western psychological theories of sexual development as well as religious precepts about marriage. In some cases, such as the following, they reject lesbianism as a possibility and encourage women to be "normal," that is, heterosexual and married. In one column a high school teacher in West Java, who had become suicidal because of numerous failed relationships with other women, told her story: "Then I wrote to Mrs. Leila Budiman (a psychologist … in a respectable [nationwide] newspaper based in Jakarta). Long time no reply. I kept writing and writing because I was so desperate, and she wrote about my case eventually [1990], after about a year! Yet, she wrote that I have to return to God and pray a lot" (Gayatri 1993, 23).

In another advice column written by Leila Budiman (2004), the same exhortation to normality appears. In this column a married woman confessed that she could love only women and had never really had any desire for her husband. Despite opportunities to leave her husband for a woman lover, however, she had refused because she felt responsible to her children. She complained that she now feels very lonely and sad because she has no love in her life. The columnist advised her to stay in her marriage, encouraging her to take up useful activities and to appreciate her good husband more. "Then your problems that in the beginning seemed as big as an elephant will become as small as an ant," Budiman declares. Her response clearly conveys the belief that "normality" through marriage is the only solution regardless of one's desires.

A 2001 article that appeared in the magazine *Indonesian Woman* offers a more complex reading of same-sex desires. The story concerns a "same-sex couple" (*pasangan sesama jenis*), working as live-in maids in Hong Kong, who threatened to kill themselves if they were not allowed to marry (*Wanita Indonesia* 2001). The photos that accompany the story show two women, Yani, who is rather handsome and androgynous-looking, and Ike, a very feminine-looking woman. In their early twenties the two women had met and fallen in love in Hong Kong. To avoid being forced into marriage with men, they made a pact that they would commit suicide if their families did not allow their marriage. According to the article, both families agreed to the marriage because the couple was sending considerable sums of money home every month and the families feared they would lose that income if they refused to allow their daughters to marry. In order to get official permission Yani's father told officials that Yani was a man. When the deception was discovered, the authorities cancelled the wedding. Both families were said to be very disappointed, but happy that the couple did not follow through on their threats to commit suicide. In this story the two are described as women, and no attempt is made to suggest that one is more male, although the photos hint at a gender difference between the two. The family does attempt to pass Yani off as a man to fool the officials, but nothing is said about Yani's own self-positioning. In this case the writer seems to be sympathetic to the women's love for each other and their desires to marry.

These and other media stories serve as unintended but important resources for an emerging understanding of being lesbi in Indonesia. A lesbi in Yogyakarta, Java, recalled reading an article about gay and lesbi in *Intisari*, a monthly magazine, when she was about ten years old [1987], which "helped her to understand her feelings" (Webster 2005, 38). Most of the lesbi I interviewed in West Sumatra in 2001 and 2004 recalled finding out about lesbi from the magazines they

FIGURE 2.2. Yani and Ike: "Lesbian couple threatens suicide if they aren't allowed to marry." *Wanita Indonesia* 2001.

read or found lying about the house, including *Kartini* and *Sarinah*, two women's magazines. One woman told me she had read many true stories (*kisah nyata*) about lesbi in magazines and newspapers. These stories were about their lives, problems, and quarrels, including one story about a lesbi who killed her lover. Similarly, several Jakartan gay men reported that they discovered a gay identity through reading magazine articles (Howard 1996).[24]

Although stories of Indonesian lesbi, gay, and waria were carried in print media and began to appear on television in the 1990s, media attention to the topic did not normalize these sexualities. A lesbian activist in Jakarta whom I interviewed in 2001 complained, "All those stories in the newspapers are biased. They all treat homosexuality as a crime or mental illness or disease." Gayatri, who tracked media representations of gay and lesbi during the 1980s and early 1990s, notes the same thing: "The print media portrayals of lesbianism never give positive images of sexuality. They show lesbian life as close to ... criminal activities, prostitution, ... drugs, free sex (promiscuity), [and] deviance" (1993, 10).[25] Media accounts of suicidal or murderous lesbians, women "acting like men," and "transvestite" men (waria) enforced the notion that such individuals were sick (*sakit*). The word *sakit* is, in fact, a commonly used term to refer to a gay or lesbi individual, and is used by gays and lesbi themselves. It refers less to their mental health than to the idea that something is "wrong" with their gender (see also Howard 1996).

Media representations that portray homosexuals as disturbed, sick or abnormal create a popular attitude of distaste and even repugnance toward same-sex sexuality and gender transgression. A Minangkabau woman who had grown up in Jakarta confessed that before she met her tomboi lover, everything she had heard about lesbi had made her dislike and fear them. At the same time that negative and sensationalizing coverage works to stabilize normative heterosexuality, media representations of same-sex couples and lesbi weddings have the effect of broadening awareness about alternative sexualities and genders, offering other ways of being that exceed the strictly normative.

Ethnic Collaborations: Minangkabau Folktales and Cross-Dressing Women

The question remains how discourses circulating in West Sumatra reflect or subvert state and Islamicist gender discourses. State policies and programs are pervasive in people's lives in West Sumatra, through, for example, education, agricultural extension programs, health clinics, village assistance programs, and regional art forms, a not inconsiderable presence that has become entwined in individual and community decision-making and *adat* practices. Both tombois' and girlfriends' conceptions of gender tends to mirror the dominant ideology represented by state and Islamicist leaders. When I asked tombois and their girlfriends what men and women are like, their responses reflect normative constructions of masculinity and femininity. I was told that women are feminine, gentle, loving, and motherly, while men are masculine, rough, and daring. Further, women are said to be easy-going, mindful of what others say, and likely to give up easily, while men are depicted as egotistical and likely to get what they want. Other differences between men and women were noted in their dress, appearance, and behavior; they said women wear skirts, men wear pants; women have long hair, men short hair; women do not smoke and drink, men do. In this section I look at shifting representations in the arts and literature of West Sumatra to demonstrate the effect of restrictive state policies and Islamic fatwa on gender expression.

In West Sumatra efforts by Muslim clerics to restrain transgressive gender practices in art performances predated the formation of the Indonesian state and have continued since. *Randai* is a form of dance-drama that is considered specifically Minangkabau. Through singing and dance movements all-male *randai* performers enact classic Minangkabau tales. In the 1930s every province in West Sumatra had several *randai* troupes. Men who played women's roles were often called *bujang gadih*, a Minangkabau term meaning feminine man or girly boy. Many of them were rumored to become *anak jawi*, a regional term for a younger man in an erotic relationship with an older man (*induk jawi*, Minangkabau) (Herwandi, personal communication, 2004).[26] The following two stories come from an unpublished article written by Anas Nafis, a noted Minangkabau scholar. During the 1930s a *randai* troupe from the province of Lima Puluh Kota became very popular, attracting the attention of media, village leaders, and ulama (Muslim religious teachers and leaders). Concern was expressed that the men who attended the all-night *randai* performances became infatuated with the performers, particularly the young males playing the female roles. According to reports, the young actors "dressed up, acted and swayed their hips like real girls. The audience became intoxicated while watching the young boys' flirtatious and erotic style" (Nafis n.d.). In 1939 a group of Islamic leaders met in Padang to discuss these performances. Agreeing on their harmful quality, they issued a fatwa on all *randai* that forbade men performing as women and women performing as men, including wearing the clothing of, moving, or acting like the other sex.

During that time a similar fatwa was issued by ulama in Padang Panjang concerning all-girl theatrical performances at the Islamic school for girls, Diniyyah Putri. The girls who played the boys' parts wore mustaches and boys' clothes, causing a great deal of consternation (*ribut*) among the ulama. The ulama declared that it was forbidden for girls to wear boy's clothes or to behave like or play the role of boys. In this case, however, the ulama agreed to allow the girls to play the boys' roles as long as the audience was all female (Nafis n.d.). These fatwa did not have the power of law but carried considerable moral weight because they circulated via local newspapers and teachers in Islamic schools in West Sumatra. They conveyed a sense of repugnance toward transvestite roles and reinforced a gender binary in which transgressive gender practices and, by implication, sexual relations with those outside of normative gender categories, were unacceptable.

During the New Order, *randai* dance became institutionalized as part of the regional art institutes of West Sumatra and was promoted as an ethnic Minangkabau art form to attract tourism (Fraser 2007).[27] As a way to promote the arts equally for all children, the state allowed girls to participate in mixed group *randai* performances, a change from the earlier sex-segregated troupes. At the same time gender representations in the performances became more stereotypical, while cross-dressing performers were completely absent. *Randai* troupes continued to perform classic Minangkabau folktales, which were told orally in the past but have themselves become subject to state efforts to control ethnic literature.[28] The contemporary renditions lack much of the flavor of older tales. One such story frequently performed by *randai* troupes throughout West Sumatra is the tale of Si Gadih Ranti, the daughter of royal parents. The comparison between the written account and *randai* performances in the 2000s offers strong evidence of the narrowing of gender expression in West Sumatra as a result of state and Islamic influence.

The tale of *Si Gadih Ranti* comes from a genre of popular Malay stories dating from the 1800s; they relate the exploits of brave noblewomen who cross-dress as men and have extraordinary adventures.[29] A version of *Si Gadih Ranti*, which was based on an oral version (date and provenance unknown), was compiled and published by Selasih in 1986.[30] The story begins with Gadih Ranti's childhood, recounting her training in martial arts and mystical knowledge as well as womanly crafts. When Gadih Ranti reaches marriageable age, a contest is arranged by her father to find a marriage partner for her. She declares that whoever can beat her in martial arts will win her hand in marriage, but after four days and many matches, not one man of noble rank is able to beat her. Following these events she slips out of the palace with six female companions, all disguised in men's clothes, and starts on a series of adventures. No one can find them because they are unrecognizable in men's clothes. Near the end of the story she is discovered by a handsome prince, gives up her disguise, and returns home with the help of the prince, whom she then marries, to her father's great relief. Her aging father decides that Gadih Ranti should become the next raja (ruler or king). She agrees after some persuasion and rules her kingdom for seven years until her younger brother is old enough to take charge. The story ends as her husband becomes king of his own land, and they move with their two children to his kingdom (Selasih 1986).

In the following analysis of this story, I take into account the ways texts are made under specific historical and social conditions in the service of situated projects. Texts change with each retelling and with each change in the relative positions of the tellers and the listeners. Once written, they are used and reused in multiple ways; by remaking texts, storytellers make meaning out of current conditions (George 1996; Tambiah 1985; Williams 1977).[31] Umar Junus (1994), one of the most knowledgeable scholars of Minangkabau literature, notes that *kaba* (folktales) are stories that are never finished; their tellers always change them to fit or comment on contemporary phenomena. In like manner, each retelling of Minangkabau folktales emphasizes certain features that reflect current events and political ideologies (see also Blackwood 2001, Kahn 1993).

In the tale of *Si Gadih Ranti* as written by Selasih, certain textual elements indicate efforts to bring it in line with state and Islamic cultural values (Knappert 1999). The story devotes numerous pages to Gadih Ranti's father and his efforts to find her a husband; to her many suitors and their efforts to win her hand; and to the young prince, who finally finds the runaway princess, convinces her to return home, and marries her. Only a small portion of the story, one brief chapter, recounts her exploits in male guise, even though for most storytellers such adventures would be the height of the action if the protagonist were a man.[32] Minangkabau storytellers typically emphasize masculine deeds, exploring the lives of heroes who leave the safe confines of a mother's house to adventure in the world (see Edwin Wieringa 1997). Gadih Ranti, however, is a feminine hero whose adventures are downplayed in favor of the stories that reflect her suitability and desires for marriage. The end of the story emphasizes her "happy marriage" to the young prince who has saved Gadih Ranti from her father's anger and with whom she lives after her short reign as king (Selasih 1986). Such is the version that Selasih published in 1986. Even that version has little resemblance to the part of the story presented in a *randai* performance for tourists in 2004.

The State Department of Culture and Tourism sponsored a dance-drama performance in Jakarta in 2004 by a *randai* troupe from West Sumatra. Contemporary theater troupes perform only a small part of a story, a part that usually reflects the interests of the state and regional leaders to present an attractive, normalizing face to tourists and other outsiders (Fraser 2007). This troupe performed the segment of *Si Gadih Ranti* in which the men try to win her hand in marriage. In Selasih's version, Gadih Ranti bests all the men who try to beat her. The *randai* performance, however, presented dramatic fights between men suitors, while Gadih Ranti was reduced to a sweet, pretty girl standing passively on the sidelines waiting for her fate to be determined by the men fighting for her hand.[33] Her participation in the contest and her skill at martial arts are absent, evidence of a reinterpretation of *Si Gadih Ranti* to fit contemporary ethnic and moral agendas that downplay women's strength and independence while emphasizing their passivity and domesticity.

The reinterpretation of Minangkabau folk literature to fit Islamic and state gender ideologies exemplifies the way knowledges are refigured to conform to dominant ideologies. Where regional arts and literature depend on the support of state and Islamic clerics, they collaborate with dominant meanings to reflect national discourses of gender difference, celebrating men's heroism and women's potential as reproducers. Those stories or characters that challenge such norms by transgressing gender or refusing normative categories disappear from view. Through these collaborations state, Islamicist, and ethnic representations intertwine to produce a normative view of gendered citizens that orients women's lives to marriage and reproduction and men's to heroic deeds and the provision of family needs.

Reflecting these gender discourses, Padang residents understand women to be primarily oriented to husbands, children, and domestic duties. Women's lives are imagined as limited to the house and in the service of their husbands, although the reality of women's lives, even in Padang, far exceeds this imagined state. When pushed to talk in-depth about women and Minangkabau kinship, interviewees mentioned women's leadership in kin groups and their ownership of land, examples of women's position and power that exceed the limited discourse of wifedom and motherhood.[34] Nevertheless, the larger expectation of gender difference inscribed in dominant representations was obvious to Danny, who said, "According to Minangkabau *adat*, women's and men's roles are different."

In these representations of marriage and womanhood, *adat* and Islam work together to construct a normative representation of domesticity and difference. As evidenced in the descriptions given by tombois and femmes, the constructs of man and woman rest on a notion of paired opposites in which each is not the other. Gender is defined in opposition to the other, part of a distinct binary system predicated on difference and recognizable in the attributes one possesses, the clothes one wears, and the things one likes to do.

57

Bujang Gadis and the Perverse Gender: Residual Meanings

The apparent dominance of a rigid gender binary raises a question about tomboi's self-positioning: If gender discourses attach gender to particular bodies, how can tombois be intelligible as men? As Butler notes, "Persons only become intelligible through becoming gendered in conformity with recognizable standards of gender intelligibility" (1990, 22). Within the dominant gender discourse, there appears to be no room for tombois; there are only females who act like women and males who act like men. And yet tombois are imaginable and to a certain extent acceptable in the context of their own locales and neighborhoods in Indonesia. Drawing on Foucault's (1978) notion of the proliferation of sexualities, which resulted from a discursive explosion surrounding sexuality (in eighteenth- and nineteenth-century Europe), I argue that the deployment of gender in Indonesia in similar manner produces a proliferation of genders that exceed the boundaries of normative man and woman, including waria, tomboi, and gay, among others.[35] This proliferation of genders also draws on residual categories of gender transgression, those cultural legacies and practices modeled in the older myths and stories about gender-switching beings and cross-dressing women and men. The intersection of these two processes is possible because, as Foucault notes, "there can exist different and even contradictory discourses within the same strategy"; a multiplicity of discursive elements may operate at the same time, so that even an act that is treated harshly may also be widely tolerated (his example is sodomy in Europe) (1978, 102).

In line with Foucault's framing, tomboi subjectivity can be understood and intelligible as a "perverse" or unorthodox expression of normative gender, the opposite of the norm, which is the "woman who acts like a man." Male-bodied waria are historically a better-known version of perverse gender, accepted as entertainers, theatrical performers, hairdressers, and experts on proper femininity (Oetomo 1996). However, according to both Gayatri (1993) and Oetomo (2001), the term *banci*, a derogatory term for waria, can refer to both males and females.[36] In fact, in the story of Bonnie and Jossie mentioned earlier, Jossie, who was born in 1956, described herself as "more male than female" and preferred to "play with toy guns and dress up as a cowboy" in childhood (*Tempo* 1984b, 5). She was called *banci* in high school, suggesting a societal awareness and presence of female-bodied men. As I noted earlier, references to "women who act like men" began to appear in the mid-to-late 1800s in colonial Southeast Asia as Islam and Christianity began to achieve dominance; such "women" were reported periodically throughout the twentieth century.

In the other highly visible story of a lesbian love affair in 1981, it was reported that from childhood, Aty "preferred to dress up and act like a boy, and also never liked playing with girls" (*Tempo* 1984a, 14). Aty, who was born in 1960, was thus understood to be acting "like a boy" in the 1960s and 1970s. Boellstorff (2005b) claims that no category existed for masculine females in Indonesia before the lesbi category became available in the 1980s. Yet, although it was much less apparent, it was present across much of Indonesia before the 1980s, at which point it was subsumed under the new categories of "lesbi" and "tomboi." Sinnott (2004) documents a similar transition in Thailand, in which the term "tom" replaces older terminology, including *kathoey*, which was used for both masculine women and feminine men, but is now associated only with feminine men.[37]

In the 1960s and 1970s in West Sumatra (and probably earlier) gender-nonconforming males and females were called *bujang gadis*, a term meaning "girlish boy" or "boy-girl." Some of the older tombois recall hearing people use the phrase *bujang gadis*, although it was not generally used or remembered by people I asked after 2000. Dayan, a tomboi who was born in the late 1950s, said that when s/he was under ten years of age, people called her BG, short for *bujang gadis*. Dayan also mentioned another term used for gender-nonconforming girls, *supik jantan*, meaning a masculine or boyish girl or manly woman (*supik*, Minangkabau, young girl), but I never heard the term used by anyone else. Another tomboi from a provincial area of West Sumatra, who was born in 1973, said s/he was called Buyuang (Minangkabau form of *bujang*) during childhood by people who lived in h/er neighborhood. Tommi, who was born in 1975, said s/he had been called "tomboi" and also *bujang* by h/er family since s/he was young. Tommi claims that older people still call tombois *bujang gadis*, but others in h/er group of lesbi friends are not so sure.[38]

In the early 1980s Indonesian media, reporting on an increasingly visible lesbian and gay movement in Europe and the United States, began using the English-language word "lesbian," even when referring to masculine females. The earliest usage and origin of the term "tomboi" is less apparent. Gayatri (1994) mentions that "tomboi" was generally used in the 1980s, but it is not clear whether she means that it was used by the general populace or among lesbians only. People in West Sumatra in the 1990s remarked on and called boyish young girls by such words as *bujang*, tomboi or *boi*. In 1990 Dayan pointed out a scruffy-looking young girl, who was about seven years old at the time and was playing alone outside a small shop, and called h/er "tomboi." When I asked about tombois, individuals readily told me stories about masculine-acting young girls. My research associate told me that a neighbor girl who liked to play with boys and had "masculine" characteristics (*sifat-sifat laki-laki*) was called "tomboi" or *boi* by relatives and friends.

Tomboi, and for an earlier generation in West Sumatra, *bujang gadis*, and in Java *banci*, were thus recognizable to most people as descriptors of a form of masculinity produced in the interstices of a binary gender system. This "perverse gender," as Butler suggests, appears only in relation to existing norms and is "constantly prohibited and produced" by them (1990, 23). In this way the binary gender system, as experienced by tombois, contains possibilities for gender transgression as long as that transgression is recognizable as a version of the dominant gender.

Proliferating Discourses on Same-Sex and Transgender Practices

The Indonesian state under Suharto's New Order regime sought to control sexuality through a deployment of gender that made reproductive heterosexuality—through marriage—the core relationship of normative social life. The properness of marriage and sexuality within marriage were and continue to be concepts supported by both the state—through appeals to "traditional values of Indonesia" (Howard 1996, 170)—and by Islamic moral precepts. For Indonesia's majority Islamic population, these moral precepts in turn are often indistinguishable from community norms. For instance, Islamic practices permeate life in Padang and the villages of West Sumatra to the extent that ceremonial lifecycle events are said to be both Islamic and Minangkabau. Despite their matrilineal practices, the Minangkabau do not believe these practices (*adat*) are incompatible with Islam; the two are said to support each other (Blackwood 2000). Likewise, the mechanisms that regulate sexuality are very much a product of the synthesis of customary practices and Islamic law.[39] As a result Indonesian Muslims almost universally acknowledge that any sexual relationships outside of heterosexual marriage are unacceptable (Bennett 2005). In this way sexuality is regulated by gendered expectations about marriage and adulthood. A properly gendered citizenry does not need strict state regulations to govern sexuality.

While the Indonesian state has been careful to define normative gender and promote properly gendered women and men, it has maintained a neutral legal stance toward homosexuality since the beginning of its existence in 1945. The State Penal Code (Kitab Undang-Undang Hukum Pidana) contains no laws proscribing transgendered practices or sex acts between individuals with the same genitalia (Oetomo 2001), except for same-sex relations with a person who is not yet an adult (*belum dewasa*).[40] This absence of law is at odds with the history of other postcolonial states that have embraced the sexual and moral codes of the colonizers.[41] Dutch laws treated homosexuality and transgender practices severely, but these laws were not imposed on the indigenous population during the colonial period, due to the Dutch policy of noninterference in the customs and laws of the colonized.[42] State policies concerning non-normative sexualities began to shift during the 1990s, however, when international pressures for lesbian and gay rights and same-sex marriage forced new responses from state and Muslim leaders in Indonesia.

Through the efforts of groups such as the International Lesbian and Gay Association (ILGA) and the International Gay and Lesbian Human Rights Commission (IGLHRC), and the efforts of lesbian and gay activists across a number of European countries to legalize same-sex marriage, in the 1990s a consortium of international lesbian and gay groups brought their demands for sexual rights and same-sex marriage to the international arena. Over the course of the decade several nations passed laws permitting same-sex marriage, while support for a universal right to sexual choice and same-sex marriage increased. Although gay, and particularly lesbi, activism was nearly invisible in Indonesia at that time, Indonesian state officials were forced to take notice of these issues and make explicit statements against the practice of homosexuality for the first time (Oetomo 2001).

At the International Conference on Population and Development held in Cairo in 1994 under the auspices of the United Nations, with 180 states participating, a motion to adopt a statement supporting same-sex marriage was presented. The Indonesian Minister of Population Haryono Suyono declared that Indonesia would not support a declaration acknowledging same-sex marriage. President Suharto himself instructed the delegation not to support the declaration, calling it "such an odd thing" (Oetomo 2001, 121). Members of the Indonesian print media took this opposition to same-sex marriage as a declaration of the state's official position against homosexuality (Oetomo 2001).

Other statements by Indonesian state officials and clerics began to address the issue of homosexuality directly. In a paper on Islam and women's rights published in 1994, Abdurrahman Wahid (1994), a highly placed Muslim cleric and later president of Indonesia, declared that lesbianism is deviant and should not be condoned. His opposition to lesbianism was based on his belief that women have a duty to be mothers and wives. That same year the minister of women's affairs was quoted in an Indonesian newspaper stating that "lesbianism is not part of Indonesian culture or state ideology" (Alison Murray 1999, 142). The reference to "Indonesian culture" obliquely calls up and asserts that the basic foundation and values of the Indonesian state are family and marriage. Using a similar argument in 1997, a well-respected member of the Islamic organization Muhammadiyah, who was running for a position in the national parliament, protested the discussion of homosexuality and casual sex on commercial television talk shows. He argued that such topics were about behavior that was "in contradiction to our culture and religion" (Oetomo 2001, 143). The minister of information joined the argument, urging that commercial television stations should censor these topics because they were providing bad examples to people.

These comments by state and Islamic officials during the 1990s reveal a changing attitude toward sexual practices deemed outside normative gender. Where the deployment of gender had worked in the past to consolidate normative heterosexuality, the international visibility of lesbian and gay rights movements seemed to call forth new tactics in dealing with "perverse" sexualities. Wahid's statement explicitly disconnects lesbianism from normal womanhood, thus shoring up heterosexuality by an appeal to gender norms. The comments by the minister of women's affairs make it clear that reproductive heterosexuality is a duty to the state. With these utterances, state and Islamic leaders position homosexuality outside the accepted bounds of manhood and womanhood and even outside culture, thus reinforcing the unnaturalness of such behavior in the context of normatively reproductive genders. Such statements stigmatized homosexuality by declaring it deviant, unnatural, and foreign (see also Bacchetta 1999). While falling short of legal injunctions, these statements provide evidence of a heightened concern about homosexuality in Indonesia.

These public pronouncements by state and Muslim officials constitute an effort to bring new tools to bear in the discursive production of knowledge about sexuality. Their statements promulgate an Indonesian sense of "family values" that affirms Islamic morals in contrast to the supposed immorality of homosexuality. If homosexuality is not Indonesian, then it can be ignored as the immoral product of Western culture. As before, gender is deployed to make the argument that reproductive sexuality is natural to women and men, thereby reinforcing the idea that homosexuality is an unnatural and deviant practice. The main focus of such pronouncements on gendered bodies ensures that women and men fulfill their so-called natural roles properly. Where in the earlier years of Suharto's New Order it was considered adequate to create and encourage normalized heterosexuality and marriage as a means to deter nonreproductive behaviors, in the 1990s the perceived threat of international gay and lesbian activists' demands for human rights—a threat to the stability of normative gender and heterosexuality in Indonesia—led to more explicit discourse about the abnormality of homosexuality for properly gendered Indonesian citizens.

Following the end of the Suharto regime in 1998, an increasingly vocal conservative Islamic minority pushed for more restrictive laws in the State Penal Code governing sexual behaviors and public morals. Their actions initiated an intense public debate on the role of the state in sexual matters. The proposed revisions call for an explicit prohibition of specific heterosexual and homosexual acts in an effort to consolidate normative heterosexuality, by strictly defining what is permissible and impermissible heterosexual sex, and threatening punishment by the state if anyone engages in sex outside of marriage. The revisions do not proscribe consensual adult homosexual relations but set a specific age limit of eighteen, below which homosexual relations are illegal. These revisions to the Penal Code suggest that a shift is occurring in state and Islamic discourses of sexuality. Whereas prior to the late 1990s the deployment of gender was sufficient to support the production of heterosexually reproductive citizens, the proposed revisions are much more closely tied to definitions of sexual acts. The revisions bring into discourse specific acts that the state will then have to repress. In the process of criminalizing behaviors that in the past were unregulated by state law, the state through its representatives has become a focal point in producing a new knowledge of sexuality in which only certain acts are legal. The assumption that normatively gendered men and women need not be disciplined sexually is gone, replaced with an explicit and restrictive list of legal sexual acts.

This new discourse brings into play, perhaps for the first time, the "deployment of sexuality" that Foucault envisioned occurring in the West with the medicalization and criminalization of sexual acts. I am not, however, suggesting that Indonesia is thereby just coming into modernity because Foucault's geographically and socially specific history cannot be applied in the same manner to contexts outside the so-called West. Ironically, the potential power of the gay rights discourse to normalize homosexuality has in its turn produced a "reverse discourse," in the sense that Foucault (1978, 101) employed it, in which the state has been forced to use the same vocabulary and the same categories of meaning to substantiate its own position. Under this new discourse Indonesian lesbi and gay may be viewed as individuals whose sexual desires are a threat to the stability of the nation. These proposed revisions represent a transformation from a civil society in which human consensual relationships are governed by moral norms expressed in notions of normative gender to one regulated much more heavily by criminal law and state surveillance of individual behavior. However, these transformations are still unfolding, their direction uncertain, as competing discourses of morality, modernity, and sexual rights struggle for dominance.[43] Even the fate of the proposed revisions remains in doubt; as of 2009, no action had been taken yet on the whole body of law.

Producing Normative Gender

A multitude of mechanisms combine and collaborate to produce a knowledge of gender during and after New Order Indonesia. The focus in this chapter has been on three lines of knowledge production—the discourses of the state, Islamicist clerics, and the media. In these discourses marriage and reproduction are dominant themes creating a knowledge of gender oriented to "natural" men and women and their god-given duties to reproduce. This knowledge contains within it sexual meanings that are assigned to each gender differently. Thus to know gender is to know one's sexuality and the proper practice of it. Rather than a deployment of sexuality, Indonesia under the New Order carried out a deployment of gender, ensuring the proper development of reproductive citizens through a rigid gender binary that obviated the need for legal restrictions on non-normative sexualities or gender transgressions. At the same time the state encouraged the marginalization and stigmatization of practices that fell outside reproductive citizenship. Discourses on sexuality were contained within the juridico-legal and moral discourses about gender. Shifts in state discourses began to appear in the 1990s, particularly after the fall of Suharto, but this period is not formative for the lesbi individuals I began to interview in 2001, hence my focus in this chapter has been primarily on the New Order period.

The discourses of gender and sexuality in Indonesia are reflected and realized in contemporary gendered subjectivities. The discourse of innate gender difference perpetuates and reinstalls a gender binary whose boundaries cannot be legitimately transgressed. For educated Muslim scholars in West Sumatra, people who transgress their god-given natures are deeply troubling. One Minangkabau scholar told me that under Islam, there are only men and women. So he asked, "What position should [waria] take? What place do they have in Islam? (*Posisi apa dalam Islam?*) They are neither men nor women and so they cannot be accepted." Although the dominant discourses create a broadly acknowledged normative gender, such ideologies are neither seamless nor all-powerful.[44] Despite efforts by the state to shore up marriage and reproduction, to bring arts, literature, and theatre in line, alternative discourses continue to appear, lingering in older versions of ethnic folktales, visible in media representations of non-normative behavior and practices, and produced anew by the very discourses that seek to extinguish them.

Gender as a subjectivity is more complex than the simple binary that state and Islamicist leaders present. Individuals may take up what is not offered because it is nevertheless there to be seen, a point I develop more fully in the following chapters. In Indonesia masculinity is apparently attached to men's bodies, yet in the light of tombois' own experiences of and pleasures in masculinity, it can be taken on and expressed by female bodies. In the next chapter I explore the processes by which tombois and their girlfriends begin to take up their gender subjectivities during childhood; in particular I demonstrate the way tombois produce a gender that goes beyond or transgresses the normative but is nevertheless intelligible, coherent, and in many contexts allowable.

Learning to Be Boys and Girls

W HEN I ASKED TOMBOIS AT WHAT POINT THEY first became aware of be- ing tombois, or of liking boys' things, their answers were generally con- sistent: "Since I was little," "since first grade," or "in elementary school." One tomboi declared, "I was always a tomboi." Another said, "Growing up, I *never* felt like a girl," disallowing any possibility that s/he could have girlish de- sires or feelings. Still another tomboi thought that s/he knew s/he was a tomboi "around four or five years old, because that's when I started to like boys' clothes, not girls' clothes." Tombois did not offer a narrative of learning to be or of be- coming tombois, but instead saw themselves as always boys. According to their stories, everything they did growing up was what boys did, a sentiment that was echoed in girls' childhood narratives about being girls.

For tombois and girlfriends, their earliest memories recall a time when their sense of reality has already been formed, a time when their practical sense of the world allows them to take for granted its social categories and expectations and their own position in it. The challenge of this chapter is to take adult narratives that situate gender as always already known and identify the processes by which children come to take up gender. Using their childhood narratives, I analyze both tombois' and girlfriends' enactment of gender and their interactions with socially significant others—their families, extended kin, neighbors, and friends.

My focus in this chapter is the intersection of childhood, gender, and sub- jectivity. Anthropological approaches to childhood are broadly concerned with the ways children learn and acquire cultural meaning, emotions, and behaviors. Although recent research on children's agency has offered new insights into the processes by which children acquire a sense of self, surprisingly little attention has been given to the processes of gendering in childhood or to cultural forms of masculinity and femininity and their consequences for the practices children en- gage in.[1] Work by feminist anthropologists has dealt broadly with the treatment of girls as they learn to become women, but few have addressed the processes by which children learn gender.[2] Debra Skinner's (1989) intriguing early research on Nepali girls finds that the process of internalizing gender is neither straightforward nor smooth, although all the girls follow the path that is laid out for them.[3] Judging by the majority of anthropological studies, and despite Moore's (1994) admonishment that individual subjects may enact multiple and competing identities, the anthropological individual appears to take up the normative gender designated for her or him during childhood to become a woman or man.

Childhood has not been a major focus of literature on male or female transgenderism in anthropological studies either, possibly due to the difficulties of assessing childhood processes from adult narrators. Nevertheless some early studies offered tentative hypotheses to explain transgenderism. In one study, male transgenderism in Plains Indian culture was attributed to the young male's failure to attain proper masculinity because of his inability to meet the rigorous requirements of male initiation (Hoebel 1949).[4] In contrast female transgenderism was not seen as a failure to attain proper femininity but the result of, for instance, having a proclivity for men's tasks or being raised as a son (Devereux 1937; Honigmann 1954). Both views reflect Western assumptions about gender hierarchies and the privileged status of masculinity. Alfred Kroeber (1940), who believed that biology was the root of such behavior, stated that Native American societies provide a niche for people who are inclined to act like the other sex. He assumed that such behavior results from an inborn state that takes the form (niche) offered by particular cultures.

More recently a solid body of work on lesbian, gay, and transgender studies has moved anthropological thought beyond notions of innate proclivities or failed learning.[5] While most of this work does not examine childhood processes, two studies I note here offer some thoughts on childhood. Don Kulick (1998) points out that girlish behavior and early sexual desire for men are formative for male-bodied *travesti* in Brazil, with the emphasis on sexual desire. While his work provides important insights into a complicated subjectivity, it leaves open the question of what prompted those early behaviors and desires. By what processes did *travesti* come to be attracted to men? Their emphasis on a growing *awareness* of desire seems to leave no room for cultural processes in the creation of that desire. Boellstorff (2005b) takes a different view concerning Indonesian gay and lesbi, arguing that they do not learn their sexual subjectivities at home because of the absence of a role model for same-sex relationships. His view assumes that gender is not a critical aspect of sexual subjectivities. By discounting the way lesbi and gay Indonesians become gendered, Boellstorff does not address childhood processes in the formation of their sexual subjectivities. In contrast, I argue in this chapter that early childhood practices are key elements in understanding tomboi subjectivities because these practices serve as the basis for their present sense of self as men who are attracted to women.

Theorizing Childhood Development

To address the way tombois and their girlfriends experience and express their subject positions as gendered children, I look at their practical enactment of gender, drawing on Moore's and Bourdieu's analyses of self and subjectivity discussed in chapter 1. Enactment as defined here is not necessarily a conscious performance but an action, constantly reinforced, that creates a practical sense of the world. Bourdieu's concept of "practical sense" emphasizes early learning through observation and reinforcement, resulting in anticipated outcomes. He argues that "the most fundamental structures of the group" take root in "the primary experiences of the body" (1990, 71). His notion of embodiment helps to connect early socialization processes and ongoing interpretations of identity and selfhood with the body. Bourdieu suggests that social meanings are "learned by the body and borne on the body," a process that tends to take place "below the level of consciousness" (1990, 73). He points to a child's silent observation of, for instance, the interactions between father and mother, that "is turned into ... a durable way of standing, speaking, walking, and thereby of feeling and thinking" (1990, 70), as evidence of the way that gendered meanings are learned and embodied, producing bodily sensations of rightness or wrongness, depending on the interaction, and creating a sense of reality. By highlighting Bourdieu's sense of rootedness, I am not thereby claiming that early gender socialization remains intact throughout life. My point is to emphasize the way culturally defined gender meanings are at first taken on, without explicit thought, and naturalized in the body, making such processes inaccessible at the time, although later experiences and exposure to other discourses may lead to new meanings.

Following this line of thinking, I start with the basic premise that within a particular class or group of people, the mutual intelligibility of the habitus, or their shared cultural knowledge (Bourdieu 1990), means that all gender discourses are available to all individuals. For example, people can say, "that's what boys are like" or "that's what girls do" and generally agree; these comments are heard and understood by children, providing what Bourdieu refers to as a "constant reinforcement" that creates their early sense of gender difference. However, children do not take up gender exactly as they see it. As Moore (1994) suggests, people have practical knowledge of how to act or not and so can manipulate this knowledge to produce different outcomes. Children learn what boys should do and what girls should do—the practical knowledge that Moore refers to—which then gives them the ability to manipulate or play with that knowledge as they take up particular gender positions, even ones not marked for them. Such a process of manipulation can be seen in the United States in young girls engaging in rough-and-tumble play or young boys trying on lipstick. Over time the enactment of gender becomes the gender of the child. It coheres as the "truth" of one's self through a process of naturalization in which the responses of significant others to particular enactments evoke feelings of rightness.[6]

I explore the enactment of gender in this chapter through the stories tombois and their girlfriends told me about their childhood years. These narratives recount their interactions with family, friends, schoolmates, and teachers, interactions that provide the context for and consequent experiences of gender. Tombois' and girlfriends' stories about growing up can be read from two different perspectives, first, as personal histories in the sense of being windows into the past that reveal the person and the social context, or second, as a set of claims oriented to and commenting on their current sense of self. The first perspective is similar to Susan Rodgers' (1995) approach in her presentation of the memoirs of two Sumatran men, which is offered as a window into their childhood years. In the second perspective, these stories act as claims to a particular subject position (offered by current discourses) through a selective framing of the past.

Both types of readings are useful here. The past is always remembered selectively as a way to align it with or comment on present conditions, a process that is noted for anthropological narrators' stories as well as the Minangkabau folktales (*kaba*) that I mentioned in chapter 2.[7] In this regard tombois' and girlfriends' narratives offer rationales for the subject positions they inhabit as adults. At the same time these narratives contain details that help to elucidate the processes by which tombois and their girlfriends began to learn how to be boys and girls. In addition the comments they made about growing up reveal the social discourses within which they are interpolated as well as the practices in which they are engaged. Finally the narratives are interesting for what they leave out as well as what they include.

In my questions about their childhood years I asked what activities they liked to do when they were little or what hobbies they had. I did not ask tombois how they became tombois, which would have demanded a childhood history that correlated with their adult sense of self, in the manner of "coming out" stories that "find" in the past incontrovertible evidence of a present sexuality while leaving out or devaluing stories of other attractions (see Weston 1991). Of course, the fact that I was interested in them because of their tomboi-ness might have led them to emphasize a history of masculinity but other answers and other stories were also possible. I assume that their childhood stories reflect the "truth" of their gender as they understand it because, like all individuals, they are situated in a gender discourse in which certain likes and dislikes function as evidence of gender (Butler 2001).

Narratives of Enactment

In Indonesia normative gender is clearly marked by the differences in boys' and girls' activities. Parker (1997) routinely observed gendered differences while studying young schoolchildren in Bali: "School age girls are nearly always at home in out-of-school time; it is expected that they will help with housework. … Boys seem nearly always to be away from home. Younger boys roam the village, fishing, hunting, playing *gamelan* [musical instruments], having adventures in all-boy bands …" (1997, 507). Similarly, groups of boys in Padang run or play games outside, while girls are nearly invisible helping out in and around their houses. Young girls are not given the same freedom as young boys. Interestingly Radjab's memories of his boyhood in West Sumatra in the early part of the twentieth century, as told in Rodgers' *Telling Lives* (1995), contain images of boys' greater freedom of movement and active lifestyle comparable to those at the end of the century, attesting to a long-established practice. These everyday practices of difference, observable at home, on the streets, and in the schools create and constantly reinforce a practical sense of the world in which gender operates in a distinct binary system.

What did tombois enact as children? Their narratives do not speak about what they thought, but what they did. Their childhood narratives were about doing, playing, and going out, about mobility and freedom, which is what boys did. Tommi, a tomboi born in 1975, said, "I liked all the toys and sports that boys liked—fishing, flying kites, playing with cars, playing soccer, playing with marbles. I really liked playing with cars." Danny's account of h/er younger years focused on playing sports with the boys. Danny, born in 1973, said, "When I came home from school, I took a nap, prayed, and then went and played soccer with the boys in the neighborhood. That's what I liked to do most." Jon, who was born in 1969 and came from a poor family, described h/er childhood as follows: "I liked to play with cars and play war with toy pistols. I never liked sewing or cooking." In these stories no mention is made of any interests other than those associated with boys and boys' things. Jon specifically says s/he did not like cooking or sewing, which are two activities strongly associated with women. Tombois' recital of their childhood interests revolves around activities that they identify as being "boys' games."

Playing boys' games meant that tombois were always around boys and hung out with boys' groups. Tommi said all h/er friends were boys. "Since I was little, I always played with guys. When we played with toy cars, I was the leader of the gang." Another tomboi said that playing with boys was one of h/er main interests in childhood. For Arief, a tomboi born in 1981, playing with boys was better than playing with girls. Robi said, "Roughhousing, being tough (*yang keras*), that's what I wanted to do." As in the games they liked to play, tombois recall being with and playing with boys only; most of their early years were spent engaged in activities with other boys. Playing soccer, playing with cars or marbles, or even just roughhousing are all very interactive activities done in same-sex groups. Tommi recalls being the leader of h/er gang of boys, suggesting that not only was s/he part of and happily engaged in these all-boy groups and activities, but s/he was successful and respected as the best in h/er gang. Robi said s/he was tough like the boys. Interestingly, tombois' stories of playing with boys and having all boys as friends did not hint at any negative interactions with those boys. Nor did they express any confusion or shame about playing with other boys. Instead they recalled their childhood days with fondness, suggesting that their interactions with boys were positive. Thus in this constant enactment of boyish behavior, of playing boys' games and being with boys, tombois solidified for themselves a sense of self as masculine, like other boys.

Another way tombois enacted gender during childhood was by wearing boys' clothes. The ideological differences between girls and boys are materially represented in children's clothing, including the uniforms that children wear to school. As I noted, children's school clothes are marked by gender, but their play clothes differ as well. Young girls in Indonesia may play in pants and T-shirts, but those clothes are more feminine than boys' in their design, color, and adornment. Several tombois mentioned that they started wearing boys' clothes at a young age. Andri said, "I've been wearing boy's clothes since I was very young, in first grade [about six years of age]." Tommi told me that s/he dressed just like h/er older brother when s/he was young and liked wearing boy's clothes better than girls' clothes. In their understanding there are only boys' clothes and girls' clothes; boys wear boys' clothes, which is what tombois recall always wearing. Because clothing is a crucial sign marking one's identity, tombois use it to normalize and make customary their identity as young tombois (*anak tomboi*, lit. a tomboi child).

Clothes were a particularly salient issue for tombois during their school years because in the public space of schools, tombois were forced to follow the clothing requirements for girls, a fact that could have complicated tombois' emerging sense of self. School administrators were uncompromising in their attitude toward dress and by extension gender. Because their "sex" was female, tombois were expected to wear girls' uniforms to school, and were thus marked as girls. Tombois had no control over the clothes that they wore to school, but outside of school they insisted on wearing boys' clothes. Masril declared, "I never wore skirts, except when I had to for school." Tombois complied with school regulations, but only for those hours during which they were at school. Lina, one of Tommi's girlfriends, who had seen an elementary school photo of Tommi in a skirt, said, "Tommi looked really cute. But Tommi only wore that skirt at school and tore it off as soon as s/he got home." Despite the requirement to dress as a girl in school, tombois did not recount stories of problems in elementary school, where school discipline accustomed them to follow the rules of the school.

Tombois I interviewed said they wore boys' clothes because they liked them better than girls' clothes. More importantly, wearing boys' clothes created a feeling of rightness that became embodied as natural and fitting with their sense of themselves as boys. Robi said, "I wouldn't wear a skirt, it didn't feel right. I wore pants even to weddings. If my parents wouldn't let me dress as I wanted, then I wouldn't go to the wedding at all." To be forced to attend a wedding in girls' clothes was embarrassing for Robi because it was not how s/he saw h/erself. Sal, whose interests in all things boyish did not develop until junior high, said, "Girls' clothes make me feel really weird and awkward." In these accounts tombois never question why they did not like girls' clothes; they just knew that girls' clothes did not feel right. Wearing girls' clothes disrupted their sense of self as boys, creating feelings of discomfort and awkwardness, of not being oneself, that made it difficult to interact with others properly. In contrast wearing boys' clothes allowed them to be visible as boys and elicited responses from others that were appropriate for boys. Consequently, boys' clothes constructed a particular feeling and experience of gender that came to be embodied physically as the truth of their gender.

Being boys, according to tombois, however, was not just about types of play or clothes but about the mobility and freedom of movement that boys have. The cultural ideal of gender difference is clearly visible in the bodily practices and experiences of girls and boys: in the classroom girls are quiet and well behaved, reluctant to stand out or answer questions, while boys are noisier, more active, and self-projecting (Parker 1997). Girls are encouraged from an early age to be modest and to carefully contain their physical activity; in contrast boys are given a high degree of spatial mobility (see also Bennett 2005). Dedi told me, "If you're a girl, you stay at home, quietly, you don't go anywhere. But boys, you know, go out a lot." An astute observer, Dedi saw what both girls and boys were like and situated h/erself with the boys. Tommi expressed the naturalness of having young boys' freedom of movement and association with other boys. "Since I was little, I hung out with guys, so my family just understood that I was more like a guy. Sleeping anywhere was not a problem because my family knew that I could protect myself." Young girls are not allowed to be away from home without supervision; tombois in contrast are proud of their ability to move freely about and associate with other boys. Their stories recount a sense of freedom and mobility that is only given to boys.

Through the enactment of gender, tombois internalize masculine responses and feelings. In Indonesia, feelings of shame (*malu*) are inculcated at an early age for inappropriate behavior. *Malu* is a complex emotion that Elizabeth Collins and Ernaldi Bahar (2000) define as a reluctance to act in a way that embarrasses one's elders, or a form of deference to one's superiors, which is expressed as shame or embarrassment. Learning to be *malu* means learning which experiences and practices are considered shameful or immodest; these differ for boys and girls. For girls, being *malu* is closely associated with proper feminine behavior, which requires girls to learn to restrain themselves by not acting in unfeminine ways. Over time this incorporation of shame into female sexual subjectivity results in a "constant, embodied sense of personal shame" that is expressed in shyness, passivity, modesty, and a reluctance to be visible in public spaces (Bennett 2005, 31). Despite these gendered expectations, girls and women may express a range of behaviors beyond the ideal of feminine modesty and passivity but they must be careful to avoid being seen as unfeminine. Boys may be made to feel *malu* for unmasculine behavior, such as crying or being too timid, but their embarrassment is expressed through anger, threats, or even violence toward the person who has shamed them (Collins and Bahar 2000). Everyday practices and interactions with children by socially significant others inculcate these feelings in children, so that they are taken on and deeply rooted as part of oneself.

Assuming that tombois may have thought of themselves at first as girls, I asked some of the tombois why they were able to do things that girls cannot. In their responses, tombois attributed their freedom to their (boyish) behavior, situating themselves as already like boys, not like girls. Rather than becoming *malu* over inappropriate (for a girl) masculine behavior, they responded to efforts to shame them in the energetic, boisterous, risk-taking way of boys. Lina's comments about one of the tombois indicates that as young children tombois learned to be *malu* in the way boys do. Lina said "Tombois like Tommi, from a very young age have acted like that and no one can stop them. They get really mad if someone tries to change their behavior, and so parents let them do what they want." In this situation a girl would become embarrassed for acting out in such a wild or boyish manner, but tombois respond with anger, as other boys would, at efforts to teach them girlish behavior or to restrict their activities. Thus, the ability to be a tomboi is not just about liking boys' things or hanging out with boys, but about embodying masculine behaviors and emotions in a way that parents are not willing to contest. A comment made about a young woman, who was attracted to a tomboi but followed her parents' wishes to get married, underscores this point. Dayan said, "She's not brave enough to talk back to her parents; the brave ones become tombois." For Dayan, the meaning was clear: those who learn to talk back and to go after what they want for themselves, who take on boyish characteristics, experience themselves as boys.

Interactions with Others

Interactions with family and kin play a crucial role in a tomboi's developing sense of self. In childhood, subjectivities are forged within the social relationships of family, kin, and community (McHugh 2002). These relationships provide not only the social context, but also the interactions that guide, provoke, encourage, or discourage expressions of gender. Within the domestic and neighborhood context, tombois first begin to enact, experience, and make sense of a binary gender and their position within it.

In contrast to accounts by transgendered individuals in the United States of traumatic experiences growing up (see, for example, Norton 1999), the only problematic childhood interactions with kin that tombois mentioned concerned parents' desires for them to wear girls' clothes. Sal said, "Even if girl's clothes were bought for me, I would never wear them." I mentioned earlier Robi's refusal to attend a weddings because s/he could not wear pants. From an early age s/he resisted h/er mother's efforts to dress h/er in girls' clothes and found support in h/er father's lenience:

> I didn't wear skirts or other girls' clothes. My mother gave me earrings but I took them off. When she gave me girls' clothes, I wouldn't wear them. Whenever we went to parades or festivals, I wanted to wear a soldier's uniform, like the one my father had; that was what I liked. I was just taking after my father. He didn't mind what I wore. He thought it was okay for me to wear boy's clothes, although my mother was stricter. My parents eventually went along and gave me boy's clothes.

In these stories, parents applied some pressure to encourage their tomboi children to wear girls' clothes, particularly at important family events, like weddings. But tombois establish a pattern of refusing girls' clothes and, like Robi, over time they are allowed to wear what they want.

Refusal to wear girls' clothes is the only instance in which tombois explicitly mention resisting their parents' wishes.[8] Their childhood stories do not contain any other accounts of direct confrontations with parents over their behavior.

Rather than experiencing isolation or ridicule for not acting like proper girls, tombois remember only easy camaraderie with other boys and (eventual) understanding from kin and neighbors. According to Dedi, "People understand, you know, because since I was little I've been like that. It's not strange anymore." Whether or not efforts to dress their tomboi children in girls' clothes were the only times parents tried to press their daughters into the realm of girlhood, tombois' refusal was the one act of resistance that they felt was important enough to mention, suggesting that the significance of clothing was more than just a sartorial statement. When tombois were encouraged to look like girls, their categorical refusal aligned them with boys and highlighted their desire to be recognized as boys. Likewise parents' sporadic efforts to change their daughters' appearance were not only futile, they served to highlight the differences between boys and girls.

Other interactions with kin helped to solidify tombois' sense of self as boys. When asked who identified h/er first as a tomboi, Andri said, "It was my parents. They saw me doing things like the boys, wearing boys' clothes, and playing with boys' toys." Danny recounted a similar experience of being told since s/he was little that s/he was acting like a boy. Danny, who loved playing soccer, said that s/he was encouraged by h/er parents and h/er older brother to take up karate. Robi's father, mentioned above, thought it was fine if Robi wore boys' clothes. An event that stood out in Tommi's memory was the time h/er uncle gave h/er a toy car without h/er asking for it. Tommi's pleasure at being given the car speaks to h/er realization that h/er boyish interests were being recognized and validated.

In addition to being told they were acting like boys, some tombois were given boys' nicknames by their families. Tommi's family called h/er "Tomboi" or "Bujuang," a Minangkabau word that means young man and is commonly used for both boys and men. Sal said that during junior high h/er family started calling h/er tomboi when they saw that s/he liked to smoke and hang out at the local coffee shop (*warung*). Dedi's behavior prompted the following reaction from h/er mother:

> My mother didn't have a nickname for me. But I didn't always sleep at home, I would sleep here or there, like a guy, huh-huh, like a boy. My mother would say to me, "You're acting like a guy (*cowok*)."

These comments and nicknames marked the boundaries of masculinity and femininity, situating tombois on the side of masculinity.

Throughout their childhood and teen years, tombois were subject to comments, admonitions, and encouragements about their behavior that constructed a world in which space, activity, clothing, and association were strongly gendered. Tombois' actions brought into play hegemonic gender discourses as adults commented on the perceived suitability of the activity for the child. Kin saw in these actions a difference in behavior and, in line with the cultural habitus of sex/gender, marked tombois' behavior as "boy" behavior, telling the child that s/he was not doing what girls should be doing. In some cases the remarks were casual or matter of fact, while other times they were made to discourage certain behaviors and carried with them implicit warnings. In their efforts to mark normative gender behavior, family and kin continually recreated and reinforced a difference between boys and girls. If tombois persisted in boys' activities, they were told, "You're acting like a boy," or they heard "Ehhh, that one's a tomboi," as kin and neighbors attempted to make sense of the "mismatch" by recalling alternative discourses, including literary representations, of women "acting like men." Through family members' repeated assertions that they were acting like boys, tombois came to understand the world as divided into two genders and to interpret their own behavior as falling into the boys' world.

Becoming Boys

Tombois did not recount stories of *learning* to become boys; they recalled having the same interests as boys and lacking any interest in what girls do. Their stories naturalized their gender construction as something that was always part of them. In recounting the past, they expressed their sense of masculinity as already given—something that was naturally present and that felt natural as well. Their recollections situated their masculinity as unproblematic; it was girls' clothes and efforts by parents to make them wear those clothes that were remembered as problematic. Tombois did not express doubts about being boys but rather expressed a bodily sense of discomfort with things feminine—clothes not fitting properly, bodies feeling awkward. Their embodied feelings of discomfort with girls' things provide evidence—beyond their own assertions—of the manner in which gender is learned and naturalized. Having been tutored in the sharp distinctions between boys and girls, and doing everything that boys do, young tombois came to feel physically uncomfortable at the thought of any behavior or action, such as wearing girls' clothes or liking sewing, that threatened to break down the distinction between themselves and girls.

Tombois' narratives pointed to the types of activities that they considered important in being boys. These activities were clearly marked for tombois as boys-only or girls-only, reflecting sex-segregated practices and discourses apparent in their homes, schools, and neighborhood spaces (the only spaces that tombois knew at that point). In tombois' stories, boys occupied a different space than girls did; boys' space was where they felt they belonged. Their presence in boys' space and their ability to do boys' activities was normalized in the context of their childhood interactions and experiences with kin and friends. Occupying boys' space was not proper for girls, but it was normal (*biasa*) if one was an *anak tomboi*.

In the process of taking up a gender, tombois interpreted their enactment of boyish activities, and its constant reinforcement, both positive and negative, as evidence that they were boys, since girls and boys were defined differently. As they produced more outgoing, tough, and aggressive behaviors, they were rewarded in their interactions with boys, by, for instance, becoming a leader, and were acknowledged by adults, who gave them more freedom in socializing with boys. As with other gendered subjectivities, this enactment of gender became embodied over time as tombois came to feel right in their boyishness and "weird" in girlish activities.

Because I do not have access to their "inner speech," tombois everyday practices and statements—about how they felt and what they did—serve as the source for understanding the processes of taking up a gender. From their childhood stories, the truth of their gender resides precisely in what they did: in the clothes they wore, the things they liked to do, and who they liked to do it with. Similarly for *calalai*, female-bodied individuals who act like men, their masculine actions confirm for them and others that they are *calalai* (Davies 2007a). By enacting particular genders, individuals provide evidence of the categories to which they belong. The enactment of gender, then, does not reflect an interior self, but creates or produces that self. The doing becomes the being, creating a transgression that moves beyond normative gender but in a way that is culturally intelligible.

Enacting a particular gender, even though it is not offered, is no different from enacting the one offered. By this I mean that, even though a child may perceive or be told that s/he does not "belong" in the gender enacted, the same processes of gender acquisition, including observation, practical experience, and social interaction, otherwise apply, suggesting that there is no inherently determined progression toward a particular gender. As Moore (1994) points out, the ability to devise an alternative strategy, which is not necessarily a consciously thought-out strategy, requires only the practical knowledge of what one should or should not do. Robi's comment speaks to h/er knowledge of what boys do. S/he said, "I was more interested when I was growing up in what boys are supposed to be like, the things they are supposed to do, their stories." Behaviors and activities that were coded as belonging to "boys" were part of the everyday habitus that was available for observation. As Robi participated in these behaviors, s/he built up h/er knowledge of appropriate boy behaviors and h/er self-confidence in h/er ability to enact them. Similarly, Jason Cromwell notes that transmen in the United States who expressed masculinity as young children were often taken as boys; these individuals created what he calls a "primary masculine identity" (1995, 286). Tombois' childhood interests, friends, and clothing all signal the masculine gender, which is read and reinforced by interactions with family and kin, both in their support and encouragement of these interests and in their attempts to bring their daughters into conformity with the feminine gender. Tombois' enactment of boyishness, whether met with approval or disapproval, makes them aware of appropriate gender behavior, enabling them to develop a sense of themselves as boys.

As children, tombois learn and enact a masculine gender in line with a New Order ideology of masculinity. At the same time tombois' interpretive understanding of their bodies conflicts with the dogma of a sex/gender system that declares a unity between bodies and genders. Their ability to create a practical sense of themselves in the world, despite their contradiction of normative social categories, comes in part from alternative discourses, mentioned in chapter 2, that imagine bodies associated with more than one gender. In addition, Shelly Errington points out that in Southeast Asia, bodily behaviors, which include posture, demeanor, and tone of voice, "are constantly attended to and read as signs of an inner moral state" (1990, 17). She argues further that regardless of how inherent a person's attributes are assumed to be in any particular cultural context, "they require social enactment to be convincing" (1990, 17). In this way, as tombois learn by observation the cultural importance attached to bodily behaviors, they come to rely on this social strategy to demonstrate their own position in the masculine gender, a point I continue to develop in the next chapter.

Becoming Girls

In comparison to tombois' narratives, girlfriends' childhood narratives were equally consistent regarding their gender attribution but much less detailed. Girlfriends' understanding of femininity closely followed dominant gender ideologies of the time. Their brief responses demonstrated that they shared the same worldview as tombois, a world populated by individuals of two different genders with their own separate interests and separate spaces.

Girlfriends I interviewed seemed to have given little thought to their sense of girlishness; their childhood stories situated them as typical little girls with girls' interests. I asked several girlfriends to talk about their childhood interests and hobbies. Out of six responses, five mentioned cooking. Other activities included sewing, playing with dolls, and dressing up. Jeni, a young woman in her early twenties, said, "When I was little I liked to play with girls' toys, like other girls. I played with dolls and played at cooking." Nila, Jeni's best friend, elaborated, "I liked to play with dolls and cook. But what I really liked to do when I was little was help my mother put on makeup and dress up. I really liked to help my mother." Epi, who was in her late twenties, gave a response that was very similar to Jeni's, "What I most liked to do when I was little was cook, just like other girls." Girlfriends saw themselves as domestically oriented, not only doing household activities but staying within the household to play with dolls and dress up.

Only Lina, who is Minangkabau but was born and raised in Jakarta, had other interests growing up. She said, "I liked sports, volleyball, badminton, and swimming. But the activities I liked the most were singing and dancing." Lina's childhood narrative was different from the others in its emphasis on playing sports, although Nila also mentioned interest in volleyball in high school. Lina's story may reflect the difference of being raised in the metropolis of Jakarta, but her narrative is not out of line with femininity in Indonesia generally. Since the 1970s, school sports have been available to young girls (Parker 1997), which has led to the development of amateur sports clubs for girls. Not all these athletes are tombois, although two of the tombois I interviewed did play on sports clubs. Singing and dancing are unproblematic for girls, particularly if the girls are performing ethnic or folk songs and dances, which have different styles for men and women. In addition, Lina did not state that her parents tried to dissuade her from these activities, suggesting that they were perceived as proper for girls. Indeed the development of sports and art venues for girls during the New Order, as noted in the preceding chapter, both challenged some of the restrictions of femininity as well as maintained rigidly gendered styles (Parker 1997; Kellar 2004).

If their activities pointed to a domestic, feminine orientation, their self-descriptions contained further clues to a childhood in which feminine traits were taken up. The youngest girlfriends, those in their late teens and early twenties, were the most shy in public spaces. Nila, who said she is very close to her mother, described herself as shy and quiet. Jeni, who said little about herself, was described by her tomboi partner, Andri, as a very patient and compliant person (*sifat mengalah*). Even older girlfriends saw themselves in similar ways. Epi described herself as "shy and quiet. I don't like going out that much in big crowds. I'm not the brave sort. And I'm really sensitive. If I get my feelings hurt, I cry a lot." These characteristics align closely with Indonesian notions of ideal feminin-ity: the person who gives in, does not fight back, and allows others to have their way.

In their childhood narratives, girlfriends did not explain their feelings and feminine interests. As in the tombois' stories, girlfriends spoke of activities that were particular to girls. They mentioned domestic activities—cooking and sew-ing—playing with girls' toys, dolls, and makeup and playing dress up. The as-sumed normality of what they did was reflected in their comments that they were doing things just like other girls, as if that explained everything. Even my asking questions about their childhood activities seemed silly to some as they struggled to come up with examples of things they liked to do. The lack of elabo-ration in the stories indicates the taken-for-granted quality of their femininity; they thought their girlhood experiences were so typical that they required no further explanation. Only Nila mentioned feeling close to her mother and desir-ing to help her, suggesting a connection, if indirectly, between liking to help her mother and learning feminine attributes.

The contrast between tombois' and girlfriends' narratives was particularly evident on the topics of clothes and friends. Unlike tombois, girlfriends did not discuss the kinds of clothes they wore or the friends they had, perhaps seeing no need to state what they considered to be obvious, that they wore girls' clothes and played with other little girls. Judging from their style of dress when I met them, girlfriends generally bear the markers of feminine appearance and probably did so in childhood as well. While none of the girlfriends had discussed the friends with whom they hung out, tombois had put great emphasis on their association with other boys.

In sum, girlfriends' childhood narratives contained few insights into the pro-cess of taking up a gender; for them it was an unremarkable process that achieved expected outcomes. Like tombois' self-attributions of boyhood, they saw them-selves as always already girls. Where tombois were proud to recount their exploits with boys and their interests in boys' activities, girlfriends saw nothing of great interest in their own childhoods. The differences in these narratives suggest that because girlfriends align themselves with normative gender, they do not feel that they have to establish their credibility as girls. For them gender is simply part of who they are as females, something that is always there. By enacting the hege-monic understanding of gender, they assume that their feelings and behaviors are reflections of their feminine nature, even though their interests and behaviors are constantly produced and reinforced by their families throughout their childhood years.

A Masculine Environment

Although tombois' earliest recollections were of their boyish behavior and clothes, it did not necessarily mean that they thought they were born men. Ontological concepts are culturally specific, by which I mean that a certain set of ideas about human beings circulate, in this case throughout much of Indonesia and Southeast Asia, to form dominant and alternative discourses. Tombois' ideas about how they became men reflect national discourses on personhood, sex/gender, and environment. As mentioned earlier, tombois' childhood narratives did not contain stories of "becoming" tombois. They did not offer any explanations for their childhood behavior other than to paint it as quite normal for them, as always already there. In other conversations that I had with some of the tombois, they volunteered their ideas about why they became tombois, relating it to the particular environment in which they grew up. This view is in line with dominant discourses about homosexuality promoted by the state and presented in Indonesian print media (lesbi, gay, and waria are generally included under the category *homoseksual* in print media). I examine newspaper and magazine articles here because the views presented in these media are familiar to and circulate among tombois, their friends and girlfriends, kin and community.

Indonesian print media generally rely on the views of expert psychologists for opinions about the "causes" of homosexuality. Because homosexual desire is equated with gender nonconformity, cases of boyish behavior or being 'like a man' are discussed in mainstream media under the rubric of homosexuality or lesbianism. These experts extrapolate from a variety of Western theories to explain causation, but unlike popular science perspectives in the United States that adhere strongly to biological explanations, they tend to emphasize psychosocial explanations over biological ones.[9] One of the primary Western sources for these psychosocial explanations appears to be Freudian psychoanalytic theory. In the early 1980s an article published in *Kartini*, a women's magazine, offered several possible factors leading to lesbianism, including penis envy, mistreatment by a father, and lack of an adequate mother figure. These factors are reminiscent of Freud's stages of psychosexual development and the Electra complex, but in this article the author explains how a young girl, upon discovering she lacks a penis, feels incomplete. If she is mistreated by her father, she will hate her father and behave like a man to get revenge (*Kartini* 1984). A later newspaper article in *Kompas* explicitly cites Freud to support the importance of a same-sex parent figure during the phase of gender identity development (see Sadarjoen 2005).

During the 1980s several articles in popular women's magazine were devoted to the topic of homosexuality. The *Kartini* article mentioned above asserted the importance of environmental factors: "A man and a woman can just become homosexual. Not because of their genes or because they are fated to it, but more because their environment makes them that way" (*Kartini* 1984, 48). An article published in *Puteri*, another women's magazine, cited a range of factors: (1) biogenic, due to hormonal imbalance, (2) psychogenic, due to psychological problems such as despair, frustration, or a broken heart, and (3) sociogenic, the result of living in an all-female environment (Wadiantoro 1984, 49).

Twenty years later such views continue to circulate in Indonesian print media. In articles published since 2000, possible sociocultural and environmental factors given for lesbianism include mistreatment by a husband or obstacles in psychosexual development, specifically an absence of or poor relationship with the same-sex parent during puberty (Pangkahila 2003; Sadarjoen 2005). In one case presented in a psychology advice column, a masculine young woman reportedly said she felt like a man and was described as dominant, aggressive, tough, and possessive. The psychologist determined that "her close emotional relationship with her father dominated her psychosexual development, so that she was likely to become a lesbian" (Sadarjoen 2005, my translation). In this case, as in others, masculine behavior was attributed to lesbianism. While allowing for the possibility of an innate homosexuality, other columnists also attributed lesbianism and homosexuality to environmental causes. For instance, in an advice column by Wimpie Pangkahila (2003), a doctor of sexology, a young woman asked why she was more attracted to women. Pangkahila responded that even if a woman is heterosexual, she can become homosexual if, for instance, she is in a close relationship with a same-sex friend. I do not cite these stories to argue for either a social or biological "origin" to homosexuality but as evidence of particular knowledge practices circulating in Indonesia, practices that assert the learned or social aspects of gender nonconformity and/or homosexual behavior. Within the dominant discourse, homosexuality and lesbianism are said to result from a variety of circumstances, among which environmental factors are given considerable weight.

The popularity of this particular view of sexuality may be due to its close fit with Indonesian concepts of personhood. As I discuss more fully in chapter 6, personhood is thought to reflect the environment or surroundings (*lingkungan*) within which a person grows up. Childhood training is believed to play a large role in helping a person achieve a properly gendered sense of self as a woman or man who knows and upholds her/his responsibilities and duties as wife, husband, and parent. The state assertion that women's child-rearing responsibilities are important to the future of the nation speaks to a belief in nurture as a necessary foundation for the development of proper citizens (Blackwood 1995b). At the same time, adulthood for Indonesians is not equated with the autonomous, bounded self that is popularly claimed in the West (see Kipp 1993). Rather, even in adulthood individuals are thought to pass through several stages as they move from being parents to grandparents; over a long process of learning and guidance they gain greater wisdom and responsibility (Blackwood 2000; Howard 1996). In Indonesia, then, personhood is an ongoing process, never completely achieved, but something that is multiple, relational, and situationally specific (Kipp 1993, 8).[10] One is not born with the necessary traits of womanhood or manhood but learns them throughout life.

In reflecting on the past, tombois emphasize the importance of particular environmental influences. I did not ask them why they thought they were boys, nor did the topic come up in their childhood narratives. The following comments were offered during other conversations. Tommi and I were discussing h/er relationship with h/er family when s/he said: "I have two brothers and two sisters, and I'm in the middle. I didn't know which way to go, so I went with my brothers" [the last part was said with a grin]. Tommi's next oldest and next youngest siblings were both male. In the context of this conversation s/he characterized the influence of h/er brothers as a key element in h/er being a tomboi. Robi's explanation for becoming a tomboi drew on the same theme, attributing h/er behavior to the fact that h/er surroundings were dominated by men. Of Robi's six siblings, five were boys. In addition h/er family's business brought in primarily men customers, so men were constantly around. Similarly, another tomboi, who was the ninth of eleven children, only three of whom were girls, explained to me that s/he is like s/he is because s/he grew up with so many brothers. Tombois' stories accentuate the influence of a masculine environment and their decision to follow or emulate their brothers.[11]

The long-term salience of this view in Indonesia is apparent from a 1968 report by a psychiatrist, who claimed that male transvestite behavior was the result of "a dominant mother, absent father, and *too many sisters*" (Peacock 1978, 215, italics mine). More than a decade later, in an anonymous magazine article, a young man attributed his homosexual experiences to his environment, including the fact that he was the only boy in a family of six children (Translation Group 1984). While media reports tend to characterize these environmental factors as unfortunate, tombois seem to value their experiences positively (except for Robi, see below) because they are proud to be like their brothers. In this way they follow dominant discourse yet at the same time appropriate it to their own meanings.

Girlfriends shared the belief that environmental influences led to tombois' masculine behavior. Noni declared that both of her tomboi lovers were shaped by their close relationships with their brothers. She told me that Diah, her first tomboi partner, was one of five children and the only daughter. She said, "Diah took after h/er brothers because that was all s/he had around h/er." In relation to her current partner, Noni mentioned that Robi's home environment was very similar to Diah's because it too was all male. Then she clarified, "Their families are all guys so they see that their brothers can do something, and they think, why can't I do that too. Eventually their personalities become like [their brothers']." Noni's view reflects the popular discourse mentioned above in the *Kartini* article in which young girls' attraction to "acting like a man" is said to be caused by the feeling that "boys are stronger, freer, and advantaged in all ways" (1984, 48). Noni also noted, "In addition, physically they [tombois] are strong too and have a supportive environment," giving credence to the plurality of possible causes presented in print media. According to Noni, becoming gendered for tombois was a matter of seeing the possibilities ("they see their brothers can do something") and over time becoming that gender because it was suitable ("they are strong too"). Noni seems to suggest that this process is a conscious choice for tombois, but she also indicates that it takes time and hence may not be something actually thought out or consciously decided on. The idea that one might perceive a certain subject position as attractive and be drawn to it echoes Moore's theory that within particular cultural contexts, alternative models are available to everyone through the knowledge of what one should or should not do. Drawing on the discourse of environmental influences, tombois and their girlfriends assert that by seeing what boys can do, enacting that behavior, and finding it rewarding, tombois learn to become boys.

Another psychological formula that has widespread currency in Indonesia attributes homosexual behavior to unfortunate circumstances. This formula apparently makes use of Freud's theory that homosexual behavior is a failure of proper psychosexual development. The gay Indonesian men in Richard Howard's (1996) study envisioned their homosexuality as a product of family relationships and histories. Several of the men Howard interviewed attributed their sexual desires for men to family disharmony or changed circumstances after a father remarried, which left them feeling lonely and uncared for. This rationale also echoes media reports mentioned above concerning the necessity of a same-sex parent to proper gender development.

Two tombois' stories draw connections between difficult family relationships and their sense of self as tombois. Robi, who had had several relationships with women, told me several times that she became like h/er brothers so h/er mother would be nicer to her. "My mother didn't pay much attention to me, except to yell at me. I got more attention from my father than my mother. Because my mother was more loving to her sons than her daughters, I thought that if I was more like my brothers, my mother would love me better." Another time s/he told me, "I had a harsh upbringing (*keras didikan*). My older brother was always mean to me. One time during Ramadan when I was only six but had already started fasting, he sent me to the store to get *sambal* [a spicy sauce]." For Robi, two factors were important: the rough treatment s/he received at the hands of h/er brother, which forced h/er to be tough, and the absence of a loving mother.

Another young tomboi, Sal, had a life history similar to Robi's, which was told to me by a friend of the family. Sal h/erself recounted becoming a tomboi in h/er middle school years, but never mentioned any relationship between h/er tomboi-ness and family problems. An older married friend of Sal's told me that Sal, who was the only girl among four siblings, became a tomboi because s/he lost h/er mother early on, and h/er aunt, who took charge, was never very nice to her, always yelling at h/er. In this case the friend attributed problems arising from the family environment, particularly the absence of a nurturing mother, to Sal's becoming a tomboi.

Whether these environmental factors are believed to produce a desirable or undesirable outcome, the similarities in the stories among tombois, girlfriends, and gay men underscore a broader Indonesian discourse on the relation of social learning to the production of sex/gender. Although tombois' childhood narratives reveal a sense of always being tombois, the narratives do not at the same time suggest that they were born that way. Tombois draw on rationales available in the larger discourse on "homosexuality" and childhood development, in this case environmental factors, to make sense of their subject positions. While the two types of narrative are seemingly contradictory, both offer ways for tombois to situate their masculinity within larger sociocultural contexts and to provide a feeling of stability about who they are.

Rewards of Gender

What accounts for a child's particular responses to the rewards and sanctions of gendered social interactions? As noted in chapter 1, in the context of everyday life normative subject positions confer a certain power or efficacy, which Bourdieu calls the "sense of reality" found in mastery of a common code or dispositions (1990, 60). If practical sense guides a child toward a certain subject position, the power of normativity, and the intelligibility and efficacy it offers, compels a child's enactment of one or the other culturally defined genders, but not necessarily in accord with the gender assigned to particular bodies. Challenges to normative positions and discourses risk social disapproval and loss of material or social benefits. But in Foucault's analysis, such challenges may result in other so-cial or material rewards because they are produced by the discourses themselves and are intelligible as negations of or alternatives to the dominant discourse. Employing this analysis for the development of childhood subjectivity, I argue that the knowledge children have of gender, with its different rewards for mas-culine and feminine behaviors, moves some females to take up the masculine subject position and its particular rewards. By taking into account non-normative as well as normative genders, this theory of childhood development offers a way to understand the different responses children make without resorting to notions of disorder or deviance.

The processes of taking up a gender follow similar paths for tombois and their girlfriends. Tombois' narratives speak of desiring everything that pertains to boys from an early age. Girlfriends' narratives are much less definitive, speak-ing only of being just like other girls. Yet as tombois and girlfriends enact gender, their social interactions inform them of proper behavior for both boys and girls. The gender binary means that two models are available, each with its own set of rewards, pleasures, privileges, and drawbacks. Children respond to the same cues in different ways and may be drawn to one set of rewards or the other, depending on their social context.

For tombois the pleasures and rewards of being boys—outdoor activities, freedom of movement, risk-taking—come to be positively valued, while the re-wards of proper girlhood—"staying at home, quietly"—become negatively val-ued. In contrast, girlfriends value things feminine, including staying home, be-ing with mother, and doing domestic activities. Tombois' responses to gendered cues, incitements, and provocations move them toward masculine behaviors, while other females' responses to the same cues move them toward feminine behaviors. In this way some children find greater pleasure in acting like girls, with the particular rewards that femininity offers in their cultural context (for instance, being coddled, protected, or treated delicately), while other children experience pleasure in the cultural rewards of masculinity (for instance, freedom of movement, competition, and daring exploits). Both are a result of observa-tions, dominant discourses, embodied practices, and social interactions with significant others that construct a particular sense of self within the terms of a culturally defined gender binary.

Doing Gender

"If the inner truth of gender is a fabrication and if a true gender is a
fantasy instituted and inscribed on the surface of bodies, then it seems
that genders can be neither true nor false, but are only produced as the
truth effects of a discourse of primary and stable identity."

—JUDITH BUTLER

ABOUT TEN O'CLOCK ON A SUNDAY MORNING my research associate and I
went to see Robi, a tomboi, and Noni, h/er girlfriend, at their new place.
They rent three small rooms in a one-story, somewhat dilapidated boarding
house (*rumah kos*). One room serves as the kitchen and bathing (*mandi*) area. In
the kitchen area is a low shelf with a single burner for cooking, a small table for
dishes and glassware, and a low rough table for preparing food. The *mandi*, iden-
tifiable by the bucket of water and drainpipe in the floor, is partitioned from the
kitchen. The middle room, which serves as the social space, is empty except for
a piece of linoleum on the floor and a small, low, roughly constructed table with
linoleum tacked on the top. The third room is the bedroom, where Robi, Noni,
and Noni's young daughter sleep on a mat.

Dedi and Tommi were just rolling up their sleeping mats in the middle room
when we arrived. Tommi had come over after closing up h/er food stall around 11
o'clock the previous night. I asked jokingly if everyone slept together in the same
room, but Noni said, "Oh no, *mami* and *papi* slept in the other room." Tommi
hadn't bathed yet, so s/he got some clothes out of h/er backpack and went to
the *mandi* to wash and change. When s/he reappeared, h/er short hair wet, s/he
had on boxer shorts (men's undergarment) and a baggy T-shirt that displayed a
drawing of a hugely muscled male bodybuilder with "body muscle" written on
it. S/he quickly put on a pair of men's pants and pulled a ball cap over h/er short
hair. Noni, who is very pretty and feminine-looking, had dressed in tight jeans

and a tight-fitting top with very short sleeves; she had already applied lipstick. Her shoulder-length black hair was pulled back in a neat ponytail. Her partner Robi, short hair slightly rumpled, had on a baggy polo shirt and long pants. Dedi wore a short-sleeved men's shirt and long pants, h/er short hair trimmed above the ears.

Although it was late for breakfast, no one had eaten yet so we decided to get some groceries and make breakfast. Tommi volunteered to go purchase the groceries with the money we provided and took off on Robi's motorcycle. When Tommi got back with the groceries, Noni started frying eggs two at a time in a small pan over the single burner. Dedi offered to help with the cooking. Noni was not interested in Dedi's help and teased h/er, saying, "I doubt you know how to cook fried rice (*nasi goreng*)!" Undeterred, Dedi started chopping up green onions. After a little while, however, s/he was kicked out of the kitchen. Noni grumbled, "They [tombois] always make such a mess when they work in the kitchen." Noni finished cooking while Robi sat in the kitchen with her. When I teased Robi about hanging out in the kitchen, Noni said, "S/he doesn't want to let me out of h/er sight, s/he's afraid s/he'll lose me." Once the food was ready, the tombois laid out the mats and dishes and helped serve the food.

After the meal, all the tombois lit up clove cigarettes, while Noni, who didn't smoke, cleaned up. Robi looked after Noni's daughter, who is five. Earlier Noni had introduced Dedi and Tommi to her daughter as "aunt (*tante*) Dedi" and "aunt Tommi," but Dedi corrected her and said "uncle" (*om*). I asked Noni what she calls Robi, and she said, "I call h/er by h/er name, or honey." That brought chortles from the other tombois who teased them about being husband and wife (*suami–isteri*).

This vignette points to the gender normativity expressed by tombois and their girlfriends, from the tasks they performed down to the boxers Tommi had on. The only overnight guests at Robi's place were the tombois, since their girlfriends were not able to stay overnight away from home except under special circumstances. Noni, the one girlfriend present, cooked for everyone. Despite Dedi's efforts to help in the kitchen, s/he was not allowed to cook because Noni claimed cooking as her womanly prerogative. She claimed that Dedi would not know how to cook, pointing out that tombois always make a mess when they try to help. The tombois did not just sit around, however, but went out to get groceries, laid out the mats, and helped bring out the food. Robi looked after Noni's daughter when Noni was busy, but that was not unusual, since most Indonesian men are capable of looking after children for shorter or longer periods of time. The terms of reference Robi and Noni used (*mami* and *papi*) and Dedi's preference for uncle reflected distinctly gendered identities. Even their clothes and hair marked them differently. The tombois wore short hair, loose shirts or men's T-shirts and pants, while Noni wore long hair, feminine clothes, and makeup. Noni's tight top revealed the shape of her breasts, while the tombois' baggy clothes revealed nothing about the female bodies underneath.

Their apparent adherence to normative gender categories raises questions about expectations of resistance for queer subjects, questions I address at the end of the chapter. Throughout the chapter I examine how tombois and girlfriends produce, maintain and negotiate their gendered subjectivities in the spaces where they socialize together. I look at tombois' and girlfriends' self-descriptions, their social interactions with each other, and the linguistic strategies they use to identify themselves and each other to understand how their subjectivities rely on and yet play with normative categories of gender. In particular I highlight the way individual tombois and their women partners identify themselves in gendered terms, drawing on the rhetoric of gender difference to make sense of themselves. "Making sense" is the feeling that things are right in relation to others and the dominant discourses of the day. As I elaborate in chapters 6 and 7, these feelings of "rightness" may shift and alter across time and space as tombois and girlfriends interact with others in different contexts.

Space and Lesbi Interactions

Because tombois' and girlfriends' social interactions vary in different situations and spaces, I deploy an analysis of space as a critical tool to help identify the particular moments in which they take up certain subject positions. I concentrate on the everyday spaces that they frequent on a daily basis, focusing on the gendered expectations defining such spaces. Because space is gendered differently for men and women, the ways that tombois and femmes use space also differs, which then becomes a way for them to substantiate and negotiate their self-positionings. To address the specificities of these everyday spaces, I forego the typical division of space into "public" and "private," as it is used in the United States both popularly and in scholarly writing. "Public" is assumed to refer to everything outside the home and "private" to everything within the home, although critics of this dichotomy point out its structural and linguistic deficits as well as the conceptual blurring that occurs.[1] Space is always more complex and ambiguous than a bicameral image of public and private suggests, although the dominant interpretation of space may remain in place due to the power of normative structures.[2] In a regional metropolis such as Padang, space can be represented as three interpenetrable and overlapping spheres, which I identify as household, community, and public spaces. By extending what Susan Gal refers to as "the carto-graphic metaphors of everyday life" (2002, 79), I am not making claims to the boundedness of these three spatial categories, nor to their sociohistorical reality. I use them as metaphors for the types of social interactions that predominate in each space. Public space refers to more or less anonymous space, such as the mar-ket (*pasar*), buses, streets, and businesses, where one's gender expression is taken at face value. Community space refers to an intermediate or neighborhood space, where one is known or has a history and natal family. This space incorporates the neighborhood mosque, social and religious organizations that one participates in, neighborhood events, and family businesses. By distinguishing a space be-tween public and domestic arenas, I call attention to the importance of kin and neighborhood communities in creating networks and fields of operation in tom-bois' and girlfriends' lives, points which are developed more fully in chapter 6.

Nearly absent from these public and community spaces are any places where tombois and their girlfriends socialize on their own; rather, their daily lives com-mingle with those of kin and neighbors, a pattern fairly typical throughout much of Southeast Asia. Alison Murray (1999) notes a similar phenomenon among lower-class Jakarta lesbians, who do not have specifically lesbian spaces, but move in heterogeneous spaces shared with prostitutes, street toughs, and others. This lack of lesbian-only space for *tom*s and *dee*s in Thailand means that they have to make do with what Ara Wilson calls "generic space," the restaurants and shop-ping malls where homosocial and co-ed groups cluster (2004, 120) and where same-sex couples can pass unnoticed. In addition Sinnott (2009) found that *tom*s and *dee*s in her study make use of female homosocial spaces, such as dormitories, factories, and schools, as safe spaces conducive to same-sex relationships.

The third space is the more conventional household space, pertaining to do-mestic contexts and family residences. This space can be quite extensive, includ-ing the households of close kin both locally and in other cities across Indonesia, which serve as temporary residences for traveling kin and job-seekers. Typically in Indonesia adult offspring continue living with their natal kin until they have saved enough money to move to their own places, which are often also nearby their parents' houses. Those who do not marry, such as tombois, may keep per-manent residence at their parents' houses.

The domestic or household space tends to be neglected in queer studies in favor of anonymous public spaces in metropolitan cities or particular spaces that queers create, such as gay ghettos or lesbian-owned land.[3] Connections among LGBT individuals and their non-queer kin and communities are often over-looked, particularly in studies of white U.S. queers.[4] By focusing on larger public contexts, queer scholars tend to miss the multiplicity of differences that exists in any one space. To redress this lack of attention Bacchetta (2002) urges a rethinking of transnational queerdom through a scalar approach that attends to micro as well as macro scales.

In Padang lesbi I interviewed have almost no lesbi-only spaces where they can socialize apart from others, except for the rare private domestic spaces away from family and neighbors, such as Robi and Noni's apartment, and public spaces where they can socialize by hiding in plain sight, relying on coded language and the conventions of women's homosociality to create a safe space. Within community spaces where kin, neighbors, and friends mingle, tombois and girlfriends make use of "generic" co-ed spaces, such as restaurants and food stalls, because these are acceptable places for women to socialize. Even in these places young women and femmes must be careful not to be seen loafing about, for fear of appearing sexually available and thus calling into question their reputations as proper women.

For one small group of friends, the food stall operated by two femmes, Jeni and Nila, became the primary space for in-group socializing. Jeni, Andri's girlfriend of five years, was operating a small food stall with Nila in 2001. Built by Andri and h/er father, it sat on the edge of a busy thoroughfare a short distance from Andri's parents' house. It was open six days a week from 9 am to 11 pm and catered mostly to middle and high school students. Because Nila and Jeni were always there, the food stall became the favorite hangout and central meeting point for the network of women and tombois of which Jeni and Andri were a part. On any particular day I dropped by, I was likely to find one or two tombois hanging out there. The odd moments when no other customers were around provided opportunity for teasing and gossip among members of the group.

The edges of household space became another location for socializing. Andri and Jeni shared a room in Andri's family home. At one time it was the preferred site for Saturday night get-togethers. Andri's room was attached to h/er parents' house, but its only door opened to the outside. People coming and going from Andri's room were visible to family members, but interactions in h/er room were less visible. Because Andri's parents and other relatives were nearby, however, they acted as a damper on any intimate behavior, including hand-holding or kissing. Even this space was not lesbi-only; other friends of the tombois, including young straight men and street toughs, often joined them on Saturday evenings. While making the space less private, the mix of friends served to disguise the tomboi-femme couples. This strategy was similar to the one used by unmarried heterosexual women in Lombok, who kept their parents unaware of whom they were dating by socializing in co-ed groups (Bennett 2005). Even though physical affection between women is customary, tombois and their girlfriends had to be guarded in their interactions with each other in family and community spaces, lest someone overhear an intimate conversation or notice a hand laid too lovingly on a tombois' thigh. By careful use of normative spaces, however, they were able to steal moments and create niches in which their relationships and friendships flourished.

Tomboi Praxis and Self-Understanding

As adults, tombois perceive themselves to have a stable subject position congruent with a masculine gender. Consistent with their perceptions of themselves as boys when they were children, they lay claim to all the characteristics and behaviors attributed to men, including their feelings, actions (*tingkah laku*), and appearance (*penampilan*). When asked how s/he sees h/erself, Robi said, "I'm masculine, a tomboi. There is no difference between me and other men." Tommi said, "My feelings are the same as a man's. There is nothing womanly about me." Describing tombois in general, Tommi said, "As for tombois, their character (*sifat*) is the same as ordinary men." In fact the characteristics they attribute to themselves are the same ones they attribute to men. Both Andri and Danny admit to being hot-headed and at times crude and uncouth (*kasar*), both defining characteristics of young men in Indonesia. Jon, who works as a parking attendant at a market, describes h/erself in the following way: "I'm tough, but I have to be. After all, I'm responsible for guarding valuables at the market (*pasar*), the cars and sometimes people's purchases. I can't be shy or timid (*lembut*)."

In these comments tombois claim that they possess all the characteristics associated with men. The truth of their claims, however, is conveyed not just in what they say, but through what they do. One evening as we were driving home on a narrow, dark road, two of the tombois swooped recklessly past our car on a motorcycle, grinning broadly at us. Noni, who was sitting in the back seat of the car, exclaimed, "Those [tombois], they're not afraid of anything! They're so tough (*jantan sekali*). They look (*tampilannya*) just like guys. People don't know if they're guys or not, and they act so tough, other guys are afraid of them. So they're not afraid to go out at night at all." As far as Noni is concerned, tombois' enactment of masculinity is proof of their status as men. This sense of the importance of "doing" or enacting masculinity was confirmed in Tommi's clever comment on an Islamic law that forbids a woman to dress like a man. "According to Islam," Tommi said, "a woman that appears like a man sins." Then s/he grinned and continued, "But we are *doing* it, not appearing like it!" In Tommi's interpretation of h/er subject position, the "doing" makes it authentic.

My discussion of tombois' masculinity in this chapter attends to the ongoing process of enacting gender, once gender has taken shape in childhood. The concept of practical enactment, which emphasizes action or doing, gestures toward Butler's (1990) concept of performance, which she defines as practices, expressed in bodily gestures, movements and styles, through which gendered meanings are constructed. Performance, as I use it, does not mean acting out a role or consciously playing at something, nor is it a representation of an interior or essential truth. As Butler states, "There is no 'I' who stands behind discourse" (1993, 225). Performance conveys deeply felt and embodied meanings materially expressed. In defining practical enactment as performance, I find most useful E. Patrick Johnson's quare theory, which he uses to theorize racialized sexuality, in its insistence that subjectivities are "viewed both as discursively mediated and as historically situated and materially conditioned" (2005, 127). Johnson, who critiques queer theory for its failure to focus on materiality, brings bodies back into "performance of the self" by arguing that the body has to be theorized in ways that address "what it does once it is constituted and the relationship between it and the other bodies around it" (2005, 136).

Importantly for this study of tombois' everyday practices, actions may be conscious or not, and meanings can be manipulated, without requiring "thought-out strategies that can be expressed in language" (Moore 1994, 76). This perspective is useful to understand tombois' agency in expressing their masculinity without necessarily requiring conscious declarations. Being a man is something that is conveyed in tombois' day-to-day activities. Indeed just as their everyday practices speak for them, and become the evidence of who they are, so they offered these practices to me as all the evidence I would need to understand them.

Enacting Masculinity

To understand tomboi masculinity, then, is to see how it is expressed in their actions, their bodies, and their experiences in interaction with others. As in childhood, tombois' appearance follows the style for men. Robi said, "My clothes are almost the same as men's clothes, like the pants I wear. And sometimes I wear a ball cap." In fact, tombois' clothes are indistinguishable from men's clothing and include not just pants and ball caps, but men's shirt, belts and belt buckles, men's watches, men's lace shoes or tennis shoes. Even the sandals they wear, if they are not just the everyday flip-flops, are the heavier men's sandals. Absent is any makeup or jewelry, unless it is men's style of jewelry. The tombois I interviewed wear their hair short, about three to four inches long, although I was told Robi used to wear h/er hair longer, but it was pulled back, like young men do. I never saw any tombois with really short hair, as some men wear it. They tend to keep their hair a little long, thereby making their appearance somewhat ambiguous, a strategic move that keeps casual observers from asking questions and placates their families, points that are discussed more fully in chapter 6.

The tombois that I interviewed perform masculinity as they move in spaces dominated by men, work in men's jobs, and take up "manly" behaviors that are disallowed for women, such as smoking and drinking. Dedi said, "A tomboi considers h/erself a man at the moment s/he joins in the men's world (*dunia laki-laki*)." The men's world in Padang is found in the public spaces predominantly occupied by men, such as cafés, pool halls, bars, and street corners. Tombois say that they can hang out in men's spaces without fear of physical or sexual violence. In fact, they move with confidence in these spaces, even in locations dominated by men, like pool halls, and are often in the company of other men, both tombois and male-bodied men, especially younger, unmarried men. Tombois demonstrate an easy congeniality with men, as evidenced on a bus ride I took with Robi. While we were on the bus, s/he yelled out the window to several guys as we went past them. When we got off the bus, Robi greeted and roughhoused with the small cluster of young men who were hanging out at the bus stop, playfully hitting and thumping one guy on the chest.

In contrast, the girlfriends of tombois have distinctly different relations to public space, reflecting the gendered discourses circulating in the nation. Girlfriends move quietly through public spaces, taking care not to bring unwanted attention to themselves. Women rarely travel alone; a woman in public is usually accompanied by another woman, a group of women, or a kinsman. Women infrequently go out late at night unaccompanied and rarely loiter in public spaces, like food stalls or cafés, like men do. In the cities women who are out on the streets by themselves or in public places, such as bars or discos, are immediately assumed to be prostitutes or low-class women (Oetomo 2001). Young unmarried girlfriends go out less often than tombois and almost never leave the house alone or without a specific reason. One of the girlfriends in her mid-twenties rarely socialized with her lesbi friends who lived and worked in the same neighborhood because she was afraid a neighbor or relative would notice her there. Young unmarried women have to inform their parents of their destination; consequently unmarried girlfriends could only manage time away from home when they had legitimate reasons, such as going to the market or to a special public event like a fair.

Work interests are a key indicator of tombois' identification with men. Robi stated, "I feel more like a man because the things I do are more like what a man does." When I asked Tommi whether there was any difference between h/erself and men, s/he said, "No, nothing." Then s/he thought about it for a little while and continued, "No, we're the same ... because the jobs I like are those that men do." Tombois avoid jobs that are typically done by women, particularly since most wage jobs for women, such as clerk, cashier, or civil servant, require that they dress in feminine clothes. Such jobs do not fit with a masculine sense of self, so tombois work in jobs such as parking attendant; furniture-maker; driver (hiring out oneself and one's motorcycle to paying customers); and cook, which in larger eating establishments in West Sumatra is primarily a man's job. Other jobs these tombois hold, such as petty trader and shop owner/manager, are jobs in which both men and women work.

The freedom of mobility associated with men is another important aspect of their masculinity. Tommi considers h/erself the same as guys because, "I can go out at night, like guys do. And I can also sleep wherever I want to, like guys." Sal, who is in h/er early twenties and keeps a place at h/er maternal aunt's house, commented, "I like my freedom and don't want to be tied down." S/he is often away from home visiting other tombois or hanging out at the local coffee shop (*warung*). In 2004 both Tommi and Dedi spent occasional nights at Robi and Noni's apartment. Dedi said that h/er family recognizes s/he is a tomboi because s/he sleeps "here and there," a reference to a common practice and privilege of unmarried Minangkabau boys and men. After they reach puberty, boys do not usually sleep at home but stay over with friends or, for the more religious, the *surau* or prayer house in which religious studies and devotions take place. For young unmarried men in Padang this pattern means that they are generally free from familial supervision and control. Dedi is an expert at maintaining h/er freedom of mobility. Although s/he has a strong bond with h/er family, no one can keep track of h/er because s/he is often away from home. One time I dropped by Dedi's mother's house, but was told s/he was at h/er sister's house. Arriving at h/er sister's house, I was told s/he was at h/er mother's. As it turns out, s/he was at neither place but was off visiting a friend.

Smoking and drinking are prerogatives of men that tombois relish. Dedi said to me once, "Everything guys can do, I can do." "Like what?" I asked. "Well, like smoking and drinking." At any social gathering, tombois always have cigarettes in hand. Even on the occasion when we went swimming in a nearby river, I saw a couple tombois in the water with lit cigarettes. Dedi's tales of h/er youth are full of stories that involve both smoking and drinking and also highlight h/er freedom to come and go as s/he pleases.

One time during Puasa [the fasting month of Ramadan] Tommi and I were out all night drinking at a café. The owner had to throw us out. We could hardly walk so we took a taxi home. When we got to my house, it was about 3 am and everyone was asleep. We tiptoed into the house as quietly as we could and went to the bathroom to put our heads in the tub (*bak*) to try to sober up. Then we fell asleep with our clothes still on.

Another time when I stumbled home very late after drinking at a party, I fell asleep in my sister's car. As daybreak arrived, I woke up and saw my sister outside the house, so I pretended to be cleaning the car. When she saw me, she was startled, 'How come all of a sudden you want to clean the car!' After she left I took my aching head and went to sleep in my bedroom.

Later Dedi admitted, "Now I don't drink so much anymore, since it started bothering my stomach. I only drink if there's a party or when I get together with friends." Aside from stories about h/er girlfriends, stories about smoking and drinking are the ones Dedi chose to recount, suggesting the significance of these events to h/er. Dedi's stories lay claim to typical behavior for young men—the heavy drinking, smoking, and staying out late without supervision that is the world of men.

Embodied Masculinity

For tombois, being men is not about trying to act like men; tombois' masculinity is deeply rooted in their bodies, in the sense of embodiment that Bourdieu (1990) suggests, producing bodily sensations of rightness or wrongness depending on how they are treated. This embodied feeling was expressed by Tommi in h/er story about riding on the bus: "If the woman next to me treats me like a woman, by putting her hand on my arm or leg, it doesn't feel right." In public spaces in Padang and elsewhere, men and women typically do not touch; in this Muslim society such contact is deemed inappropriate and unseemly. Casual contact between women, however, is perfectly acceptable. But Tommi does not see h/erself as a woman and does not like being treated as if s/he is. In this situation the depth of Tommi's self-positioning as a man produces a bodily feeling of discomfort that Tommi reads as evidence of h/er masculinity.

The discomfort that tombois feel at being in the wrong place or situation with women was further evident at a gathering at Robi's house.

Noni had been sick for a couple days and was too tired and achy to get up. Robi sought out an old friend who had knowledge of herbs and healing rituals and asked him to put together an herbal remedy for Noni. Several of us were gathered in the room where Noni was lying as Robi prepared the mixture, which had to be applied directly to the body. We were there to lend our support; the focus of our thoughts is said to improve the success of the ritual. Once the preparation was ready, Robi took off Noni's sarong to apply the herbal concoction. Noni lay on the mat in her tank top and pair of boxers borrowed from Robi. Dedi, who had been sitting nearby, suddenly jumped up and left the room, saying, "I'm a guy!" (*awak jantan*, Minangkabau). S/he didn't return until the ritual was finished.

Given h/er response, it appears that Dedi was uncomfortable seeing Noni with so few clothes on. Unrelated men in this Islamic society should not be in intimate contexts with women other than their wives. It may be that Dedi was aroused by seeing Noni undressed, a feeling that led to h/er discomfort. Whatever the reason, and I did not ask Dedi why s/he left, s/he made it clear that s/he was leaving because s/he was a guy, implying that it was improper for h/er to be there. Leaving, however, was not just a matter of propriety, since other tombois chose to stay in the room, but of h/er own level of discomfort. In making such a comment, which was apparently intelligible to the others, s/he identified h/er gender ('I'm a guy') as the source of h/er discomfort. In this situation h/er identification with men and masculine practices produced bodily feelings of pleasure/discomfort at seeing Noni's body, and these caused h/er to walk away.

On another occasion Tommi's response at being treated like a girl was not discomfort but anger. This event occurred when Tommi, Dedi, and two other tombois were sightseeing in a popular tourist spot about two hours by bus from Padang. Dedi recounts the story:

As we were walking down the street a guy bumped into Tommi and poked h/er chest with his elbow. He thought s/he was a girl. Tommi grabbed him by the shirt and angrily challenged him to a fight. The guy got real nervous because there were four of us, so Tommi told him to go and get his friends if he wanted, and we would wait for him to return. The four of us waited there for about ten minutes, but when he still hadn't come back, we left. He must have been too scared to come back and fight.

Women who are harassed by men in public usually do not challenge them or even respond to them. To confront a man about such behavior would only make the situation worse because it could provoke further aggression on his part. These responses are associated with the concept of *malu* in Malay societies, discussed in chapter 3. Women, who are taught to be reticent, modest, and self-restrained, are ashamed if a man harasses them because they may be accused of having invited his attentions. In contrast, as Collins and Bahar (2000) note, any behavior that causes a man to feel *malu* may prompt an aggressive response. The young man who accosted Tommi apparently assumed Tommi would act like a girl and avoid further confrontation. "But," Tommi said gleefully, "he made a mistake this time and picked the wrong person, so he got what he deserved (*kena batu*)." Both Tommi and Dedi laughed when they recalled how the young man ran off after being challenged. In this incident Tommi's aggressive response to the other man's action reflects masculine understandings of *malu:* the disrespect shown by the other man is instantly met with anger and a challenge to fight.

Tombois I interviewed said that they embody masculinity in their physical movements as well as emotional responses. When I asked Andri to describe other tombois, s/he said, "You can tell by the way they walk, like a guy, and the way they talk, which is coarser and firmer." Sri asked Robi if s/he was ever taken for a man. Robi said, "I am often called *abang* (elder brother) or *mas* (sir), very often, because of the way I walk. For instance, if I go shopping [at the open-air market], I'll be asked, 'What do you want to buy, Bang?' I don't say anything" [meaning s/he does not correct the person]. "Bang," shortened from *abang*, is a form of address for a man. "Shopping" here is not a domestic or feminine task, since both men and women are sellers and buyers in markets in West Sumatra. On other occasions I noted how one tomboi, when seated on a crowded minibus, had h/er legs spread wide in the way men do, instead of held close together as women generally do. At get-togethers tombois sit cross-legged on the floor, in the style men use, rather than with their legs to the side, as is the women's style. In this performance of masculinity, bodily gestures and movements as well as vocal styles are all part of the gendered practices that mark tombois as men. In public spaces their proper performance of masculinity is read as masculine, resulting in them being hailed, like Robi, as men.

Even though tombois embody masculinity, they make a distinction between their physical bodies and male bodies. When I asked Dedi if there was any difference between tombois and men, s/he said, "Only in physical matters (*hanya fisik saja*). Men are stronger. And they can give their partners children." Robi, however, said s/he was as strong as men. When I asked Tommi if there was any difference between h/er and men, s/he grinned and said, "Here and here," touching first h/er chest and then h/er pubic area. As far as Tommi is concerned, only their bodies differentiate them from men, and the difference is limited to genitalia. According to the dominant ideology of sex/gender in Indonesia, physical genitalia and the ability to father children are considered part of one's sex/gender. Lacking these attributes, tombois distinguish their bodies from men's, seeing their own bodies as female to a certain extent, while at the same time minimizing the difference as much as possible.

In addition to appearance, behavior, and bodily movements that mark them as men, tombois see themselves as possessing a masculine spirit (*jiwa laki-laki*), a term that several of the tombois used to emphasize their identification as men. Like the older butches in Saskia Wieringa's (2007) study, Dedi said, "I have a man's spirit (*jiwa laki-laki*)," while Tommi said that one of the reasons s/he is a man is "because I can't present a feminine spirit (*jiwa perempuan*)." When asked how s/he saw h/erself, Andri stated that s/he sees h/erself as a *jaka*, a slang term for young man, and then said, "because of that I am friends with guys who are like me (*cowok yang sejiwa*)." *Jiwa* can be translated as soul or spirit, or the animating spirit behind something (Stevens and Schmidgall-Tellings 2004). I understand tombois' use of *jiwa* to mean "having the spirit of" something, such as someone who has a warrior spirit or heroic spirit. This meaning is somewhat different from a translation of *jiwa* as "soul," which in English refers to a distinct entity separate from the physical body, the essential or fundamental part.[5] *Jiwa* translated as "spirit" is more in line with tombois' own descriptions of becoming boys due to a masculine environment. In this sense *jiwa laki-laki* refers to a set of attributes and a masculine way of being that develops through experience over time, rather than something that is part of one's nature from the beginning.

Girlfriends' Self-Positioning

In line with their childhood narratives, girlfriends see themselves as indistinguishable from other adult women. They express interest in feminine tasks and occupations, such as cooking and handicrafts, and wear clothes and makeup like other women. Being "the same as other women," as they declare it, includes the attributes they possess and the occupations they take up. Girlfriends, like other women, Jeni said, "are refined, loving and polite. *Cewek* like a lot of attention, they like to be loved and spoiled." The types of jobs that girlfriends take reflect their identities as women. Nila and Jeni manage a food stall, for which they do all the cooking themselves. Another is a maid, a fourth a seamstress. The other girlfriends I interviewed are either still in high school or college, unemployed and living with their natal families, or at home raising children. Epi, who lives at home, makes and sells handicrafts to earn some income. Nila applied for a job as salesperson at one of the large shopping centers in town but did not get the job. Jeni briefly worked in a small café, and then worked as domestic help before she started selling food with Nila.

In addition to their occupational pursuits, girlfriends claim domestic interests. The things Epi likes to do are similar to her interests growing up. "I like to cook a lot," she said, "things like cake and cookies (*kué*)." Jeni said she likes to take walks, cook, and read popular magazines when she is not busy. Nila prefers to play volleyball and read in her spare time, although she has little time for either with her work schedule. As noted at the beginning of this chapter, Noni, who is unemployed, cooks for her family as well as any houseguests who stay over. She considers the kitchen her domain and prefers not to have tombois interfere. None of these occupations or interests set the girlfriends apart from other women.

Asked to describe their appearance, girlfriends do not have much to say about the clothes they wear, except to mention that they sometimes wear skirts. Their lack of comment, as in their childhood narratives, suggests that they do not see any need to point out the obvious. Asked to compare tombois and girlfriends in terms of their appearance, Jeni said that girlfriends' clothes are more feminine and that girlfriends wear more makeup than tombois. Based on my own observations, girlfriends' clothes without exception are the style worn by other women. Even if they wear jeans and T-shirts, these clothes are marked as feminine by their tighter fit, shorter sleeves, brighter colors, and feminine motifs, such as Hello Kitty. If girlfriends wear jewelry, the items are generally delicate and small. Earrings in particular separate them from tombois, who do not wear such jewelry. These feminine practices align the girlfriends with norms of appearance for women.

Girlfriends embody their understanding of femininity in their actions as well. At social gatherings with others of their group, girlfriends tend to sit quietly with their tomboi partners, laughing occasionally at the antics of the tombois. They do not smoke or drink beer at these gatherings. They only drive motorcycles if they are alone or with another woman; otherwise they ride behind, while their partners drive. I noted other differences between girlfriends and tombois at an outing I organized at the river a few miles outside of town.

> As we arrived at the river for a picnic and swim, the tombois made sure that we found a secluded spot away from curious onlookers. They chose a spot where the river ran about six feet lower than the bank. The river's edge was nothing but rocks and only gave us a few feet between the bank and the water. The river here was quite broad so that people on the opposite bank couldn't really see us that distinctly. Everyone quickly removed their outer layers of clothing and went into the water. Tombois kept their baggy T-shirts on and stripped to loose shorts, while the femmes had a mix of tight and loose underclothing they wore in the water. The river was shallow at that point and full of large, slippery rocks. While everyone got wet, the tombois were much more boisterous and energetic, splashing, clowning around, and threatening to dunk their girlfriends under water, while the

girlfriends moved more carefully in the water and tried to just dip in to get wet rather than splash around.

The physical embodiment of feminine gender is clear in girlfriends' restrained and careful movements, called for by dominant expectations of gender and taken on as appropriate to their gender as women. For girlfriends, their behavior speaks to a gender ideology that limits women's behavior and actions to careful and measured movements and disinterest in calling attention to themselves.

Same as, Different from: A View from the Gender Binary

The gender binary does not just inform the behavior of tombois and their girl-friends; gender as difference is the foundation of their self-identities and relationships. To the extent that tombois see themselves the same as men, they also see themselves as different from women. In this regard the behaviors and feelings tombois take up are all in conversation with what tombois see as their opposite, women. As Jon, the parking attendant, said "I'm tough. … I can't be shy or timid. I'm a forthright kind of person—my yes means yes. I'm quick to make friends, but I'm not easy to fool." "Like women" went unsaid. Sal said, "I like my freedom and don't want to be tied down," like women. Describing the differences between men and women, Sal was more explicit, "Women are gentle and easy-going, where guys are more to the point." Andri's description of the difference echoed Sal's, "Guys are rough, while girls are gentle and motherly." In these descriptions the comparison for tombois' behavior is women's behavior.

The tombois I interviewed cite attributes of their girlfriends that are dis-tinctly different from their own. In talking about h/er partner, Jon summed up Upik's personality by saying she has a motherly spirit (*jiwa keibuan*). Upik has not had children, but she is the one who takes care of domestic tasks in the house they share, such as cooking, cleaning, and laundry, and she looks after Jon's son when Jon is at work. Jon describes h/erself as having a masculine spirit. Andri said h/er girlfriend "is quiet, easy to get along with. As long as we've been to-gether, she has always been patient with me even when we have arguments." S/he said girlfriends have a feminine style and soft voices, not the "coarse voices" that s/he attributes to guys. When Danny described h/er girlfriend, s/he said, "Epi does what she is told; she can't refuse her parents or talk back to them." When I asked why, s/he said, "Because that is the way women are (*sifat perempuan*). They are more under their parents' control." In these descriptions all the attributes as-signed to their girlfriends differ from those they give to themselves.

103

For their part, girlfriends see tombois as distinctly different as well. Epi described Danny, her partner, in a manner opposite to Danny's description of her, "Danny cannot be forbidden from doing anything." Jeni called tombois "energetic and lively," while Nila went further and said, "They are hot-tempered, wild, whereas girls (*cewek*) are loving." In contrast Nila sees herself as timid. Noni, who declared tombois are not afraid of anything, said of herself, "I'm very afraid to go out at night alone. I'm a woman! Someone might try to rape me." In their descriptions, girlfriends attribute characteristics to themselves that match the normative model of womanhood. Epi described that model in the following way: "Women are gentle and feminine, not at all tough, whereas men are just the opposite; they're tough and resolute in everything."

Tombois' and girlfriends' views of each other join together in supporting their differences, a product of a distinct gender binary. I was struck by the way tombois are called *berani* (brave), while girlfriends think of themselves as meek and soft-hearted (*lemah lembut*). *Berani* conveys the sense of someone who is brave, courageous, daring, even reckless or a bit foolhardy, the opposite of someone who is gentle, easygoing, and mild mannered. These terms signify the way men are expected to take the initiative, be aggressive, and make decisions, while women are expected to follow along or go along with them. Lina said, "Women give in easily or leave it up to their partners (men)," which she attributes to the fact that women "always follow what people say," that is, they will heed other people's advice or do as they are told. Women are said to be more concerned about what people say about them and are careful to maintain their reputation by not doing things that will cause gossip. In this pairing of brave and meek, tombois are unruly, women are ruled.

The conception of gender held by tombois and girlfriends mirrors the dominant ideology represented by state and Islamicist leaders. By demonstrating that they are not what women are, tombois feel confident in their self-positioning as men. At the same time girlfriends do not need to question their own desires because they feel their self-presentation of femininity properly contrasts with that of the tombois. By evoking a shared sense of the world based on the gender binary, they set the framework for interactions and negotiations in their relationships.

Fantasies of Gender

In considering the interactions between tombois and girlfriends, I find Moore's concept of "fantasy" useful. Moore uses fantasy "in the sense of ideas about the kind of person one would like to be and the sort of person one would like to be seen to be by others" (1994, 66). This notion of fantasy appears to be a very conscious process, but Moore highlights its "affective and subconscious nature." Tombois' and femmes' understanding of each other constitutes a deeply held fantasy about the difference between men and women. Their world only makes sense in terms of those gendered understandings. The depth of this fantasy was expressed by Lina, one of the girlfriends, when she asked me, "Uni, what position [tomboi or femme] are you?" Sal thought I must be a tomboi because of my short hair but was confused by my earrings, which suggested I was femme. When I showed Sal a photo of my girlfriend in her firefighter uniform, s/he knew s/he had the answer. My partner fit the tomboi category, making me unquestionably a femme.

The question "What are you?" was asked or whispered of anyone new or foreign who did not quite fit the parameters of tomboi or femme. When an Australian friend of mine, who had very short hair, came to visit, everyone was curious to know "what" she was.

> The two of us went to Tommi's café one evening with Dedi, Robi, and Noni. We had been chatting and smoking clove cigarettes for a while (except for Dedi and Noni), when Dedi pulled me aside and whispered, "Is she the same as us?"
>
> I nodded yes, thinking that Dedi meant, does she desire women. A little while later, Tommi came up to me and asked more directly, "Is she tomboi or femme?"
>
> "What do you think?" I replied.
>
> "It's hard to tell with foreigners, but I think she's probably a tomboi," Tommi said.
>
> Dedi finally got up the nerve to ask my friend directly and was rewarded with an even more confusing response, "I'm mixed (*campuran*)," meaning she was a little of both, masculine and feminine. That response was completely unsatisfactory to Dedi, who remained unsure of how to interact with this foreigner.

In their frame of reference, my friend's appearance (short hair), behavior (smoking), and apparent freedom of mobility (traveling alone in West Sumatra) identified her as a tomboi. But, knowing that foreigners are hard to read, they persisted in trying to establish whether she was tomboi or femme. The answer, however, gave them nothing to work with and only confirmed how problematic foreigners can be.

The photos and postcards I brought from the United States were equally perplexing to them. Having been unable to discuss my personal life when I conducted research in a rural village in West Sumatra in 1989–1990, I wanted my friends in Padang to have some sense of who I was and how I lived my life. By bringing photos of my lesbian friends I wanted to provide information on the everyday lives of lesbians in the United States, a space up until that time for them occupied by such internationally famous lesbians as Martina Navratilova and Melissa Etheridge. I also hoped that such knowledge would provide support for the particular obstacles they faced. My lesbian friends, residents of a small university town in the Midwest, reflected a white, middle-class, androgynous lesbian style popular in the 1970s in U.S. urban lesbian communities and still popular in less metropolitan areas. I hoped the photos would allow them to see that we shared a commonality as "lesbi," the term that I used to describe myself to them.

The photos of my friends, however, were disappointing both to the tombois and the femmes. Everyone in the photos had short hair. Robi, who said jokingly as s/he looked at the photos that s/he wanted to find an American girlfriend, could not find anyone who seemed attractive to h/er. "I want someone feminine," s/he said. "Two tombois together would not be good." Lina examined the photos, trying to determine who was tomboi and femme, and gave up, complaining that it was too hard to identify them properly. Other than having short hair, most of the women did not look masculine enough to her.

My collection of U.S.-made "lesbian" postcards was equally disappointing, but more so for the femmes. I showed Jeni the postcards and told her to pick one to keep. She looked through the cards and finally, with little evident delight, chose one with a picture of a woman in a leather jacket and cap, who was standing next to a slightly shorter, softer-looking woman in casual clothes. I finally realized what was happening. The woman in the leather jacket was the only one in all the cards who came close to resembling a tomboi-type person. Most of the pictures on the postcards would probably appeal only to the tombois because all the women in the photos were attractive in a feminine-looking way with thin, graceful bodies and longish hair. The only contrast between the women in some of the cards was in hair color (light or dark) and length of hair (shorter or longer). The cards I had chosen showed "lesbians" in a narrow range of femininities, alluding to differences only by contrasting hair color and length.

To the lesbi in Padang I interviewed, couples are comprised of tombois and femmes; anything else seems strange and unappealing, because it does not resonate with their understanding of the lesbi world. They did not doubt that I was lesbi, although they were eager for me to bring my partner to Padang so they could see her for themselves, but they assumed all lesbi fit the binary mold. They were as perplexed with my rather androgynous friends as I was when introduced to a very feminine girlfriend on my return trip in 2004. Despite knowing the categories of tomboi and femme, I still found myself wondering if she was "lesbi" or not because she looked just like an ordinary woman (*cewek biasa*). If she had not been with a tough-looking tomboi, I would not have "seen" her as a lesbi. The world makes sense when it fits the appropriate fantasies of gender; otherwise there is neither intelligibility ("what are you") nor sexual attraction.

Negotiating Gender: Tombois' and Girlfriends' Interactions

In the preceding sections I discussed how tombois and girlfriends take on a sub-ject position, how they see themselves and come to their own meanings, in rela-tion to the structures and discourses that frame their understandings. If a subject position is always in relation to others, as Moore (1994) notes, then interactions with others on an everyday basis, whether family, kin, friends, or strangers, and through them the institutionalized discourses and practices that each engages, become an important part of the production of lesbi subjectivities. Social interac-tions convey sanction or reward for the particular positions taken up. One's self is confirmed (as well as challenged or negated) by other selves. I explore in this section the way identities, meanings, and categories are continually rehearsed, interrogated, confirmed, disclaimed, or elaborated through social interactions among tombois and girlfriends.

I draw on Moore's (1994) use of the concept of "investment" here to at-tend to questions of power and identity in the negotiation of tomboi and femme subjectivities. Having taken up a particular subject position, individuals become invested in maintaining their position because of the socially defined pleasures or rewards consequent on that position. One of the problems with using a term such as investment, however, is that it smacks of rational choice or calculated decision-making. To counter such a criticism, Moore (1994) argues that invest-ments can be made through practice and need not be done consciously. A further criticism of the term stems from the concept of social reward, which may seem to be relevant only for those in dominant subject positions, with power to control others' lives. Social rewards, however, do not come in just one form but take dif-ferent forms in different contexts and even different interactions (Moore 1994). Individuals may find pleasure in some contexts or social interactions, such as tombois' in-group interactions, which become highly valued, and these outweigh the displeasures found in other contexts, such as with disapproving kin.

Although tombois and girlfriends narrate their genders as coherent and fixed both in their childhood narratives and their stories about themselves as adults, they constantly monitor and judge each other's behaviors in relation to the standards of normative gender. For tombois these interactions can reinforce or call into question one's masculinity. One time when I visited Robi and Noni at their place, we decided to play dominoes with the other tomboi who was hanging out with them that day. As play progressed, I began to notice a clear difference in playing styles. Each time the two tombois played a domino, they took their turns quickly and decisively, solidly smacking the domino down on the table. When Noni and I took too long to play or tried to duplicate the smack of the domino on the table without success, there were snickers and teasing about being *cewek*. These comments reinforce the differences between tombois and femmes in the same way that displays of drinking and smoking, or for girlfriends, working in the kitchen preparing food, reaffirm those differences.

At other times tombois challenge each other to live up to their identities as men. Tensions occasionally arise because of the need to guard their intimate relationships from kin or from competition with other tombois. In these moments failure to maintain one's proper self-identity threatens the edifice of gender so carefully constructed, provoking strong responses. The following story, based on Dedi's account of events, took place at a New Year's Eve party:

> Dedi attended the party with a woman s/he was interested in. As the party went along, Dedi got very drunk and started making embarrassing comments to the woman. Things got tense when Danny got involved because Danny didn't like how Dedi was treating h/er date. Finally Danny yelled at h/er, "Hey man, you're nothing but a cunt!" (*Dasar pepek ang!*). The femme joined in the verbal attack and told Dedi, "You're a coward (*jiwa penakut*)! You don't even have the nerve (*tidak berani*) to say how you feel about me!" After that they got into a war of words until one of the tombois, who was also interested in the femme, punched Dedi in the head. Too drunk to retaliate, Dedi tried to enlist the help of h/er friend Tommi but to no avail because Tommi was also very drunk. So Dedi left the party and stumbled home alone.

In this situation Dedi's failure to treat h/er date decently, as a gentleman should, brought the wrath of the other tombois as well as the femme. Danny's derisive outburst, *dasar pepek ang*, is an insult that refers to Dedi's genitals (*pepek*, a vulgar term for vagina) as female. *Pepek* in this phrase is contrasted with *ang* (you, masculine), which is the Minangkabau second person masculine pronoun *wa'ang* (shortened to *ang*). I translate it as "Hey, man," since English has no comparable pronoun. Tombois frequently use this pronoun when talking to each other, particularly if they are joking or, as in this case, disciplining someone. The statement pointedly reminds Dedi that s/he is not acting like the man s/he professes to be and thus is in danger of losing h/er credibility and becoming what is the base or foundation (*dasar*) of h/er identity, female. The argument ends with a physical blow from another tomboi, an expression of masculine aggression that reflects tombois' willingness to fight. In contrast to that masculine act, Dedi is told by the femme that s/he is no better than a coward, which is certainly not a manly attribute, and, worst of all, that s/he is lacking in bravery, that quintessential quality of manhood.

Dedi's efforts to police h/er date result in h/er verbal and physical disciplining by both her date and by other tombois, an intervention that attempts to ensure Dedi's proper behavior as a tomboi. By responding harshly, the other tombois shore up the particular investments they have in their subject positions, even at the risk of creating disharmony among themselves. In fact, Dedi told me that after the incident s/he refused to talk to the tomboi who hit h/er, even though s/he was an old friend, because Dedi thought the treatment s/he received was unfair. In this situation Dedi was shamed, not for being drunk and out of line, but for not acting like a man. H/er behavior threatened the stability of the tombois' sense of masculinity, leading to adverse consequences for Dedi and a stinging reminder to keep the border between genders intact. By scrutinizing and commenting on each others' behaviors and actions, tombois learn to live up to and maintain proper gender codes.

Enforcing Normality

Tombois' careful maintenance of hegemonic masculinity extends to their interactions with their girlfriends, who are expected to uphold proper femininity. Robi told me, "Femmes are almost the same as ordinary women, in their character, clothes, and the way they act, so it's rather difficult to tell the difference between a femme and other women." Underlying Robi's declaration of femme equivalence with women is the expectation that femmes should act like women. Andri said, "Women are feminine; they wear their hair long and wear skirts. That's why I told Jeni to grow her hair long. I don't like girls with short hair." Andri here rehearses the dominant norms of gender difference for women and confirms h/er own attraction to feminine traits, such as long hair. Because of h/er own investment in these norms, s/he insists that h/er girlfriend maintain them as well.

Tombois I interviewed feel that it is very important for women to behave properly, a point that femmes generally agree with. According to Tommi, "Unlike tombois, young women are always asked where they are going, and with whom, and told to be home by a certain time. Parents fear for their daughters, so they set limits." Dedi said, "If a woman acted like that [like a tomboi], it would be bad, people would think badly of her." Because of social norms of femininity, women are strongly discouraged from going out alone at night, a practice that tombois supported by escorting their girlfriends home in the evening or refusing to let them go out at night unaccompanied. If Lina visited Tommi at h/er food stall in the evening, Tommi made sure that Lina either got home before 8:30 pm or that s/he gave her a ride home on h/er motorcycle, thereby guarding Lina's reputation as a proper woman. Similarly, Robi said, "I don't want Noni out late at night. It doesn't look good." The interaction between Robi and Noni over serving tea, described in chapter 1, also speaks to this rehearsing of proper femininity. In this instance, Robi insisted that Noni should make the tea, while Robi should sit with h/er guests as a man would in the same situation. Noni's quickness to comply and her expression of chagrin at forgetting showed her investment in the norm as well. By encouraging womanly behavior, tombois police the boundaries of femininity for their girlfriends and at the same time reinforce gender normality.

Girlfriends in most cases concur with these actions because they, too, endorse the notion of womanly propriety. At that fateful New Year's Eve party, one of the things Dedi said to h/er date was that she should not drink, but h/er demand went unheeded. The fact that h/er date did not conform to proper feminine behavior and drank despite being told not to, disrupted generally agreed-on gender codes and created serious repercussions among the tombois over how to manage the situation. In the contest over the unattached femme, Dedi's abusive verbal behavior was punished, while the femme's refusal to do what she was told was supported by the other tombois. Dedi, however, felt that h/er date's behavior reflected poorly on h/erself and h/er position as a tomboi. A properly feminine girlfriend works to consolidate and reinforce tombois' own masculinity and vice versa. Through each normalizing interaction, tombois and femmes reclaim and reproduce their genders in opposition to each other and in line with dominant ideological formations. Their desires to maintain the norms reflect an investment in the subject positions they have taken up. I am not suggesting, however, that tombois and girlfriends consciously accommodate the gender binary. They remain largely uncritical of the way gender discourses reinforce ideas of binary gender because for them the binary is the natural expression of gender and sexuality.

Linguistic Strategies and the Production of Gendered Selves

Because social interactions are structured by communicative practices, I now turn to the linguistic strategies employed in the creation and negotiation of tomboi and femme subject positions. I asked Robi how the tombois address each other when speaking. S/he said, "We just use our names to speak to each other. But sometimes if we're fighting (*berantam*), I'll call [a tomboi] *wa'ang* (you^m)." *Wa'ang*, as noted, is the masculine form of second person singular "you" in the Minangkabau language (Moussay 1998). In an article on linguistic gender-bending, Anna Livia (1997) suggests that the same devices, such as pronouns, that limit gender expression can be used to reverse or exceed gender. Livia argues further that these devices create gender identities, a point I take up to explore linguistic conventions among tombois as they work to substantiate and reinforce their gender identities as men.[6]

In addition to calling each other "guy" (*cowok*), tombois frequently use Minangkabau masculine pronouns when speaking to each other. Minangkabau is the language learned at home in West Sumatra and a marker of Minangkabau ethnic identity. Although children become fluent in the national language of Indonesian (*Bahasa Indonesia*), which is the language used at school, Minangkabau remains the preferred language at home and in everyday contexts. Many Minangkabau speakers are more expressive in their first language and feel more comfortable using it. In Minangkabau the second person singular has a masculine form, *wa'ang* or *ang* (you^m), and a feminine form, *engkau* or *kau* (you^f), which are used for persons of equal or lower status (see Table 4.1). Third person singular is gender neutral in Minangkabau, as in Indonesian (Moussay 1998).

Use of *wa'ang* in speaking to another tomboi depends on the context. *Wa'ang* may be used in ordinary conversation between two tombois, as in the following two examples.

"*ang* Di" (Dedi^m): the speaker uses *ang* as a masculine modifier when addressing Dedi

"Kawan model apo *ang* bawo ko Dedi?" (Minangkabau) (What sort of friend did you^m bring, Dedi?"): the speaker uses the masculine pronoun *ang* when asking whether the woman with Dedi is a femme or tomboi.

TABLE 4.1 Indonesian and Minangkabau pronouns

Pronouns		
Indonesian	English	Minangkabau
aku	I	*awak*
kamu	you	*wa'ang* (masculine)
		engkau (feminine)
dia	he/she	*inyo*

As Robi mentioned, tombois also call each other *wa'ang* when they are fighting or joking around. This usage was evident in the phrase *"Dasar pepek ang"* (Hey man, you^m're nothing but a cunt!) uttered during the altercation at the New Year's Eve party. This phrase acts as a form of verbal discipline to warn against improper tomboi behavior. During the same event, Dedi turned to h/er close friend for help and finding h/er too drunk to be of use, said, *"Seperti iko namonyo bakawan awak, katiko kawan ditinju wa'ang indak mambantu!"* ("What kind of a friend are you when I'm getting knocked around, and you^m don't help!)?!) Here the masculine "you" is thrown out as a challenge to rouse the other tomboi to join in the fight. In another instance, when a tomboi was grilling my research associate about her interest in studying tombois, Tommi intervened by saying, "So, dude [you^m], what do you [name] think about … ?" as a way to cut off questions that were becoming somewhat impolite.

Both waria and tombois engage in pronoun-switching. Waria in Padang call each other *kau* (you^f), particularly when they are arguing, according to Robi. Waria use of feminine pronouns may have provided the model for tomboi usage, given that many of the code words used by tombois and their girlfriends come from waria vernacular and practice, a point I discuss further in chapter 7. Unfortunately, there are no histories of these practices. In Padang, tombois' use of *wa'ang* may be following and emboldened by waria usage, which in turn reflects the way tombois see waria as having an analogous position outside gender normative categories. Waria use of *wa'ang* when addressing their tomboi friends likewise suggests a feeling of solidarity with tombois.

Switching gender pronouns is not a linguistic strategy used only by tombois and waria, however. Danny told me that some of h/er men friends use *wa'ang* when addressing h/er or other tombois they know, a fact that also offers some indication of the acceptance of tombois as men within (certain limited) men's circles. Nor is gender-switching used only in reference to those outside of gender normative categories. Normatively gendered Minangkabau youth also engage in gender-switching, using opposite gender pronouns to tease each other. According to Sri, some young women she knew, who were tomboi-ish but not lesbi, would sometimes call each other *wa'ang* in jest

Use of these pronouns is context-specific. *Wa'ang* is only used in spaces where other tombois, girlfriends, and, on occasion, men friends, are present, and are avoided when kin or family are present. Livia (1997) sees many possibilities in using linguistic gender against normative meanings. When used by gay or transgender groups, it may "express in-group solidarity, or outsider status, sympathy, or antagonism," or then again it may express gender fluidity by its ability to move one outside of normative gender (Livia 1997, 365). Livia suggests that these uses are both paradoxical and ironic, meaning that they seem to support the gender system at the same time that they play with and perhaps challenge such systems. The same devices that limit gender expression—pronominal gendering and gender concord—can be used to reverse or exceed gender.

In like manner tombois' use of *wa'ang* in certain contexts can be meant as a challenge to another tomboi to act like a man or a put-down for not acting masculine enough. As a practice shared among tombois and waria, it may express solidarity within and across these two groups. Finally, and more critically, tombois' use of a masculine pronoun dissociates the speaker from gender normative constructs in which the expected pronoun is feminine. As Livia points out, pronoun-switching suggests that linguistic conventions can be used in the creation of gender identities. For tombois, using the Minangkabau masculine "you" as a sign of masculinity is a verbal strategy that creates the desired gender. I take Livia's explanation farther, however, to suggest that such conventions among tombois work not just to create but to substantiate and reinforce their gendered positioning as men. Thus, the act of shifting gendered pronouns, as Livia (1997) notes, paradoxically calls into play the very binary system that excludes certain speakers who then use it to generate their own meanings. This ability to make use of linguistic conventions for different ends suggests the agency of speakers in creating their own vision of the world (Livia 1997).

Tombois' assertion of masculinity through the use of a masculine gender pronoun in certain contexts is even more noteworthy in light of the fact that in the Indonesian language, pronouns are gender neutral. For instance, the third person singular is *dia* regardless of the gender of the person being spoken about. Being proficient in Indonesian, tombois could use *dia* to avoid marking each other as masculine or to mask gender identity. Still another set of Indonesian pronouns are available to mask gender identity. *Aku/kamu* (I/you), which are gender neutral, are used in informal speech in certain areas of Indonesia, more so in urban areas as well as in popular songs, and are the preferred pronouns among teenagers in flirtatious or romantic contexts. Indonesian citizens are adept code-switchers, but in general conversation tombois do not call each other *kamu* as a way to avoid using the Minangkabau you[f], *engkau*, although I have heard *kamu* used in personal conversations between partners. Instead they rely on the Minangkabau convention of using first names in place of pronouns. In West Sumatra it is common for a speaker to replace first and second person singular nouns with personal names or terms of address, so that for instance, "I" is replaced with the speaker's name, and "you" is replaced with the name of the person being addressed.[7] Use of the gendered *wa'ang* among insiders, including men friends, then takes on particular significance as a critical aspect of tomboi linguistic practices that serves to emphasize, highlight, and leave no doubt as to one's masculine gender.

Girlfriends' and Couples' Speech Practices

Both tombois' and girlfriends' conversational speech practices construct and index their gender positions. A comparison of tombois' with girlfriends' speech practices reveals certain key differences between them. Tombois perform masculine styles of speech, which include speaking more coarsely and crudely, as their use of *wa'ang* in some contexts suggests. In group settings they are likely to engage in verbal taunting and teasing, practices that show off their aggressive masculinity to their girlfriends. Loud joking and roughhousing are properly the domain of men and tombois, especially young men and *préman* (street toughs). Such behavior is not something that women engage in with men. Likewise girlfriends do not engage in the boisterous wisecracking or name-calling of tombois, preferring to perform the speech practices of other women, particularly in public or familial spaces.

Girlfriends express their femininity through careful avoidance of conversational practices, such as use of coarse language and vulgarity, that would label them as loose women. I have no record of girlfriends using *wa'ang* when talking to tombois, although it may occur in one-on-one conversations or arguments. They generally avoid using second person singular in conversations with their tomboi partners, preferring the Minangkabau convention of calling others of the same age by their names. For instance, when I asked Noni what she calls Robi, her tomboi partner, she said, "I call h/er by h/er name, Robi or Rob, and sometimes honey." "Honey" would be used only in private contexts. This naming convention is considered a more respectful way to address another person. For their part, girlfriends' speech practices signify their membership in the category of normative woman and indicate an ongoing desire to be seen as proper women.

In private or intimate contexts couples make greater use of gender-specific terms of endearment and kin terms. Girlfriends call their partners *papi* (daddy), or in some cases, *abang* (older brother), a common form of reference used by heterosexual married women for their husbands. Depending on the context, tombois may call their girlfriends *mami* (mommy) or *adik* (younger sibling [gender neutral]). *Adik* is a term that husbands use for their wives regardless of age difference. In calling their partners *papi*, girlfriends show their allegiance to dominant gender norms for intimate partners by placing their partners in binary opposition to themselves (*mami/papi*). Since this term is only used in private, however, girlfriends do not employ it in an effort to pass as heterosexual women but as a sign

114

of support for their partners' sense of self, a sign that also positions girlfriends properly within the ideological gender binary. While girlfriends' use of terms of endearment accords with their self-positioning as proper women, at the same time, by calling their partners *papi*, they help to bring into being and participate in a vision of the world that ignores the (culturally constructed) incongruity of the tomboi's body to h/er masculine self and creates a space for relationships that contradict the dominant constructions of gender and sexuality.

In line with the normative gendering of intimate relationships, tombois and their girlfriends sometimes speak of their relationships as that of husband and wife. Noni said to me, "I consider Robi my husband, and I am h/er wife." When Tommi showed me a photo of h/er current girlfriend, s/he looked at me with a twinkle in h/er eye and said, "Wife," grinning broadly. Tommi could have said "my wife" or "the wife" but said simply "wife" (*isteri*). Because we were at h/er workplace when s/he showed me the photo, s/he uttered only one word softly, making a claim about their relationship while at the same time endeavoring not to be overheard. Another time when a group of us were together at Robi's place, Dedi showed me a high school photo of h/er girlfriend that s/he carried in h/er wallet. When I asked who it was, s/he said with a broad smile, "The wife" (*isterinya*). I take Tommi's and Dedi's smiles to mean that they are playing with and yet participating in a normative discourse that delegitimates their relationships with their girlfriends. At the same time they are willing to imagine and desire just such a relationship for themselves, that is, to be husbands and wives.

While the juridical terms "husband" and "wife" are not used as terms of endearment, the more affectionate terms *mami* and *papi* are used, as well as other kin terms, both between partners and among group members. Noni told me that everyone in their group of friends calls her *mami*. Another woman, who is older than her tomboi lover, is called *mami* by all the tombois. Both these women have children and are older than several members of the group. Creation of family through kin terminology extends beyond the use of *mami* and *papi*. Within h/er group of lesbi friends, Robi is called affectionately "uncle" (*uncu*), a Minangkabau term for one's mother's younger brother, signifying h/er place as elder in the group. As mentioned in the opening vignette, Dedi wanted to be called uncle by Noni's daughter.[8] Dedi did not insist on being called uncle, however, because children cannot be trusted to know the right times to use such terms. Instead Dedi was making a point that in this context and family, s/he occupies a masculine kin category.

On another occasion, Danny and Andri were trying to figure out the appropriate kin terms for each other and their girlfriends.

Danny said, "Andri is my *ipar*." Andri looked quizzically at h/er. Danny thought for a second and then said "Oh, no, Jeni [Andri's girlfriend] is my *ipar* because Jeni is married to Andri, my younger brother (*adik*)."

Danny explained to me that *ipar* means sister-in-law, the one married to your brother. S/he said, smiling, "That makes us family (*bersaudara*)."

In this conversation Danny extends kin terminology not only to h/er best friend Andri, whom s/he identifies as h/er younger sibling (*adik*), but to Andri's girlfriend Jeni, whom s/he calls sister-in-law (*ipar*). Andri does not object but is confused that Danny might be calling h/er "sister-in-law" and therefore female. Danny's confusion about the proper use of the term *ipar* suggests that it is not a term often used within the context of the group. By assigning these kinship terms to h/er friends, with me as witness, Danny purposely extends the concept of family and kinship (*bersaudara*) to those who share the same understanding of lesbi relationships. S/he also asserts h/er vision of Andri and Jeni's relationship as a marriage, laying claim to the normative heterosexual category. In these instances tombois take the available kin terms for heterosexual couples and use them creatively to define their own gendered relationships. By extending the idiom of kinship beyond individual couples to other group members, they also create, or to use Deborah Cameron and Don Kulick's (2003) phrase, materialize through language kin ties among those whose relationships are excluded from normative family ties.[9]

Although these speech practices and terms of endearment participate in normative categories, I do not see them as efforts to imitate dominant categories of meaning. Rather, by making use of available gender and kin constructs, including those that circulate translocally, these practices lay claim to and substantiate a particular sense of self and of kinship that does not completely align with normative categories. Through their speech practices tombois and their girlfriends assert particular gendered subjectivities that on the one hand rely on normative gender constructs and yet on the other hand move beyond binary gender because they disregard normative body assignments.

Resistance and Queer Subjectivities

Visible in their interactions and linguistic strategies are the meanings and dimensions of tombois' and girlfriends' gendered world. In their relationships they move within the terms of a binary gender discourse, using difference to assure themselves of their proper places. Deeply rooted, this discourse produces a sense of reality in which only two options are possible and assumed to occur naturally. Behavior that muddles a clear binary is not tolerated. As Noni recognizes, a *woman* who exceeds the bounds of femininity by going out alone at night risks social retribution, but as Robi demonstrates, tombois can move safely in the men's world because they are seen as men and not as women.[10] In their everyday interactions with each other, tombois and femmes work to ensure that the boundaries of binary gender are maintained.

By drawing on hegemonic ideologies of gender difference to make sense of their lives, both tombois and their girlfriends reproduce state and Islamic gender discourses, even as their lack of perfect fit with those ideologies positions them somewhere on the margins of social space. The pervasiveness of the hegemonic ideology is reflected in the fact that they offer no explicit critique of the femininity or masculinity of their partners; in fact, they are attracted to just those qualities in their partners. If a tomboi flirts with a woman who considers herself heterosexual, then within the context of their cultural paradigm, the tomboi *makes sense* because s/he has positioned h/erself as a man. At a certain level s/he neither challenges nor unsettles h/er girlfriend's subjectivity as a "normal" woman who is attracted to men.

Tombois' and girlfriends' claims to normative gender trouble U.S. queer studies discourse, which assumes that to be queer, subjects must resist normative ideologies of gender and sexuality. Tombois enact the gender binary in a way that tends to maintain the differences and inequalities between themselves and their girlfriends. But by enacting hegemonic masculinity, are tombois simply reproducing the dominant discourse? Are they conformists to mainstream dictates, using their masculinity to avail themselves of men's power and privilege, as Janice Raymond (1979) claimed in her railings against a supposed "transsexual empire"? (Her diatribe is unfortunately still felt by U.S. transpeople thirty years later.) Does the apparent conformity of tombois to hegemonic masculinity exclude them as queer subjects? Speaking to this point, Grewal and Kaplan warn that "we cannot think of sexual subjects as purely oppositional or resistant to dominant institutions that produce heteronormativity" (2001, 670). Nor can Western queer scholars demand that all forms of queer sexuality adhere to the same strategies and representations of sexuality. Such demands serve only to reimpose binaries—of gender and sexuality—that tombois' positioning, even while apparently conforming to masculinity, works to destabilize through their performance of a contingent masculinity, a point I develop in chapter 6.

Tombois cannot be positioned simply as members of a dominant gender; such contentions fail to take into account the complexities of gendered subjectivities. To paraphrase Butler (1993, 219), tombois stand under a sign to which they do and do not belong. In shifting masculinity to their female bodies, despite the depth of embodiment of this subject position, tombois at the same time understand that they are not just the same as men, in light of the dominant gender discourse that links bodies to genders. Terms used by tombois and girlfriends to describe normative men and women as "real" or "ordinary" (for instance, *laki asli* or *perempuan biasa*) underscore their awareness of and participation in difference. At the point at which socially defined meanings of bodies intervene, tombois acknowledge their difference from normative categories of men and draw on alternative discourses of perverse genders that enable masculinity for female bodies. They become in that moment the articulation of the ideologically imposed category "women who act like men." Tombois' self-positioning with its apparent acquiescence to normative codes of masculinity is more than an act of conformity; it comprises both compliance with and difference from gender norms.

In this chapter I have focused primarily on tombois' and femmes' sense of self as men and women in their interactions with each other. In the context of their relationships their narratives reveal subject positions that appear relatively uncomplicated; they see each other and position themselves as opposites. They make no attempt to complicate these gendered understandings and in fact work to ensure that the borders of gender are clearly marked and maintained. In the following chapters, however, as I turn to other social contexts within which tombois and femmes move, the multiple and apparently contradictory subject positions that they occupy become more apparent.

Desire and Difference

ONI, WHO IS DIVORCED AND HAS ONE CHILD, has been with her tomboi lover, Robi, for nearly two years. When I asked Noni about her earlier relationships, she told me the following story:

> My first relationship was with a guy, but he used to drink all the time. I told him to quit drinking, but he threatened to find another girlfriend who was nicer to him than me, one who would give him more freedom and understand him better. So he broke up with me, which really hurt my feelings. [Noni was sixteen years old then.] Then in my first year of high school, I met Diah. We lived together in the same boarding house with other girls who were also attending school. We used to bathe (*mandi*) together, but I didn't think anything of it. Diah was very supportive and protective toward me if there were any problems at the boarding house. I became so attached to Diah that wherever we went, we were always together. After a while the girls at the boarding house started gossiping, so Diah decided to find us another place to stay. H/er family had money so s/he was able to get a place at another boarding house.
>
> At first I thought we were just friends, but I started having questions when Diah got mad at me for bringing a guy to the house. We lived together for six months before Diah finally got up the nerve to tell me how s/he felt about me. I was shocked because I wasn't aware that I had entered the lesbi world (*dunia lesbi*). Up to that point it just felt nice (*nyaman-nyaman saja*) with Diah. But part of me was also thinking, if I'm friends with another girl, well, I won't get pregnant, you know, because that's something teenagers are really afraid of. After that we lived together for three years.

Noni's story recounts a gradual strengthening of her attachment to Diah, a tomboi, while at the same time dating boys. Tommi's story shows a somewhat different transition with a little more drama:

> In the fifth and sixth grade I liked a girl who was in the same school, but it was just a crush. When I was in middle school, I had a boyfriend for a

while [three months]. One day we went to the river together, and we were splashing around in the water when he tried to kiss me. Just then a piece of wood came floating by. I grabbed it and shook it at him, telling him he better not kiss me or I'd hit him. He called me a lesbi because I refused to kiss him. After that we broke up. Then I had a girlfriend for a little bit in middle school, but I was still somewhat afraid of dating a girl. In high school I had a boyfriend again. But he was really more like a friend than a boyfriend. By the end of high school I started seeing a girl.

These stories raise questions about the meanings of sexual desire and the relation of gender to desire. How is it that a tomboi first dated a boy or that a femme was unaware of her feelings for a tomboi? What convinces tombois of the rightness of their feelings for women? How do femmes compare their relations with men to their relations with tombois? In this chapter I discuss how tombois and femmes come to understand their sexual desires by looking first at their emerging desires during their youth and then at their relationships in the lesbi world.

"Checking It Out": Tombois' Emerging Desires

Adolescence for tombois, particularly during their middle school years, is a time of transition that challenges the simple gender binaries of childhood. Girls are expected to rein in boyish behavior and conform to the expectations of proper womanhood. In West Sumatra adolescent girls are closely watched to ensure they maintain a good reputation. Religion and school are dominant forces pushing Minangkabau teenage girls to be chaste and virtuous (Parker 2009). At the same time youth magazines and movies are full of romantic stories of young love, exemplifying the contradictory streams of discourse about sexuality in Indonesia (Bennett 2005). For most students the middle school years are the time of first crushes and romances, of passing love letters and declaring undying love. According to Linda Bennett, attraction begins for both boys and girls around the ages of ten to twelve. She describes these attractions, colloquially referred to as *cinta monyet* (monkey love), as a period "marked by a growing awareness of one's sexuality, yet also characterized by sexual naivety [sic] and social immaturity" (2005, 56). Like their schoolmates, tombois had crushes and began dating during this time period. For tombois, however, this period is fraught with confusion and questions about their attractions, made more difficult by the fact that they have to wear girls' uniforms to school and so are seen as girls by others, even if they do not see themselves that way.

120

No one story captures this process of emerging sexuality for tombois. In fact all their stories differ, yet they do contain a few common threads. Several tombois had crushes on girls in elementary school, following which some dated girls in middle school while others dated boys. Others vacillated between boys and girls. One tomboi reports that s/he had one boyfriend during middle and high school and did not develop feelings for a woman until s/he was twenty-three years old. To make sense of their emerging desires, I look first at tombois who dated both boys and girls and then at those who only dated girls.

Four of the tombois, including Tommi, whose story opens the chapter, had boyfriends during their middle and high school years, mostly for short periods of time, but in some cases for a year or more. Sal, who in comparison to the other tombois did not categorize h/erself as a tomboi until middle school, remembered, "Since I was little, I liked pretty women (*wanita cantik*)." But in middle school Sal dated a boy for about three months. "We broke up because I didn't like it when he kissed me. I was just checking it out (*coba-coba aja*)," s/he said. "It wasn't serious." Sal quit school after middle school and started hanging out with Danny, Andri, and other young men. The following year, when s/he was sixteen years old, s/he became infatuated with an older woman and started seeing her whenever s/he could.

Dedi remembered that s/he began to idolize girls in the sixth grade and wrote them love letters, but then she had a boyfriend for a year in seventh grade.

> We wrote love letters to each other, like that, but we never kissed. In the beginning it was nice (*enak*), he paid attention to me. But I was also seeing a girl at the same time and paying attention to her. With boys, I was just going along with it (*ikut-ikutan saja*). After I broke up with that boy [in middle school], I dated a girl for a couple years who was in the same school as me. Then my first year in high school I dated another girl for about a year. After that I had a boyfriend for a couple months, but the result was the same as before, so I thought it was better to go 100 percent for girls (*full ke cewek*).

These stories suggest that some tombois had not yet made sense of their sexual desires and were following along with expectations others had of them as girls. What becomes very clear later on—that if they act like men, then they love women—seems less clear while they are still in school. In trying to figure out their sexual desires in the school environment, when other girls are dating boys, these tombois also try dating boys to see if it fits. As Sal said, s/he was checking it out, *coba-coba*. Dedi was "just going along with it," implying that s/he did not have any great interest or desire in the relationship, although writing love letters back and forth suggests a more active role and interest than Dedi admits. Dedi's attempt to date a boy in high school was not any more satisfactory ("the results were the same"), but this second effort suggests that s/he was still trying to see if it fit.

In these accounts, problems arise when boyfriends try to initiate kissing. For instance, Sal broke up with h/er boyfriend because s/he did not want to be kissed. In the story in the opening section, Tommi's reaction to h/er boyfriend's attempt to kiss h/er was instantaneous and forceful. Being on the receiving end of sexual attentions did not fit with the way Tommi understood h/erself. Tommi said s/he had a crush on a girl in fifth and sixth grade, but in middle and high school s/he dated boys while secretly liking some girls. Tommi's effort at dating a boy in high school was more about being friends, s/he said, suggesting that there was nothing sexual about it.

Dedi's statement about kissing versus being kissed is instructive. After h/er second boyfriend, Dedi realized, "It's better when I'm the one kissing rather than being kissed." Implied in h/er statement is a growing understanding that being a boy and having another boy make the moves does not feel right. By taking the subject position of a girl, and getting kissed, Dedi was taking a passive feminine position. Tombois see boys as the assertive ones and, having laid claim early on to being a boy, Dedi does not feel comfortable when the situation is reversed, that is, when s/he is expected to be passive. Dedi said that during this period s/he began to wonder about being with a boy when s/he was like a boy h/erself. For Dedi, the practice of masculine desire was becoming clear: boys kiss and girls are kissed; boys take the initiative and girls receive. In a normative world of sexuality in which opposites attract, one's desires must be directed toward the opposite gender, boys. Understanding this, Dedi feels the rightness of h/er desires and goes "100 percent for girls."

Crushes and Dating Girls

While some tombois recalled dating boys first, other stories of emerging sexual desires do not follow the same trajectory. For these tombois the feeling of sexual attraction to difference (girls), not sameness (other boys), becomes clear at an earlier age than it does for others. Robi mentioned liking girls when s/he was in elementary school, but said, "I didn't think anything about it." For h/er these early crushes are not anything unusual; they are just a feeling that had little significance at the time. Yet in contrast to Tommi, Robi never mentioned dating boys. Instead s/he said, "In the second year of junior high, I began to be attracted to girls," marking exactly the particular time period in which this attraction began. Robi recalled watching movies that had subplots "about same-sex friends. I looked at myself, because I was still in middle school, you know, and I looked at how I was interacting with my friends." Through these stories Robi tries to make sense of h/erself and h/er attractions to girls, and eventually starts dating girls.

Some tombois never dated boys, or never mentioned it to me, but their stories reveal a certain amount of questioning when they first began dating girls. Andri said s/he had a crush on a "very pretty" little girl in fourth grade and then started dating Jeni when s/he was fourteen or fifteen years old.

> Jeni was my first girlfriend who liked me back. That was in sixth grade [Andri had been held back in school]. At first it was Jeni who was interested in me. I was surprised that she liked me. I didn't understand anything yet about who I was, but I was attracted to her. I just didn't admit it at first. So when Jeni was trying to get close to me, I responded in the opposite manner and that made Jeni even more interested in me.
>
> When I was in middle school, a guy named Boy wanted to date me. Jeni introduced us. This guy told my parents that he liked me, but I didn't like him so we didn't date. Since then no guy has ever asked me out.

In this narrative Andri discloses that h/er initial reaction to Jeni's interest is surprise. Although Andri had always played with boys and had early crushes on "pretty girls," it confused h/er at first that Jeni was attracted to h/er. Andri's statement that "I didn't understand anything yet about who I was" suggests that s/he was uncertain about h/er attraction to girls; it did not yet make sense. In fact, in Jeni's telling of the story, "Andri's response was just the opposite. S/he acted as if s/he was completely uninterested in me and was always making fun of me, even to the point of calling me '*poyok malam*' " (lady of the night, Minangkabau slang for prostitute). At the same time Andri apparently lacks any interest in dating boys. Although Andri does not mention why s/he did not like boys, which was perhaps due to being taken as a desirable *girl*, h/er developing interest in Jeni deflects any further sexual interest in boys. Finding girls more desirable, s/he begins a relationship with Jeni.

In fact, similar to Robi's reflection on movies, Andri recalls a story that s/he read growing up that made h/er rethink the given categories of the world.

> I can't remember the name of the magazine, but it was a true story about a woman. In the story the woman falls asleep, and suddenly a bright light streams through the window and illuminates her so that her whole body glows and is purified. Afterward she no longer has breasts but has the genitals of a male.

123

Andri understands this contemporary story of perverse gender as a true story. The transformation from female to male in the story reflects a broader folk tradition, mentioned in chapter 2, in which mythological figures are able to change their bodies to have sex with the object of their desire (see also Blackwood 2005a). In thinking about this story, Andri begins to reimagine h/erself and the possibilities of having a relationship with girls.

Arief, a friend of Andri's, is another tomboi who did not date boys. Arief recounted h/er impression of Jeni, Andri's girlfriend, and h/er own early dating, as follows:

> When I met Andri, I was surprised to see that Jeni was h/er girlfriend. 'How can they be involved,' I said to myself, 'when they're both girls?' But then I met Nila, and the same thing happened to me. When I was in middle school, Nila was in the same class so we got to know each other. We started dating in the ninth grade. In high school we were in different schools. We broke up for a year because Nila was jealous of me when I was around another girl at my school. We got back together the last year of high school with the help of Danny, Andri, and Jeni.

Despite tombois' sense of themselves as boys, like Andri, Arief experiences confusion over h/er attraction to girls. In Arief's narrative, she asks h/erself what two girls (Andri and Jeni) are doing together. Even though s/he knew Andri was a tomboi, s/he thought of them both as girls and wondered how they could be attracted to each other. Arief was still embedded in the nexus of "boy-girl" dating, which was reinforced every day at school in interactions with students and teachers. Both Andri and Arief relied heavily on their mutual friend Danny, when they first met, to understand their interests in girls. In Arief's narrative h/er own developing interest in Nila resolves the confusion, and s/he begins dating girls.

I am not suggesting here that through this process tombois discover their "true" sexuality. Rather I suggest that their sexual desires come to align with their feelings of being boys and their understanding of what masculinity entails in this particular historical and social context. In this scenario, the masculine position they have taken on entails active, aggressive behavior rather than passive, receptive behavior. Not being habituated to a receptive position, the tombois who dated boys feel more and more uncomfortable, even threatened, when they found themselves in that position with other boys. For some, their growing feelings of discomfort in the sexual role assigned to girls leads them to question their relationships with boys. Over time this feeling of discomfort is resolved by going "100 percent for girls." For other tombois, while at first their attraction to girls is confusing, as they come into contact with other discourses through media or conversations with friends, they come to understand the sexual prerogatives of the subject position they have taken up and lay claim to this desire.

Adolescence is a period of trying on what feels right and what does not, learning the *gender* of sexuality, even as one negotiates one's gender. As I see it, the quandary of tombois' emerging sexual interests lies in the tension between their own bodies—defined as female and marked as such by school officials and the very clothes they wear to school—and heteronormative dictates that construct "natural" desire only between differently sexed bodies. These dictates and the apparent naturalness of gender binaries necessitate for some a period of dating or "trying out" boys. As tombois become more secure and confident in their masculinities, the sex/gender conundrum is resolved by asserting their gender, their self-positioning as men, as the operative factor in directing sexual desire. Still upholding the heteronormative dictate that opposites attract, they come to align their desires with their sense of being men. As Robi stated, "Because I consider myself a guy (*cowok*), not a girl, I'm attracted to ordinary girls (*cewek biasa*), like guys are attracted to girls."

For these tombois, sexuality shifts out of (its ideologically determined) place and is no longer connected to their girlish bodies, but to the gender they perform. Tombois' interpretation of masculinity is possible because, as Moore suggests, "dominant structures and discourses involve a high degree of indeterminacy" (1994, 83; see also Bourdieu 1990). Dominant constructions of gender and sexuality, like other hegemonic processes, are never seamless, never occupy the landscape alone, and are themselves shifting and reformulated through a range of disciplining mechanisms. In this new cultural habitus that coalesces around stories, conversations, feelings, experiences, and the continued salience of gender difference, the category of masculinity entails a sexuality defined by the dictum "opposites attract." In their intimate relationships, tombois come to learn what fits with their sense of themselves as masculine—of desiring girls, of wanting to be the active, dominant partner, and of not wanting to be desired by boys—a desire informed by normative gender.

Gendering Desire

In analyzing tombois' narratives I foreground the importance of gender in producing sexual desire. But the complexities of emerging desires are hard to tease apart. Can sexual desires be distinguished from gendered desires? Does gender alone drive tombois' sexual desires? Some might argue that tombois' early crushes on girls provide evidence of pre-existing sexual desires, which are then hidden as the tombois try to date boys. Lesbian coming-out narratives in the United States from the 1970s and 1980s posit such a scenario of adolescent conflict and denial. In these narratives lesbians recall pretending to have an interest in boys, or even having boyfriends in high school, so no one will know of their "true" desires (see Weston 1991). I am not equating U.S. lesbian narratives with tombois' adolescent experiences, but rather I mention them because their accounts of hidden desires are absent in the narratives of tombois who dated boys. In the tombois' narratives, none of them mention that they were pretending to like boys as a way to hide their "true" desires. Sal's "checking it out" (*coba-coba aja*) suggests that s/he was open to dating boys until the point that it began to conflict with h/er understanding of h/erself as a boy. Dedi as well seemed to enjoy having a boyfriend, although some of the tombois' dating experiences were less welcome than others.

At the same time tombois' stories of being afraid to date girls at school implies the necessity for hiding desires. Tommi mentioned in the opening story that s/he was too scared to get involved with girls in school. H/er first serious relationship with a girl happened after s/he graduated from high school. S/he said, "It's hard at school because everyone knows what everyone else is doing and who they're seeing. It's not safe." Tommi's fear of discovery suggests that s/he may have been hiding h/er desires for girls when s/he dated boys. Robi also mentioned that it was risky to make h/er desires known in high school, even though girls were chasing h/er, s/he said. Further, tombois' avoidance of the term "lesbi" in general conversation suggests that one has to guard against others knowing one is lesbi. Danny told me that h/er parents do not know s/he is lesbi, but they do know s/he is a tomboi. In fact most of the tombois began to think of themselves as "lesbi" only around the time they had their first relationship with a girl. "Lesbi," then, is more closely associated with sexual relationships that must be kept hidden, whereas gender-marked behavior associated with being a tomboi is recognized and visible in public. "Lesbi" marks a sexual practice that exceeds the boundaries of normative sexuality and cannot be openly claimed in public spaces in Padang.

And yet despite their fear of being known as lesbi, I think that for tombois, learning one's desires is a more complex process than simply knowing and hiding them from others. In contrast to those who expressed fear about dating girls, other tombois quickly entered into relationships with girls while still in school. Danny, Andri, and Arief all started long-term relationships during middle school and never dated boys. Yet Andri's and Arief's stories both reveal an initial sense of uncertainty about dating girls. Their hesitancy points to uncertainties about their bodies and their genders at that moment, suggesting that they saw themselves as boys and not as boys at the same time. The constant social iteration that they are "girls" reminds them that they are different from other boys. Despite enacting masculinity, when they first begin dating girls, they do not have the confidence of boys, who are constantly reinforced in the rightness of their normative gender positions and sexual desires.

For Andri, Arief, and the other tombois, inconsistencies lurk between the cultural meanings of bodies and genders. Representations of normative sexuality are part of everyday life, between mummies and daddies, as well as in the romance novels and movies available to a young Indonesian audience. Early on they are unaware of other forms of sexuality, or of stories that might make sense of their desires for women. Then, as in Andri's case, s/he is struck by the report of the transformed woman and begins to imagine other possibilities. Is their hesitancy at the cusp of adolescence due to a naiveté about sexual acts and body parts that make it difficult to imagine sexual desire without physical difference? In fact a variety of scenarios take place in the process of negotiating gender and desire. For Robi, in enacting boyhood, and finding girls attracted to h/er, s/he is assured of h/er masculinity and of h/er desires for women. For Andri, Arief, Tommi and Dedi, in enacting boyhood, and seeing themselves as boys and yet not boys, finding boys undesirable helps to confirm their feelings for girls. Or, like Danny, in enacting boyhood, s/he finds girls attractive as the opposite which attracts.

Kulick (1998) asserts that in the childhood stories of Brazilian male-bodied *travesti*s, desires for men are given greater prominence than desires for girlish things. He argues that these stories provide evidence of the priority of sexual desire over gender in forming *travesti* subjectivity. In contrast sexual desire does not figure in tombois' narratives of their early childhood years. As their stories in chapter 3 reveal, the early years were all about being boys, about doing, playing, and going out like boys. According to Robi, h/er first attraction to a girl occurred in middle school and was not part of h/er self-description about h/er childhood years. Similarly, Danny said, "I was aware I was a tomboi in elementary school. I became aware I was attracted to girls when I started dating [a girl] in middle school." In their accounts attraction to women is not presented as a formative moment in becoming tombois, but something that develops later. Robi's statement suggests that attraction to women follows from the recognition that s/he was like a guy. Following Kulick's line of reasoning, tombois' childhood stories indicate that becoming a boy is primarily a gendered process that precedes their sexual desires for women.

In contrast to *travesti*, tombois claim a masculine gender that then leads them to desire women, asserting the priority of gender in understanding and making sense of desire. Within a system of gender duality, loving women is an attribute of masculinity. Similarly female-bodied *calalai* in Sulawesi describe a childhood devoted to doing what boys do but do not mention sexual desires (Davies 2007a). Saskia Wieringa recounts that older butches in Jakarta became aware of their sexual attraction to women only after the realization that they had a "masculine soul" (2007, 80). However, the problem of asserting the priority of gender over sexuality, or vice versa, in transgender narratives, lies in the danger of positing a dichotomy where none may exist. The weight that tombois give to gender, or *travestis* to sexuality, in explaining their sexual subjectivities does not rule out the co-construction of gender and sexual desire in childhood. By this I mean that in particular social and historical contexts gender and sexuality are co-constructed in the very processes by which prepubescent boys and girls learn to establish and maintain their differences from each other. As boys learn to be brave, assertive, and take risks, and girls learn to be timid, modest, and desire protection, the preconditions for desiring the other are created and deeply embedded. If girls are not what boys are, they are as surely what boys (will) want in a context in which attraction of opposites has been constructed for them as the "truth" of their gender and their desire. A culturally defined hierarchy of gender is reproduced in a hierarchy of sexuality, which is learned even as gender is being learned.

To return to those early crushes, if, at first, sexual attraction to "other" girls does not make sense for tombois ('I didn't know who I was yet'), it means they have not yet found the available discourses to fit with those desires; they are still embedded in a heteronormative world that requires opposite bodies in sexual embrace. As tombois traverse adolescence, as they begin to make sense of their interest in girls and are supported in it through interactions with other tombois, they learn that the truth of their gender—which lies in their performance of masculinity—is also the truth of their sexuality. Irrespective of body parts and the cultural meanings assigned to those parts, they assert the rightness of claiming men's normative desires for women and men's sexual privileges. In this way they conform to the sexual meanings of normative masculinity, but not of normative bodies. For even as they embody normative gender and sexuality, tombois continue to see their bodies as female based on both the unrelenting dictates of the sex/gender system and the perverse category of "women who act like men." Their female bodies thus furnish mute evidence of the arbitrariness of these categories, providing a critical perspective on the normative and its opposite, which opens the way to navigate multiple subject positions, a point I pursue in the next chapter.

Loving Women

When I asked Tommi if there was any difference between h/erself and men, Tommi replied, "No, we're the same. When I fall in love, it's with a woman." In line with h/er self-realizations as an adolescent, Tommi makes sense of h/er sexual desire by aligning it with h/er gender. Falling in love with a woman means not only that tombois are the same as men but that they adhere to men's sexual prerogatives. In the same way that tombois have different attributes than girlfriends, they also lay claim to sexual prerogatives not accorded to their girlfriends.

Men are said to have greater sexual drive, a broadly accepted idea across much of Indonesia. This idea was expressed both in the village of Taram, where I conducted research in 1989–1990 (see Blackwood 2000), and in Islamicist pronouncements about sexuality, despite the fact that such notions sit uneasily with the dominant Islamicist perspective that men have greater self-control (see Brenner 1998). For men the deployment of gender entails an expectation of marriage and family that also tolerates extramarital affairs. According to Bennett (2005), men's sexuality is much less closely regulated than women's; men are assumed to desire and to have extramarital liaisons, and they are not generally condemned or punished for them. Fatwas (religious opinions) concerning marriage and men's right to take more than one wife reveal an underlying assumption that men have stronger sexual needs than women. For instance, a fatwa regarding marriage counsels women to be prepared to sacrifice a little happiness and agree to additional wives, if requested, for the sake of their husbands' souls (Hooker 2003). This Muslim form of polygamy, in which men may have up to four wives, is viewed as a safeguard for men against adultery (van Doorn-Harder 2006; Hasyim 2006; Hooker 2003). Thus the sacrifices of women enable their husbands to rise above their nature and maintain the moral code.

The perception of men's greater sexual desire and freedom is apparent in tombois' and femmes' narratives about their relationships. I was chatting with Danny about my partner when s/he asked me, "How can you be away from her so long without *it*? I can't be without it for that long. When I was away from Epi for a month in Medan, there was a girl that was interested in me, although I didn't do anything about it." In this case Danny passed up the opportunity, but clearly felt a desire for sexual relations due to Epi's absence. Similarly, Andri admitted with apparent nonchalance that in the absence of h/er girlfriend, s/he started seeing another woman. "Jeni and I were together for about a year when she went away to work for a couple months. I couldn't stand being without her, so I started dating another girl. When Jeni came back to Padang, we got back together again."

Tommi and other tombois, including Danny, told me they had dated other women at the same time they were involved with their primary partners. In some cases it was the sister of the current girlfriend. Tommi's girlfriend Lina often complained to me that Tommi is not very faithful to her. Lina said, "I've been faithful to Tommi." Then she poked Tommi, who was sitting next to her at that point, and said, "But not this one. This one is always getting other girlfriends. Tombois are quick to seduce (*menggoda*) women." Because men are thought to have greater need for sex, normative expectations of fidelity that attach to women are not enjoined as strongly on men. Suryakusuma (1996) demonstrates that among high-ranking civil servants, it is generally the norm for men to have extramarital affairs. Similarly, tombois do not hold themselves to the same standards of fidelity that they expect of their partners, allowing themselves greater freedom to have more than one relationship at a time.

Tombois I interviewed take up and reproduce the code of masculinity, and its attribution of greater sexual need and desire, by having multiple partners. Femmes in their turn participate in this understanding of tombois' sexuality by assuming that their partners will act like men and be less than faithful. This expectation leads femmes to put up with the behavior despite their feelings of jealousy, a response also noted among married Javanese women, who tolerate their husbands' infidelities because it is expected (see Brenner 1998). Tombois see their sexual privileges differently than their girlfriends, a view that accords with the ideology of sexual difference and underscores tombois' masculinity.

At the same time tombois and girlfriends' sexual relationships are fraught with tensions and contradictions as a result of their tenuous connections to normative sex/gender. Thinking of the risks incurred when tombois pursue apparently normatively inclined women, I asked Lina, "How can it be so easy for them [tombois] to get other girlfriends?" She said, "It's easy. Tombois are quick to make friends and are thoughtful, considerate, and easy to be with. They understand women better, so women like that and want to be with them." In fact on another occasion Lina had admitted to me, "As far as giving love and affection, Tommi is better than any man." In this narrative, tombois are and are not just like other men in their performance of sexuality; they take up certain masculine privileges, but, as Lina attests, they are more loving and attentive than men. According to Sinnott (2004), Thai *tom*s, who are appreciated by *dee*s for their greater attentiveness in lovemaking, are therefore not simply reproducing heterosexual dynamics.

Falling into the Lesbi World

As noted above, dating is a prominent aspect of school life, although actual physical contact, including holding hands and kissing, are strongly discouraged (Parker 2009). The young women I interviewed who dated tombois are no different from their peers in having numerous relationships during their school years. But unlike other girls, girlfriends recount dating both boys and tombois in middle and high school. Some of the girls had boyfriends first; others were involved with tombois first, yet all of them dated both boys and tombois. In some cases their behavior came under increased scrutiny from kin and schoolteachers who were fearful that their sexuality was not being properly directed in a heterosexual manner.

Noni, whose story of high school romances appears at the beginning of this chapter, first dated an ordinary guy, to use their terms for a male-bodied man. After her break-up with her boyfriend, she experienced a gradually intensifying friendship with Diah. Even after they moved in together, Noni did not think anything was different about their relationship and continued to date guys. When Diah told her how s/he felt, Noni expressed surprise and then remained with Diah for three more years. Their relationship ended tragically when Diah was killed in a car accident.

In contrast to Noni, Nila's first boyfriend was a tomboi who was in the same class as Nila.

> Arief was my first love. When we were still in middle school, we fought a lot and broke up several times, then got back together. During high school we were in different schools, but we always met at 11:00 every day at the local café. We broke up my second year in high school because Arief was rumored to have another girlfriend. After we broke up, I had three boyfriends in succession. Then when my grandmother passed away, Arief came around because s/he wasn't dating that girl anymore. I had decided not to go back with h/er because my heart was closed to h/er. But my friends Danny and Andri worked hard to get us back together again, so we finally did. When we got back together, I was still dating a guy. We broke it off but not right away.

In this narrative Nila relates only the personal problems she had with Arief; she does not mention any qualms about dating a tomboi, even though she was warned both by her teacher and indirectly by her mother early on in the relationship.

> My teacher [in ninth grade] had a conversation with me, warning me about being in a lesbi relationship. Then someone told my family about Arief, so my mother went and read my diary. Upon learning the truth, she wrote in the margins of my diary, "Child, the road you have taken is the wrong road," but she never confronted me directly. I'm still very close to my mother, but my younger sisters are not very nice because they don't want me to see Arief, sometimes to the point of really hurting my feelings because of the things they say.

Nila continued to see Arief despite the warnings, maintaining silence about her relationship with a tomboi. In telling me her story she does not deny having an interest in the other boys and, in fact, implies that she really liked the last one because she continued to see him even after she got back together with Arief. Her ready return to boyfriends after breaking up with Arief suggests that dating boys was not a subterfuge on her part to keep her family unawares.

Like Nila, Epi's first boyfriend was a tomboi, but she was not immediately attracted to h/er.

> I met Danny in the eighth grade when we were schoolmates. We were in the same group of friends together. At first I was afraid of Danny because s/he was really wild, always making fun of me and bothering me. S/he chased me for about a year, and then we started dating. In high school we were in different schools. We had some trouble and broke up because Danny had another girlfriend. I started dating a guy, but after high school we broke up, and I got back together with Danny.

Epi told me that after she began dating Danny, she read lots of stories about lesbi in newspapers and magazines. "They were real stories (*kisah nyata*) about their lives, problems, and quarrels. There was even one story about a jealous lover murdering her girlfriend." Like Robi and Andri, Epi found alternative discourses in print media that provided evidence of other sexual possibilities.

Each of the girlfriends recounts alternating between dating ordinary boys and dating tombois. Unlike tombois, who seemed to be trying on boyfriends, the girls do not mention that they dated boys to check it out, nor did they wonder about their attraction to tombois. Their efforts to find out information on lesbi suggest that they did see their relationships with tombois differently from those with their boyfriends, yet their accounts of adolescent affairs seem fairly simple and straightforward. Any break-up with a tomboi is quickly followed by dating ordinary boys. In Jeni's case, she dated an ordinary boy first, who was a friend of Andri's. When this boy graduated from middle school, she pursued Andri. Lina was the only femme who never dated tombois during her teen years.

Girlfriends' stories of adolescence claim an unchanging heterosexuality beginning from the time they started to date. Being with a tomboi does not rule out desire for ordinary boys (*laki-laki biasa*) or vice versa. In the same way that girlfriends do not question their femininity, they do not question their developing sexual interests, but rather fit themselves into the hegemonic ideology, which requires that girls like boys. They make sense of their desires as a normative attraction to boys that fits with their own sense of themselves as girls.

Femme Desires

If adolescence is a time of questioning and finding what one likes, how do girlfriends resolve their desires for both tombois and men as they move beyond adolescence? In their attraction to tombois, girlfriends could be interpreted as desiring female bodies as well as male bodies, but they understand their own sexuality as consistently oriented toward men. Bisexuality is not part of this discourse (but see chapter 7). What happens in the lesbi world, then, as femmes begin to understand themselves as women attracted to tombois?

Girlfriends such as Nila and Jeni define their sexual attraction within normative terms. Nila recently graduated from high school; Jeni stopped school after middle school and has been working for the past five years. Jeni said, "I'm the same as other women because I'm still attracted to ordinary guys. If Andri left me, I would start dating ordinary guys again." Nila, who began dating Arief in ninth grade, said, "I consider myself the same as other women. Although I'm attracted to Arief, I consider h/er like other guys. I've dated ordinary men and in my opinion Arief is the same as them." In describing their relationships, these women both explicitly state that they are no different from other women and that they consider themselves "normal." "Normal" is the term they use for normative sex/gender, meaning that they are feminine women who date men. This term draws on the dominant discourse, which contrasts normatively gendered individuals with those who are non-normatively gendered or sick (*sakit*) (see chapter 2).

Having grown up with certain accepted expectations about normative femininity and their own place within that norm, girlfriends look for attributes in tombois that fit with and support their own feelings of femininity. As I explained in the previous chapter, all the girlfriends I interviewed feel that they possess feminine traits. Jeni, who describes herself as quiet, shy, and insecure, said, "With Andri, I feel safe and protected." Where opposites attract, and men are expected to be courageous protectors of women, Jeni finds those qualities attractive in her tomboi partner. Noni similarly liked the way her first tomboi lover, Diah, supported and protected her. Lina likes many qualities that Tommi has. "S/he definitely has a certain charisma that other people don't have. S/he gets along well with people, with whoever, rich, poor, down on their luck, she isn't picky about h/er friends. Because of that, since we started going together, it's been very difficult to break up with h/er." Nila, whose desires for Arief developed slowly, said, "I like h/er cheerfulness, sense of humor, and the way s/he is always to the point." Being outgoing and sociable, like Tommi, or direct and sure of h/erself, like Arief, are all attractive qualities in men that balance girlfriends' own qualities. Epi likes the way she and Danny can talk about everything and discuss their problems. Then she said, "We are very different. I hide my feelings whereas s/he has an open disposition." These descriptions underscore the sense that girlfriends have of being feminine and of desiring the qualities of the "opposite" sex/gender, that is, those masculine qualities that appeal to their feminine senses.

Girlfriends I interviewed generally claim a normative heterosexual attraction to men, which makes them the "same as" other (heterosexual) women. Since tombois position themselves as men, girlfriends make sense of their attraction to tombois by pointing to their masculine qualities. This perception of femme sexuality is consistent with other (but not all) femme lesbi in Indonesia, including the older femme partners that Saskia Wieringa (1999, 2007) studied in Jakarta. These femmes identify as women because they are "primarily attracted to the masculinity of their partners" (2007, 80). Wieringa notes further that femmes are mistrusted because their partners fear they will return to men, and in fact many do have husbands or boyfriends. The similarity to Thai *dees* is instructive, although the cultural and national dynamics are different. Partners of masculine *toms*, *dees* are identified as "ordinary" women. According to Sinnott, "All 'women' (that is nonmasculine women) are potential dees; never having had a tom lover before is no reason to discount a particular woman as a partner for a tom" (2007, 131). *Dee* identity is conditional to their relationships with *toms*. In contrast, femme partners of hunters (*calalai*) in South Sulawesi feel like women, but are not sexually attracted to ordinary men, according to Davies (2007a). Even though many of these femmes are married to men and have children, Davies positions them as women who sexually desire "females who have the style of men" (2007a: 58). The versions of femininity represented in these studies point not only to the complexities of each location, but to the problems of blanket categorization.

Lesbi Women?

Although the femmes I interviewed acknowledge the term "lesbi" for themselves, they see themselves as only loosely attached to that label. During interviews I asked girlfriends when they became aware that they were lesbi. In their answers all the girlfriends pointed to a particular moment in time, which was the moment when they began to date or be attracted to a tomboi, and not before. Epi, who had not liked Danny at first, stated simply, "I realized I was lesbi when I started dating Danny." Lina's account of falling in love with Tommi was similar to Epi's. She said, "When I first met Tommi, I didn't like h/er, I felt strange around h/er. But Tommi kept giving me lots of attention, and after a while I started to like h/er." At the time I interviewed Noni, she had had three tomboi lovers. Noni's account of her first relationship with a young man does not hint at any prior inclinations, thoughts, or desires for tombois. As did Lina, Noni credited the attention and care she received from Diah as reason for their relationship.

"Coming out" in the United States, at least during the 1970s, is often portrayed as a process of growing awareness or discovery that one's sexuality is different from others, followed at some, usually later, point by sexual experiences with the same sex (McNaron 2002).[1] Girlfriends' accounts of their first experiences with tombois are quite different from these coming out narratives. In Noni's case, her first relationship with a tomboi came as a shock to her. It was as if she was caught unaware. For her it was an external event, something that happened to her, not an internal process of coming to realize already present feelings. Becoming lesbi meant entering into a different world, one of which she had no knowledge beforehand. Rather than a "coming out," in which her own identity is revealed, this experience for Noni is about coming into another world, the world of lesbi (*dunia lesbi*), which she joined because of her relationship with Diah.

In these accounts, being femme is not articulated as a sexual orientation or a core aspect of one's being that is unchangeable, as it was defined at one point in time in the white lesbian community in the United States (see King 2002). For instance, Noni's attraction to Diah arose in a particular situation, suggesting that for these women, becoming a femme lesbi is a conditional subjectivity rather than an enduring identification or sexual orientation. Boellstorff (2005b), who positions femmes (he uses the term *cewek*) in Indonesia as lesbi women, suggests that being lesbi for femmes is a persistent sexual identity, but he does not take into account the femmes who move into and out of a lesbi subject position. From the point of view of femmes I interviewed in Padang, "lesbi" is what they are only when they have a tomboi partner. Jeni, who sees herself the same as other women, said, "While others see me as lesbi, the only difference I can see is that I am attracted to Andri." Lesbi as a category does not seem to resonant strongly with Jeni. She is not sure she wants to be identified with that term because she sees herself as a normal woman attracted to men.

Epi, who is older and has been with her tomboi partner for over ten years, allows for a little difference between herself and other women. Epi said, "The differences between femmes (*lesbi cewek*) and ordinary women are not at all apparent. Sometimes there actually is no difference at all." The difference that is "not at all apparent," according to Epi, seems to be based primarily on the quality of her relationship and how close she feels to her partner. I asked Epi, who had dated an ordinary guy after high school during one of her break-ups with Danny, if there were any differences between Danny and her former boyfriend. She said, "The feeling is different. I didn't feel as close to him as I do to Danny." Despite my further prodding, she did not offer anything else. Nila was adamant that they are the same as women, "Femmes (*lesbi cewek*) are the same as normal girls (*cewek normal*)." Unlike Epi and even her close friend Jeni, Nila insists that it makes no difference for her to be with a tomboi.

Adding to the sense of femme lesbi as a conditional construct are the girl-friends who declare that they would not take another tomboi lover. For Epi and Lina, there has only ever been one tomboi in their lives. When I asked Epi if she would look for another tomboi if she and Danny broke up, she said, "NO! I don't want that again. If Danny broke off our relationship, I would return to being an ordinary woman. That's my nature (*kodrat*)." For her, becoming an "ordinary woman" again means dating men. One's sexuality follows from one's gender in Epi's understanding; neither her gender nor her sexuality is in question as far as she is concerned. Epi uses *kodrat* in this context to (re)align gender and sexuality, perhaps hinting at her discomfort with, yet acknowledgement of, a culturally defined misalignment between the female bodies of tombois and femmes. Returning to ordinary men is not seen as a big change, particularly for Nila, who denies any difference between ordinary men and tombois. Despite the depth of their feelings for and attachment to their tomboi partners, these women do not imagine being with a tomboi as a permanent choice or a fixed sexual orientation. Lesbi for these femmes, then, is a temporary state. If at the moment they are lesbi, later on they may not be. What they understand to be fixed or stable is their gender identity as women and their attraction to men. They just happen to like men who are tombois.

The assumption that femmes are similar to other women is shared by tombois. According to the tombois I interviewed, the only way to tell the difference between ordinary women and femmes is in the way women react to tombois' advances. Danny said, "A femme will act all shy, but right away it will be obvious that she's interested in the tomboi. Ordinary women will not react at all to a tomboi's efforts to attract their attention." Tombois assert that when a girlfriend first becomes involved with a tomboi, it is not certain what she is or will be. I asked Dedi if h/er girlfriend, who at that time was eighteen, would consider herself a lesbi. Dedi said, "I couldn't really answer that. She is still young and doesn't know what she wants out of life yet. Who knows what she will choose in the future." Tommi added as further clarification to Dedi's statement, "[She] has just fallen into the lesbi world" (*terjun ke dunia lesbi*), meaning she has just become a part of it since she started seeing Dedi, so it is not possible to say if she is lesbi or not.

These comments reflect the shared understanding that being lesbi for girlfriends is something that happens through the process of becoming involved with a tomboi and not something that was always there inside them waiting to be discovered. It also suggests that if a girlfriend stays with her tomboi partner, then she will be considered lesbi, but she may also choose to leave later on and end her association with that world, in effect returning to the normative heterosexual world, where men have male bodies. Similar to girlfriends' descriptions of their relationships, Howard's (1996) study of Indonesian gay men in the early 1990s found that these men did not think of "gay" as an essential aspect of their identity and were likely to abandon the identity and the "gay world" when they married, evidencing a temporary and contextual sexuality. Tombois may be permanent denizens of *dunia lesbi* and provide entry into it for their girlfriends, but girlfriends are not likely to stay forever. As Lina said, "Being with a tomboi depends on how long you can stand the situation of not having a typical life and getting married."

Desiring Men

Although femmes I interviewed assert an uncomplicated attraction to men, they position themselves (if temporarily) under the label "lesbi," which points to a difference that is non-normative. If they claim an attraction to men, then their desires should be for normatively defined male bodies and male genitalia as well as masculine characteristics. But their tomboi partners do not have the normatively defined bodies that women should be attracted to. I am not arguing that femme desire for tombois positions them as sexually attracted to women, for in this point most femmes are very clear—they do not desire women. Rather I want to explore how normative categories of sex/gender fall apart in light of femme desire.

Through the following stories of two femmes, I analyze how femmes deal with the tensions between heteronormative categories of sex/gender, in which bodies and genders must be the same, and their perceptions of their partners, who, according to Nila, are just the same as men. I lay out the discourses that substantiate and shore up femme positioning as normative women, both in the broader sociocultural context and amongst themselves, while also accounting for the generation of new femme subjectivities. For femmes, does the power of normality prevail even at the point where bodies touch? Is there some slippage in femmes' understanding of the category "woman" or of their partners' female bodies? What happens to sexual constructs if genitalia are irrelevant?

The answers differ somewhat for each girlfriend, depending at the very least on their own experiences, the length of time with their partner, and the types of discourses they are exposed to. Let me state again, however, that I do not imagine these processes to be necessarily consciously thought out. Rather, I suggest that in the frictions produced through the daily process of living and enacting certain subject positions, or what Anzaldúa (1987) calls incompatible frames of reference, femmes, like tombois, may be moved toward other ways of perceiving their relationships. Their altered perceptions generate slight shifts in understanding and performing normative categories of being, as the stories of Upik and Noni demonstrate.

Upik's Story

In regard to their sexuality, most girlfriends I interviewed do not speak of desires for their partners' bodies or mention any physical qualities that they like about their partners. In fact they are generally silent about their sexual desires, allowing their stated desire for men to speak for itself. As noted above, the young unmarried girlfriends are attracted primarily to their partners' masculinity and disregard the physical aspects. Some of them stated that they were not attracted at all to their partners when they first met but over time developed strong attachments to them. Only one unmarried girlfriend mentioned her sexual desire for her partner. I present her story here, gleaned from interviews with both Upik and her partner, Jon.

Upik, a young feminine woman, has no significant experience with male-bodied men and five years with a devoted tomboi lover. As with other femmes, her feelings for her partner developed gradually over the time they have known each other. She has been with only one tomboi, Jon, who is more than ten years older than she, and has not had contact with other lesbi in Padang. Upik is from a very poor family living in coastal West Sumatra and has had to work since before she completed middle school. When she met Jon, she had been living in Padang with her mother's sister and family and working as a maid. Jon and Upik now rent a small three-room house, which they share with Jon's young son from a previous marriage and one of Upik's younger sisters. Upik works as a domestic servant, while Jon, also from a poor, working class family, works as a parking attendant.

When they first met, Jon was in need of someone to help care for h/er son. "I was doing everything, working, cooking, washing, and taking care of my son," s/he said, "and I didn't have any help, so I took Upik in." Upik's family at first thought Jon was using black magic to control Upik, but despite their initial concerns, they now accept Jon and appreciate what s/he has done for Upik by providing a house for her and taking care of her needs. Their style of relationship may be analogous to an earlier form of mentoring/erotic relationship reported between Minangkabau men, mentioned in chapter 2, in which an older established man (*induk jawi*, Minangkabau) takes on a younger man (*anak jawi*, M.) to help him. This type of relationship is also apparent in the 1939 report of two women, a widow of eight years and a young, unmarried woman, seeking to get married (Alhamidy 1951).[2] The invisibility of an older generation of female couples in this region, however, makes it impossible to be certain.

When I talked to Upik, she appeared to be very happy in her relationship with Jon, although she mentioned some initial misgivings. When Jon first tried to attract Upik's attention, Upik thought Jon was crazy because h/er hair and clothes were always so dirty and disheveled. Jon persisted in h/er attentions, however, and after some time the two moved in together and eventually began a sexual relationship. Jon said, "Upik can't go to sleep unless she is in my arms and I'm caressing her. She likes that a lot." Upik smiled broadly at that, indicating her complete agreement. Jon and Upik have some knowledge of lesbi through films and videos—they like to see women kiss in the videos, Jon said. But they are isolated from other lesbi in Padang and the meanings that circulate through those networks. Upik did not seem to know what lesbi meant when I asked her if she defined herself as one. Jon explained it for her, saying, "You know, when we do it together (*melakukan baduo*, M.)," equating the term "lesbi" with sexuality, and clearly indicating that their relationship is sexual.

Surprisingly, however, Upik had just recently married a man at Jon's urging. The husband works for a fishing trawler and is away most of the time, but stays with the couple when he is on shore. When I asked about this new husband, Upik said, "I don't enjoy it with my husband; I don't have any desire (*nafsu*) for him, not like with Jon." *Nafsu* in this context refers to sexual desire. I asked how long she had dated her husband before they got married. She wrinkled up her nose as she responded, saying, "It was three years, but I rarely saw him during that time." Upik is clearly very loyal and devoted to Jon, who has provided her with support, protection, and tender loving care, even to the point of finding Upik a husband. As Jon told me, s/he wanted to make sure Upik would have a happy life. In comparison, her new husband has shown none of the careful attention and love that

Jon has given Upik. Jon told me, "I tried to teach him how to treat a woman right sexually. He needs to get close first, flatter her, give her some loving, and then make love, but he doesn't want to do that. All he wants to do is have sex, and then he's done." While it is possible that Upik's lack of interest in her husband is due in part to the stark contrast between Jon and the new husband, at the same time she articulates a sexual desire for Jon, not for her husband.

Upik's story reflects the hesitancy of some of the young femmes in their initial interactions with their partners. Although she felt no attraction to Jon in the beginning, her feelings changed over time and suggest a love for Jon that is both emotional and physical. Jon's efforts to ensure that Upik has a husband reinforce their shared understanding that Upik is a woman who will want to have children. Nevertheless, although Upik said she wants to have children at some point in the future, she is little interested in changing her situation and would prefer to stay with Jon. Upik's desire to remain with Jon rather than live with her husband differs from other young girlfriends who pronounce their willingness to date and marry ordinary men. In her desire to stay with Jon, Upik's story hints at some slippage as heteronormative categories are met with alternative forms of desire.

Sexual Proscriptions

Men's and women's sexuality in Indonesia are viewed as god-given attributes that are carefully controlled to maintain family honor and community order, although men's sexuality is under much less surveillance than women's (Bennett 2005). Women who are known to have had sexual relations outside of marriage are considered disreputable, poorly brought up, and a great shame to their families. Young women must guard their reputations by avoiding places and situations in which their good name can be compromised. As discussed in chapter 2, sexuality is proper and permissible for women only within marriage and under the control of a husband. Further, women are not thought to have any sexual desire "independent of the desire for children" (Bennett 2005, 31).

The proscription against sex outside of marriage falls heaviest on young unmarried women, who generally are expected to be virgins at the time of marriage. While young women's desires are apparent in their investment in dating, their need to remain virgins complicates these relationships. Tombois are aware of and participate in the proscriptions regarding women's sexuality to the point that they are unwilling to have penetrative sex with their unmarried girlfriends. Tommi admitted to me, "I have never had sex with a lover, like husband and wife, only kissing and hugging. That girl will get married someday," meaning that s/he does not want to spoil her girlfriend for marriage. Upik's partner, Jon, also was concerned about protecting h/er partner's virginity and said to me more than once in an interview, "I would never damage an unmarried girl." Tombois' participation in the ideology that enforces virginity on young women in some cases means that their intimate relations are quite limited, particularly if the tombois themselves do not allow femmes to touch their bodies.[3] By avoiding more intimate relations, femmes can overlook the (culturally defined) incongruities of their partners' female bodies with their masculine presentation and thus remain fairly secure in their own desires for men. Sinnott (2004) notes a similar de-emphasis of sexuality in *tom* and *dee* relationships, along with an expectation that kissing and hugging are sufficient, but in this case these practices derive less from cultural expectations of virginity and more from cultural constructions of women's sexuality as lacking in desire.

Sexuality and sexual desire for tombois and their girlfriends are constituted and filtered through heteronormative assumptions. Dayan told me that because femmes are attracted to men, they obviously prefer sex with a man who has a penis. *Tom*s in Thailand had the same perception of *dee*s, whom they assumed would be more satisfied by "real" men because of their ability to penetrate women with a penis (Sinnott 2004). Such assumptions maintain the fusion of normative sex/gender and the expectation of femme desires for men. For femmes, a limited sexual repertoire, combined with strong reinforcement of their normative femininity, means that sexuality does not shift out of place, although some slippage is possible. The meanings of their experiences and desires continue to make sense within a dominant discourse that positions them as always already heterosexual women attracted to men and male bodies.

At the same time couples find room to maneuver within the shared parameters of sexuality, which in some cases appears to exceed hugging and kissing. Jon expressed quite a bit of confidence in the intimacy s/he and h/er partner Upik share. "We kiss on the lips and more," s/he said, "we give to each other, and we both want it." Exactly what "it" involves was left unsaid. Andri had a well-formulated understanding of sexual relations between h/erself and h/er girlfriend. "In principle, couples want to please and to be pleased by each other in everything, including sexual relations. When we have sex, it depends on who wants it. It could be Jeni who starts it or me." Although not explicit about their lovemaking, Andri's and Jon's comments suggest that they do have sexual relations with their partners and that their partners have active sexual desires as well. These stories point to the complexities of femme subject positions and the possibility of slight shifts in meaning as their enactment of proper femininity engages with non-normative sexuality, that is, a sexuality between bodies culturally defined as the same sex. The question remains how femmes view tombois' bodies. For *dee*s

141

in Thailand, who prefer emotional relationships over sexual pleasure, they do not reciprocate their partner's sexual attentions. By not engaging with their partners' bodies sexually, they can thereby maintain their normative position as women. Sinnott (2004) associates this practice with hegemonic constructions of proper femininity.

Marriage Trouble

Marriage looms as a troublesome prospect for many young lesbi couples, particularly for the femmes. All Indonesians are expected to marry. The deployment of gender through state and Islamic discourses creates and perpetuates norms of sexuality in which marriage is the only possible place and future for sexuality.[4] The properness of marriage and sexuality within marriage are concepts supported by both the state, through appeals to "traditional values of Indonesia" (Howard 1996, 170), and Islamic moral precepts. For Indonesia's majority Islamic population, the requirement of marriage is embedded in the nexus of community norms, customary practices (*adat*), and Islamic precepts. I was frequently told that marriage is a requirement of "custom" (*adat*) and "religion" (*agama*, but more specifically Islam); one becomes an adult and fully functioning member of one's kin group only if one is married.[5] In essays by leaders of the national Islamic organization Nahdlatul Ulama, several writers emphasize the "natural" connection between women and marriage (Munir et al. 1994). Within marriage woman's most important task is to educate children, therefore a woman must marry someone who can enable her to fulfill her "natural" function to have children (Wahid 1994). In this way sexuality is produced and regulated by gendered expectations about marriage and adulthood.

Consequently, Indonesian Muslims generally acknowledge that any sexual relationships outside of heterosexual marriage are unacceptable to the moral code of Islam and customary practices (Bennett 2005).[6] For women, failure to marry and bear children means failure to achieve full adult status. The strength of this normative prescription results in intense pressure on women to marry a man and have children. Marital status reflects not only on oneself, but on one's family. As one of the tombois explained to me, parents feel strongly their responsibility to ensure their children's marriages; if any of their children do not marry, their feeling of shame is equally strong. A good son or daughter will follow their family's wishes and marry someone of the appropriate social status. Getting married, then, is tangible evidence of respect for one's family, for the cultural order, and for the nation state, a point I take up again in the next chapter. The force of this ideology is found in the social and material consequences for unmarried individuals, who over time become marginalized within their kin groups and communities because they lack the requisite bonds to create socially legitimated families and cannot produce future generations to provide support in later years.

Marriage expectations are strongly integrated into young women's identity as "normal." Unlike Upik, other unmarried girlfriends tend to portray their relationships with tombois as detours from the normative life course for women; breaking up with their current partners would send them on their way to marriage. The younger girlfriends, Nila and Jeni, averred that they expect to marry a man at some point, especially if their current relationships fall apart. Lina said if she breaks up with Tommi, she will look only for someone she can marry. Even Epi, as noted earlier, is quite firm about not wanting another relationship with a tomboi. In this way the force of normative gender buttresses their own self-positioning as women and its entailment of marriage and child-rearing.

Tombois participate in this normalizing discourse of heterosexual marriage and motherhood by assuming that their girlfriends will want to marry ordinary men and have children. Dedi said, "If my girlfriend wants to get married, I'll let her. I won't prevent it." S/he explained, "Tia [her ex-girlfriend] is normal. She should have a life with her own family and house and children. I can't give her that kind of life, so I have to let her do what she must do." Dedi does not question the dominant discourse that portrays women as desirous of marriage and family. Dedi went on bravely,

> It's better that I'm the one who is brokenhearted. It's enough that she knows I love (*sayang*) her. When I was with Tia, I was close to her family. So her mother approached me and told me she wants Tia to get married. 'Would you help me find a husband for her?' She asked my help in persuading Tia to get married! In my heart I thought, who would agree to their lover marrying? But in my head I knew that I couldn't marry her.

In this conversation Dedi appears conflicted about losing h/er girlfriend to marriage, but s/he went along with it because s/he thought it best for h/er girlfriend. Dedi finds h/erself in the same situation with h/er current girlfriend, who is dating a young man. Again s/he told me, "It's okay with me as long as I know what's going on. I don't want my girlfriend to be ignorant of guys on my account."

Andri is of the same mind regarding Jeni's future. Andri said, "I won't oppose it if Jeni's family finds her someone to marry." Some of the tombois encourage their girlfriends to find husbands. Tommi introduced a man to Lina as a possible suitor, but Lina was not interested. As noted in Upik's story, her partner Jon encouraged her to marry. When I asked Jon why, s/he replied, "Well, Upik's parents were concerned that she should get married, so I told Upik about it. Besides, it would be a pity if she didn't have a child." Although Upik was not eager to marry and disrupt her current situation, Jon was convinced that with Upik's motherly nature, she would want and need to be married.

Tombois' concern for their partners' reputations and marriageability, and femmes' concurrence with that view, provide evidence of the power of normality. I use the term "normality" here to refer to Bourdieu's habitus, "an acquired system of generative schemes" that produce mutually intelligible meanings beyond conscious intent or thought, a shared sense of reality that harmonizes peoples' experiences (1990, 55ff). Within this shared reality femmes and tombois understand that women "by nature" will want to marry and have children, with the result that tombois do not try to prevent their girlfriends from marrying and may in fact encourage it. As Dedi notes, since tombois cannot give their girlfriends children (and do not consider adoption a viable strategy), they do not want to ruin their girlfriends' prospects for marriage and children.

Thai *tom*s express a similar resignation over their girlfriends' desires to have a normal family life, which Sinnott (2004) suggests arises from Buddhist-inflected cultural discourses of karma as well as a desire to confirm *tom* difference from *dee*s. In a slightly different vein, tombois' willingness to allow girlfriends to marry can be read as chivalrous, a way of protecting the girlfriend's reputation, and thus, for tombois, an inherently manly act. Through sacrificing their own happiness for that of their girlfriends, tombois, like *tom*s, confirm their masculine standing. In this case the norm, as well as its social and material effects, powerfully conditions certain practices and expectations for the future. Bourdieu calls this process of agreeing to the only apparent possibility, "a virtue made of necessity" in which "agents refuse what is anyway denied and ... will the inevitable" (1990, 54). Bourdieu does not mean here that agents have no recourse or ability to change, and in fact recognizes the importance of praxis in shifting meanings, but insists that the weight of past experiences (in a class-limited habitus) tends to guarantee that certain practices appear inevitable and will continue. Since marriage to their partners is denied them, tombois' actions to preserve their partners' marriageability becomes a virtue of sacrifice in which they will their own unhappiness in the face of what appears to be inevitable.

And yet the denial of their own possible futures seen from another angle may be a strategic move by tombois, whose ability to shift masculinity to their own bodies comes in part from their participation in and maintenance of the dominant gender binary. As I noted in the previous chapter, tombois secure their identity not only by their proper performance of masculinity, but by policing their girlfriends' performance of normative femininity. Acquiescing to dominant

expectations that women should marry may work to secure one's own positioning. Because tombois do not seriously disturb community norms of marriage and
family, they ensure the partial legitimacy of their position on the margins of social convention. In this apparent collusion, tombois acquiesce to dominant gender norms by maintaining an attitude of understanding and sympathy to their
girlfriends' desires to marry and to fulfill family expectations.

Shifting Femme Desires

After falling into the lesbi world, some femmes in long-term relationships were
moved to reconsider the meanings of their desires for tombois. This situation is
somewhat different from the one Bourdieu imagines for his notion of habitus.
Given his focus on the homogeneity of habitus, the number of possible generative schemes that can be invoked is in fact limited. However, with the availability
of subdominant or alternative discourses in a globalized world, and the mediation of their own subjective experiences, some femmes are able to rework and
recast their definition of womanhood and their desire for a relationship with a
tomboi.[7]

In contrast to younger femmes, the older and more educated femmes, Epi
and Lina, had longer experience in the lesbi world and had greater access to
alternative discourses. Of her group of friends, Epi was the first to "fall into the
lesbi world" in the early 1990s at the age of sixteen, then Lina in the mid-1990s.
Epi, Jeni, and Nila had been friends through their tomboi partners for about
five years by the time I met them in 2001. Lina was friends with both Tommy
and Dedi and their friends. All of these women were careful to maintain proper
appearances, but Epi was the most careful about guarding her reputation. She
rarely socialized at the food stall that Jeni and Nila ran and only interacted with
the others on public occasions.

Despite the fact that Epi and Lina have both broken up with their partners
several times over the years, they have never found boyfriends they wanted to
be serious with and have always returned to the same tomboi partner. Epi dated
a man during one of her break-ups, but said he was boring, so she eventually
patched up her relationship with Danny. Lina turned down a man Tommi had
introduced to her. Both women voice the expected desire to marry and have children, but neither are making much effort to do so. In considering the prospect
of marriage, Epi decided that if she had to marry, she would have a child and
then leave her husband to return to her tomboi partner. She sees this temporary
compliance with marriage as a strategy to fulfill her familial responsibilities and

preserve family harmony. "Once I have a child, I can do what I want, and my parents won't be able to stop me," she said. Lina, who first had a boyfriend for nine years and has been with Tommi for seven years, said in 2001, "I still want to marry but not as much as I used to, maybe because I'm getting older." Three years later Lina was still *thinking* about marriage and leaving the lesbi world. But her doubts were growing. She said, "I don't know, I still have strong feelings for Tommi. You know, s/he is so charismatic, s/he's hard to resist. And we've been together for a long time now." For both Lina and Epi the depth of their relationships and their histories of being partnered with tombois enable them to imagine staying together despite family pressures to marry.

In moving between two worlds, the "normal" world and the lesbi world, Epi and Lina engage in practices and discourses that contradict the normative model for women. Lina, who said she did not know anything about the lesbi world before she met Tommi, and had negative images of those who were called lesbi and "homo," now pays attention to media discussions of gay and lesbi but from a different perspective, one that recognizes the possibility of lesbi relationships. Epi reads stories about lesbi in women's magazines. In addition newspaper stories about famous lesbians in the United States, including Melissa Etheridge's marriage to another woman, convey the possibility of long-term relationships outside of heteronormative marriage. In fact Epi and her partner Danny had exchanged rings in the same manner as normatively married couples. For Epi and Lina, their reluctance to marry suggests that the definition of "woman" as someone who marries and has children is in flux.

The lesbi world presents both an alternative discourse and, to bring Bourdieu back in, a different habitus with new possibilities, although these possibilities are conditioned by past experiences and discourses. The subjective experience of being lesbi and the practical enactment of an intimate relationship with a tomboi offer these femmes a critical perspective on marriage. Epi can justify her disinterest in men by saying that her date was boring, that is, not like Danny, who has won her heart. Neither woman will say that she refuses marriage, but in this lesbi world other measures of satisfaction have become possible that support a reworking of their subject position as "women." Similarly Upik's investment in her relationship and its tangible benefits—the ability to meet their daily needs and rent their own house together through sharing incomes—provides her with a critical platform to resist heteronormative expectations and imagine a possible future with Jon despite the fact that their relationship falls outside social norms. These new satisfactions, however, must be reckoned against the risk of never gaining marital status. Heteronormative gender requires that a proper woman desires not just a man, but a man who will become her husband and give her children.

In desiring tombois, girlfriends move a step away from normative desires, at first perhaps without thinking, as in Nila's insistence that there is "no difference" or Noni's surprise at finding she had fallen in love with a tomboi. But through time spent in the lesbi world, their subjective experience of being "women" begins to shift as they become aware of other possibilities.

Noni's Story

The shifts in meaning that femmes experience as they inhabit the lesbi world extend beyond the question of marriage to the meaning of femme desire itself. As noted earlier, the term "lesbi" for femmes takes on meaning only in the context of a relationship with a tomboi and does not identify a fixed sexual desire for "other women" because femmes claim an attraction to men, ordinary men and tombois. Noni's love life, however, suggests other possibilities and more complex desires.

Noni, an older divorced woman with one child, has experience with both men and tombois. After Noni's first relationship with a tomboi, described in the opening to this chapter, she married the man her family had found for her. In describing the following years, she said:

> I didn't like being with a man. I'd been with Diah [her tomboi partner] and was used to h/er. From the time I was married, I did not want to have sex with my husband. When we had sex, I tried to keep my body covered. One time while I was reading a book, my husband forced himself on me. I really didn't enjoy sex with my husband. Although it gave me a child, I didn't like being a housewife. My husband complained that I wasn't fulfilling my wifely duties. I got sick and tired of the situation so I started hanging out with some lesbi friends. They were all friends of Diah.

Noni left her husband for one of the tombois she met during this time, but when that relationship soured because the tomboi was abusive, she returned to her husband. Eventually Noni met Robi and left her husband for a second time. Noni said she considers Robi her husband, but when I asked if she would want Robi to have sex-reassignment surgery, she said, "No, I don't want a man. I don't like being with them. I like women (*perempuan*). Yes, Robi is a tomboi, that's the way it is here, tomboi/femme, but Robi is still female (*perempuan*)." Noni then described a "lesbi" in the following manner:

> Lesbi, indeed, we are only attracted to women (*perempuan*). Although we partner with tombois, we don't need or desire a dildo (*alat bantu*). Just the way they are satisfies me, I don't need anything else. I can come without

having to use a dildo. I had one lover who wanted to use a dildo when we made love. I said, "You should love your body as it is. I am perfectly happy with that, so why use it [a dildo]?" S/he answered, "So we're not bored."

Noni is one of the few femmes I met who had had more than one tomboi lover. Her status as a wife and mother gives her a somewhat different view of her sexuality than the younger unmarried girlfriends. Noni never voiced any concerns about being a woman; she was secure in her femininity. Yet she was equally clear that she enjoyed the female body of her lover. As far as she was concerned, tombois may be like men, but they are still female.

Noni's view reflects her access to multiple discourses circulating in Indonesia about gender and sexuality, including "blue films," erotic foreign-made videos of women making love to women. Noni said she had purchased a number of those videos while still married, much to the disgust of her husband, who had looked at them to see what she had bought. He complained to her that the videos were just "two chicks going at it" (*tempé sama tempé*, a slang phrase).

Noni's attraction to tombois and to their female bodies is not in line with the attractions cited by younger femmes. Those femmes desire men and are comfortable with men; in their minds tombois are types of men. Indeed, Noni perceives the gendered construction of tomboi and femme as something that is necessary, given the cultural context, but she feels comfortable seeing her partner as female. In her experience heterosexual intercourse is unsatisfactory; sex with a tomboi "just the way they are," that is, without a dildo, is what she prefers. Here Noni disputes the assumption that femmes can only be satisfied by having sex with a man, that is, sex which includes a penis or penis alternative. Although her partners have been tombois, the female bodies of her partners are important to her, suggesting that she does not see tombois as men but as masculine women.

Noni's view aligns somewhat more closely with lesbi activists in Jakarta, who define lesbi as women who love women, a point I discuss in more detail in chapter 7. To the extent that this discourse may become dominant in the lesbi world, it has the potential to alter tombois' own views of the relation between their masculinity and normative female bodies, apparent in Robi's shifting desires for sex-reassignment surgery. In 2001 Robi told me s/he had seriously considered having surgery when a former lover offered to pay for it. By having the surgery s/he hoped to be able to marry h/er lover. By 2004 Robi and Noni had been together for a couple years. When I asked Robi that year if s/he was still interested in surgery, s/he said, "No, not anymore. Before I was only thinking emotionally. It was only because I wanted to keep [my lover] so bad that I considered having surgery." H/er attire at the river picnic I organized in 2004 may have reflected h/er change in attitude as well. Robi's swim clothes revealed the outline of h/er breasts in a way that none of the other tombois' clothes did. Robi's apparent comfort with h/er female body may reflect Noni's feelings about tombois' bodies, although Robi's view of h/erself as a tomboi, that "there is no difference between me and a man," has not changed. For other tombois the discourse of femaleness creates tensions in their self-understanding, as I discuss in chapter 7, but not a discernible shift in their views of themselves as men.

Intimate Strategies

In this chapter I have explored how subject positions inform desires and how those desires shift over time as individuals encounter and take up other discourses and practices. Couples' praxis concerning marriage and their own relationships demonstrate a range of strategies and imaginings that reflect their individual experiences, histories, and family contexts. Like the single heterosexual young women in Bennett's (2005) study, tombois and their girlfriends simultaneously uphold expectations of normative gender while seeking ways to maintain long-term relationships. In Bennett's study, single women in Lombok, Indonesia, engage in backstreet romances (*pacaran backstreet*), a term referring to secret relationships with men. She argues that such relationships are pragmatic responses to family expectations that preserve women's reputations and the dominant gender ideology, while at the same allowing women to engage in premarital relationships.

Tombois' and their girlfriends' efforts to maintain their relationships, whether by physically living together, postponing marriage, or, for girlfriends, marrying in order to return to their partners, are similarly pragmatic responses. As I discuss in the next chapter, evasion and circuitousness, while deemed inappropriate strategies by U.S. LGBT activists, allow the relationships to persist and avoid possible serious repercussions from family or kin (see Quiroga 2000). At the same time these responses point to changes in their self-positionings as interpretations of normative categories of gender and desire shift.

These stories bring me back to the question I asked earlier about the relation of gender to sexual desire. Can femme desires for their partners be separated from desires for the bodies of those partners? In Jackie Kay's novel *Trumpet* (2000), a story of a transgender jazz musician, Joss Moody's wife Millie loves his body, irrespective of his genitalia, because she loves Joss. She imagines his body as male because she does not see him as anything other than a man. Like Joss's wife, do girlfriends love the bodies of their partners and imagine their partners' bodies are male? Whatever girlfriends' initial responses were to their tomboi partners, those in long-term relationships, such as Upik, Epi, and Lina, express a strong attraction for their partners. Upik said that if Jon, her partner, dressed like a woman, s/he would look like a man in drag, a statement that reveals how much she thinks of and sees Jon as a man. For these femmes their experiences in the lesbi world offer them a different view of gender and sexuality, one in which a meaningful, loving relationship is possible apart from heteronormative structures of marriage. For Upik, whose only experience of this world is with her very masculine partner, she is desirous of her tomboi partner but not of men, at least not men such as her new husband. In Noni's case she speaks of a desire for her partner's female body and is comfortable thinking of h/er as female. For other femmes, like Jeni and Nila, who also love their partners, they remain invested in normative structures and the possible future of being wives of and having children with male-bodied men.

The differences between Noni's and Upik's stories and those of other femmes may reflect their different histories and family connections, as well as the instability of normative categories of sex/gender. The "normality" of womanhood dominates younger unmarried girlfriends, who feel that they cannot refuse their families and must eventually live as women are expected to live. If these femmes see their attraction as one directed toward men, not all who position themselves as femmes lay claim to the same desires. For Noni, who has already fulfilled her obligations as a woman by marrying and having a child, the power of normality has weakened. Who and what is desired are shifting and complex. Noni's assertion that she desires females with female bodies speaks to the presence of competing discourses that enable her to reimagine her desires as those of a woman who loves a masculine woman. Not all femmes travel the same route as Noni, however, but find their greatest satisfaction in loving the masculinity of their tomboi lovers.

Ambiguities in Family, Community, and Public Spaces

While discursive categories are clearly central sites of political contestation, they must be grounded in and informed by the material politics of everyday life.

—CHANDRA T. MOHANTY

TOMBOIS ARE FEMALE-BODIED INDIVIDUALS who lay claim to the social category "man," by which I mean the ideologically dominant conception of manhood that circulates through much of Indonesia. In this chapter I look at the particular practices they perform in relation to socially significant others across household, community, and public spaces. Despite articulating a sense of self that they consider to be nearly the same as other men's, tombois take up different subject positions in different spaces, engaging with and reproducing a version of femininity when they move within family and community spaces. Thus I ask in what moments and by what processes do tombois take up particular subject positions. I examine issues of body knowledge, tomboi praxis, and space, focusing on moments of interaction in particular spaces, to develop a theory of contingent masculinities that accounts for the multiple subject positions tombois take up and raises questions about the meanings of normative gender. Further, I explore concepts of female masculinity and mestiza consciousness as a way to think about the relation between transgender identities and normative constructions of gender.

My analytical focus on bodies and spaces in this chapter leads me to examine how tombois respond to and manage expectations of gendered practices in different cultural spaces. As tombois move through household, community, and public spaces, they engage in practices and behaviors that produce apparently contradictory subjectivities. Within household and community spaces, tombois'

151

female bodies are visible, called on by family members and recalled by tombois. By exploring the particular contexts in which tombois' female bodies become visible, I address how tombois understand that visibility in light of their own subject positions as men. Further, I seek to "queer" the household context by foregrounding the tensions and accommodations between families and tombois, a context that creates key linkages with theorizing by queers of color regarding multiple subjectivities. The processes that I began to hint at in the last chapter—of multiple subject positions and complex desires—come into full play here. Tombois' ability to navigate different spaces recalls Anzaldúa's (1987) formative work on mestiza consciousness, a point I return to at the end of the chapter to make sense of how tombois embrace multiple and apparently conflicting subjectivities.

Family Space and Female Masculinity

Despite the fact that kin think of tombois as female based on their knowledge of tombois' physical bodies during the period when they were growing up, they do not force tombois to appear in feminine attire within familial spaces. The tombois whom I visited at their homes do not change their appearance around family but wear the same clothes they always wear, the pants, T-shirts, belts, and shoes that are common attire for young men. The first time I was invited to eat at Dedi's house, however, I was not sure what to expect. Dedi met me at h/er family business and then took me to h/er mother's house, which was outside the center of town in a small group of houses nestled next to rice fields. Dedi was dressed in h/er typical men's attire and appeared to be quite comfortable around h/er family. H/er mother and older sister had prepared the meal for us without Dedi's assistance. S/he and h/er close friend Tommi carried the food to the half-finished house next door where we ate. The food was laid out on banana leaves, which were placed on mats on the floor. Dedi's niece, who calls Tommi "Uncle," joined us for the meal. When we were done eating, Dedi and Tommi cleaned up by tossing the leftovers out the window for the cats, dogs, and chickens to finish off. On this occasion as well as other times when I visited Dedi at home or at the family business, I saw no change in Dedi's appearance, although s/he was more tempered in front of h/er elders.

The tombois I interviewed explained that they have the same privileges as their brothers in terms of mobility and autonomy. Dedi said, "My family doesn't restrict me. I'm free to hang out with whomever I want. At home I'm the only one who has this much freedom." In this statement s/he contrasts h/erself with h/er unmarried sister and sickly brother. Tommi, who also lives at h/er family home, told me, "My family trusts me not to get in trouble. If I am out at night, they know I can protect myself and would not embarrass them." It would be embarrassing for a family if an unmarried daughter became pregnant, but, as Tommi declares, they are not shamed by tomboi behavior. While unmarried women's movements are closely monitored by their families as a way to protect their reputations, tombois' ability to navigate public and masculine spaces (*dunia laki-laki*) without problem helps to confirm for their families that their performance of masculinity is fitting and permissible. By performing masculinity, tombois enunciate a self that comes to be recognized by their families. It is not through discursive claims that tombois are recognized as such, since tombois do not speak about their gendered selves to family; rather their performance of *proper* masculinity creates a space for them within the family context.

Although this form of queer praxis lacks a public declaration of identity, which is and has been one of the political acts of greatest import for the lesbian and gay movement in the United States (see Armstrong 2002), it nevertheless effectively conveys certain meanings to tombois' families that are received and understood without comment or criticism. Families recognize the masculinity performed as an intelligible practice, even though it is embodied in a female body, and thus ignore in everyday practice the gender transgression of tombois. Ara Wilson (2004) argues that *tom* economic contributions to their families account for family toleration of *tom* gender transgression in Thailand, a suggestion that has merit in relation to tombois as well, since some tombois give part of their income to their families. Andri, whose relationship with Jeni is accepted by h/er family, contributes substantially to h/er family's meager income. However, tombois point out that their families have been accustomed to their behavior since childhood, which suggests that family acceptance is a process that begins before any economic contributions are made. In Martin Manalansan's work on gay Filipinos, one of his subjects remarked that his family knows about him without anything being said. As far as he is concerned, silence on the part of family means neither denial nor complete acceptance. Silence "was indicative of a kind of dignified acquiescence and, more importantly, of abiding love" (Manalansan 2003, 30). Similarly, the fact that families in Padang do not confront adult tombois about their behavior signals their acknowledgment of tombois' personhood.

Evading Marriage

Despite the legitimacy tombois have within family spaces, they face certain obstacles in enacting their masculinity. Although they see themselves, as they say in their own words, "the same as men," at the same time cultural understandings of female bodies situate them somewhat precariously within the social category "man" because the dominant gender ideology in Indonesia equates sex with gender. Tombois' kin may respond to and treat them as men in many ways, but they retain knowledge of tombois' female bodies by virtue of having raised them or having grown up with them. Similarly, Davies (2007b) notes that the families of *calalai* (masculine females in South Sulawesi) never forget that they are female. In fact, in the community where one *calalai* and h/er woman partner live as husband and wife, visitors are informed that the *calalai* is female, thus ensuring that h/er culturally designated female body remains visible. In Padang this knowledge means kin have certain expectations about tombois' behavior and social positioning related to their female bodies.

Tombois' everyday performance of masculinity does not erase for their kin the gendered expectations assigned to female bodies, in particular the duty to marry a man and bear children. As noted in the last chapter, the importance of marriage is supported by both the state, through appeals to supposedly traditional Indonesian values, and Islamic moral precepts. Boellstorff (1999, 2005b) positions marriage as a modern choice, a national imperative that cements one's belonging as a citizen. Becoming a wife (or husband) is necessary to fulfill familial duties and obligations as well as to gain the full respect of society and national belonging.[1] Consequently, families seek to provide marriage partners for their tomboi daughters in the only way that they understand—by finding husbands for them.

According to Boellstorff, many Indonesian gay and lesbi have no opposition to marriage, finding it "a source of meaning and pleasure allowing them to enjoy homosexual relationships while pleasing their parents ..." (2005b, 111). For tombois, however, marriage positions them irrevocably in the social category "woman" and forces them to constantly perform a feminine gender as a consequence of interactions with husbands and in-laws. Marriage is the most troubling challenge to their positionality as men. The prospect of tombois marrying evoked the strongest reaction from Dayan, one of the tombois, who asserted that it is just wrong for a tomboi to marry a man. Although Boellstorff (2005b) recounts instances of tombois marrying in the city of Makassar, Sulawesi, if only temporarily, Davies (2007a) reports that a *calalai* she met in Makassar was repulsed by marriage and had avoided it, while another married a waria (a male-bodied individual who acts like a woman) and so maintained h/er masculine position.

In Padang girlfriends are the ones much more likely to marry and in general are thought to be unable to resist the marriage imperative. In contrast efforts by families in Padang to marry off their tomboi daughters are met with varying degrees of resistance. The one exception in Padang that I knew of was Upik's partner Jon, who had been married briefly in h/er early twenties and had a son before s/he met Upik. When I asked Jon why s/he married, s/he attributed h/er desire for marriage to Islam, stating, "According to the Qur'an, one must have a husband." Jon married a Javanese man because, s/he said, "they are more easy-going and tractable (*lunak*). But the trouble with him was he wanted more wives, so he left after two years." It is not clear in Jon's case what role h/er family played in the decision to marry, but from h/er brief statements about it, it appears that marriage to a man, even an easy-going one, was not suitable to Jon.

Tombois I interviewed understand that their families would be ashamed (*malu*) if they do not marry, yet most tombois told me stories about finding ways to put off marriage indefinitely. When I met Danny in 2001, s/he was facing a terrible dilemma. S/he was panicked and stressed out because her parents had found a man, who was younger than Danny and worked as a tailor, whom they wanted h/er to marry. Danny said, "I feel like I'm being forced into a corner, like I have no options left. But I'm very close to my family." Danny was caught between wanting to please h/er parents and maintaining h/er sense of self and re-spectability as a tomboi. At first she decided to make them happy by going along with their plans. Danny said to me, "I'll travel this road first, and if it doesn't work, I'll ask for a divorce." Another time, however, s/he said s/he would marry and stay with h/er husband for a month and then leave him. S/he talked to h/er girlfriend Epi about it, and Epi agreed that s/he should go along with the plans for now. "If you can't take it, then you can get a divorce later after a few months," Epi told her. Others in their group of friends were not as sympathetic. Jeni de-clared that if Danny got married, s/he would have to leave the group, a boundary maintenance statement that underscores the threat to femmes' identity as normal women if a tomboi should become a "woman" by marrying. Clearly Jeni did not want Danny to be part of the lesbi world, if s/he, a tomboi, married a man.

Unlike their girlfriends, however, tombois are more successful in avoiding marriage. When Danny met h/er prospective groom, h/er sister told h/er to wear a skirt, but Danny refused and just wore what s/he always wears, hoping that would make him lose interest. After several months of persistent efforts by Dan-ny's family, Danny still had not agreed to the wedding. Before I left that year, s/he talked about finding a place to live away from h/er family. S/he said, "I'll just come home once in awhile, and if they ask where I've been, I'll just say I was stay-ing with friends. That way, they won't know where to find me, and so hopefully I can avoid getting married." Three years later s/he was still unmarried. When I asked what happened, Danny laughed and said jokingly, "He lost interest in me," a clever comment, particularly useful around Danny's family because it puts the blame on the prospective groom and exonerates Danny. What was left unsaid was, "I did everything to make him not like me," so he lost interest. Danny was still in a relationship with h/er girlfriend Epi as well. In this case the strength and sense of rightness of Danny's self-positioning as a man enabled h/er to avoid a marriage proposal.

The threat of marriage produces various strategies of resistance. I asked Tommi how s/he deals with h/er family's efforts to marry h/er off. S/he said, "I just tell my mother, if you want a marriage so much, you marry him! So they leave me alone." Faced with such resistance, families are reluctant to force their children into anything that they do not want to do. In the midst of Danny's anxieties about h/er potential marriage, s/he had turned to Andri to help find a place where they could live with their partners away from the scrutiny of family. They were very excited about making this move, but they faced some serious obstacles. Although the plan might have worked for Jeni, who no longer lives with her family and could have moved with Andri, it would have been more difficult for Epi because she lives with her mother and would not be able to spend many nights away from home. By 2004, however, neither Andri nor Danny had been successful in their plans to move away from their families and live with their partners, due in part to a lack of money to pay rent.

The potential negative consequences of marriage for tomboi self-positioning leads tombois to seek ways to outmaneuver marital expectations, either by seeking their own living arrangements or by allowing girlfriends to marry, in hopes that they will eventually leave their husbands and return. The struggle over marriage takes tombois beyond the shared reality of normative gender, with its expectation of marriage, into conscious realization of the effects of living under the norm's rule. This realization moves them to resist its demands and work toward other possibilities. In this case normality's inability to reflect tombois' own experiences and desires creates an opening for them to perceive and, if only momentarily, to exceed its control. This moment, and others like it, recalls Anzaldúa's (1987) sense of double consciousness that moves her to make sense of incompatible frames of reference.

A "Woman" at Home

While expectations of marriage create the greatest problems for tombois, and are consciously resisted, it is not the only instance in family space in which expectations associated with femininity and female bodies recall their culturally designated sex/gender. Most of the tombois have close relationships with their families. In addition to living at home, they help with family matters and assist with or attend the frequent lifecycle ceremonies held by kin and neighbors, including those for marriages, births, and deaths. In the context of everyday life with their families, tombois I interviewed accommodate kin expectations by engaging with and reproducing femininity to a certain extent despite presenting themselves as men. In these instances tombois do not insist on a proper performance of masculinity.

Dedi was talking about h/er family one day and commented that at h/er mother's house, s/he is "a woman at home" (*wanita di rumah*). Struck by that comment, which I thought was so out of character for a tomboi, I asked h/er to explain what s/he meant. Dedi said, it means "doing feminine duties around the house, like washing dishes, sweeping, keeping my room clean." At the same time that Dedi is careful to perform some feminine tasks, s/he is not just like other women at home because there are limits to what s/he feels comfortable doing. When I asked h/er if h/er feminine duties included cooking or washing clothes, she said, "No. I won't do that." In West Sumatra, the mantra of womanhood, as told repeatedly to me, is "a woman cooks, sews, and takes care of her husband and family." In light of these expectations, Dedi's lack of knowledge about cooking would not be interpreted simply as a lack of interest or ability but as a lack of femininity. Dedi proudly told me that s/he is asked to do repair work and painting around the house, which are considered men's jobs. Tommi used the same phrase as Dedi to describe how s/he acts at home. S/he is "a woman at home and a man outside." But Tommi also said, "I am never asked to do women's jobs around the house—only if I want to." Being a "woman at home" appears to mean that s/he is more careful at home in how s/he presents h/erself.

The expectations of femininity at home, coupled with tombois' desires to express their masculinity, lead to a certain level of subterfuge. Dedi, who took up smoking and drinking in high school, recounted with much laughter what happened when s/he first started smoking. "One time I was in my room [at home] with [three other tombois]. We were all smoking. After they left, there was so much smoke in the room I had to use mosquito repellant to cover the smell so my mother wouldn't notice." In this account Dedi's efforts to cover up h/er smoking points to h/er ability to manage disparate subject positions, the rowdy young man and the polite daughter.

The care taken at home to perform some feminine practices and to hide those practices that are not considered appropriate for women is meant to show respect for and preserve relationships with families. In recounting these stories Dedi never suggested that s/he felt burdened or angered by the need to conceal h/er masculine behaviors. By being "a woman at home," Dedi said, s/he is able to maintain a good relationship with h/er mother. Dedi's story is indicative of the feelings expressed by other tombois I interviewed. Tombois asserted the importance of upholding kin expectations to a certain degree because loyalty and duty to family and kin carry a great deal of weight. In Indonesia kin ties provide individuals with a social identity and sense of belonging that they rely on throughout their lives. In addition kin are a source of emotional and financial support, paving the way for future opportunities by paying for education, extending loans, and helping find jobs.[2] To act in a way that would create a rift between oneself and one's family is neither advisable nor acceptable. Thus, couched in the context of maintaining good relations at home, Dedi acts in ways that are congruent with h/er concerns about family and kin.

Despite the fact that most tombois have been pressured at one point or another to marry a man, they are unswerving in their loyalty and sense of obligation to their families. Danny said, "Family is number one. You have to protect your relationship to your family." When asked what h/er family and h/er girlfriend meant to h/er, Dedi said, "Others are second after family. I told my girlfriend, family business is number one. In fact, no matter what, family stays number one, a girlfriend is number two. That's the agreement I have with my girlfriend." Because I was surprised at the depth of Dedi's loyalty and devotion to h/er family, I questioned h/er still further about h/er feelings for h/er girlfriend. Dedi responded, "Ya, my girlfriend is everything to me. But the possibility of [the relationship] ending is definitely there. As for family, there is no such thing as ex-family, but there are ex-lovers." Both Danny and Dedi are uncompromising in asserting the importance of family; being without family or losing family support is to them nonsensical ("there is no such thing as ex-family").

Feelings of loyalty and respect toward kin, evidenced in forms of bodily emotion and sentiment, are, as Bourdieu suggests, firmly embedded in bodies; they are, as he notes, "expressed and experienced in the logic of feeling (filial love, fraternal love, etc.)" (1998, 39). Take, for instance, the fondness Indonesians express for being with others or being in a large group of kin. The Indonesian word *ramai*, which means lively or bustling, is used positively in reference to large gatherings and signifies the pleasure of being immersed in a crowd. This preference for being in a group is an indicator of the importance of relationality (McHugh 2002). For Indonesians, being surrounded by a large group of kin produces a sense of happiness and security, while solitude is seen as undesirable and, in fact, suspect. The unattached person bereft of family or kin is to be pitied. Durably embedded, these feelings about one's kin link to broader cultural processes of social identity and belonging that make family and kin ties irreplaceable, despite the tensions they may produce.

By acting with restraint and politeness within the house, Dedi demonstrates respect for h/er mother, as would be expected of a daughter. Dedi's feelings of respect and loyalty are expressed materially by washing dishes, keeping h/er room clean, and sweeping floors, duties that sons typically would not perform. At the same time, h/er refusal to perform certain tasks, such as cooking, which would position h/er uncomfortably as a woman, suggests that h/er feminine performance can only be taken so far, beyond which it begins to seriously challenge h/er masculine subject position. H/er relationship with h/er family is managed by maintaining some aspects of femininity, while refusing others. Like Dedi, tombois perform a version of femininity within household space, taking on some tasks that are considered feminine and avoiding certain markers of masculine behavior, such as smoking. In other words, tombois' actions at home speak to the contingency of their subject positions.

Gender theorists such as Judith Butler (1990) and Esther Newton (1972) talk about gender as normative or non-normative and drag as the performance that points to the artificiality of gender. But what of an everyday masculinity that incorporates feminine practices? What of the *calabai* (male-bodied woman, Sulawesi) who walks with a swaying feminine gait, but when s/he is accosted by a man is ready to protect h/erself by fighting if necessary (Davies 2007a)? How to address the complexity of subject positions that queer gender? I want to push these gender theories further to consider how gendered individuals, such as tombois, may take up subject positions that move back and forth across the ideological boundaries of normative sex/gender systems through the performance of both masculinity and femininity.

A first step in this direction is to examine the concept of personhood within the Indonesian context. The Western idealized concept of self as an autonomous, cohesive, and integrated entity, distinguishable from all others, differs from notions of personhood in Indonesia, where the self is defined by and through one's kin and community of origin, as well as age, social status, and rank.[3] One's social position and behavior are relative to the person with whom one is interacting. Further, the variety of kin terms by which one is denoted signifies the contingency of self and the toleration of discontinuity (McHugh 2002). In this context personhood is never something finally achieved in the sense of a coherent, fixed identity.[4]

The notion of personhood as contingent, that is, not fixed, but relative, dependent on something else or a prior condition, points to the contextual, not just the multiple, aspects of subjectivity. Ernestine McHugh (2002), whose work focuses on Buddhist society in Nepal, uses the concept of the contingent self to highlight this relational aspect of selves. In her view the contingent self is neither bounded nor coherent but conditioned by circumstances, a process rather than an entity. McHugh's view is important for understanding the relational aspect of tomboi subjectivities, in which maintaining family relations is as important as and, in fact, structures who one is. Dedi may be a pragmatist who recognizes the difficulties of long-term relationships ("there is always the possibility of relationships ending"), but family relations are highly valued as far as s/he is concerned. At the same time that Dedi expresses very strong feelings for h/er girlfriend ("she is everything to me"), s/he does not see any contradiction between those feelings and h/er feelings for family ("family stays number one"). Bringing this view of contingent selves together with the concept of body knowledge suggests that tombois' subject positions, as daughters, friends, and lovers, which are conditioned by the material effects of particular spaces and gendered expectations, are experienced in relation with others and in relation to the logic of feeling, or embodied knowledge, that structures tombois' sense of being.

Tombois' efforts to balance their sense of loyalty with their sense of masculinity resonate with the modes of praxis of queer Latino Americans in Cuba and Mexico. José Quiroga (2000) points out that for Latino queers to choose family exile by asserting their queer identity is too much to ask, underscoring the importance of maintaining the social fabric of family life.[5] Likewise tombois can neither deny their families nor deny their femme lovers. For one they perform a certain version of femininity and for the other, as Tommi said, they act even more masculine (*lebih jantan*). Quiroga (2000) notes that circuitousness, evasion, and avoidance, which tombois evidence by avoiding certain masculine behaviors in front of family, are not necessarily forms of denial but particular ways of saying something. Tombois' evasiveness and desire to avoid being seen in ways that would embarrass their families can be interpreted as a particular way of, in this case, expressing filial love through acknowledgement of parents' concerns. It can also be interpreted as a continuing claim on the benefits of that relationship. In this manner tombois enact a certain version of femininity that maintains family ties and the sense of belonging that such ties offer without losing the possibility of relationships with femme lovers.

I want to build on Quiroga's argument concerning the importance of family to queers of color to examine briefly the place of kinship in subject formation. Dorothy Holland and Jean Lave (2001) define subjectivity not simply as the meaning that individuals give to it but as something formed through the collective work of positioning, improvising, and refusing participation, thereby emphasizing social interaction with others. One aspect in the process of subject formation that has been undertheorized is the importance of what I call kin collectivities. Ortner (2006) refers to a similar idea briefly in her discussion of the "good" embeddedness of agents in relations of solidarity, which include family, friends, and kin. I define a kin collectivity as a particular set of social relations organized around the idiom of kinship, constitutive of everyday life, and holding material and social consequences that may be as meaningful and potent as the disciplinary practices of state, religion, and capitalism. By using this term, I am not invoking kinship as a set of universal or "natural" relations based on blood ties, or a biological grid, but as a set of relations that become meaningful in particular contexts. I offer this anthropological riff as accompaniment to the meaning of family life theorized by queers of color because the question that lingers unasked is why family is important.

I suggest that kin collectivities act as a critical force in collectively producing certain subject positions. Collectivities, such as kin groups and families, and the productive power such groups possess, have been antithetical to Western thinking. The Enlightenment Self, the rational, autonomous thinker, was constructed in part in opposition to what was perceived as the self-abnegating, unthinking practices of kin collectivities, or culture writ small. Émile Durkheim (1984) used the term "mechanical solidarity" to refer to a context in which the goals and needs of the kin group far outweigh the "individual" desires of its members. His use of the term "mechanical" signifies his assumption that its members act for collective purposes, automatically following the wishes of the group. As recuperated in the twentieth-century United States, kin collectivities are equated with tyranny, greed, immorality, and irrational behavior. Popular tales, such as *Romeo and Juliet*, *The Godfather*, and the storied feuds of Appalachian clans, attest to the evils perpetrated in the name of "family." These narratives uphold the value of individualism and the valor of the heroic rebel, who breaks from "family" to become his own "man." In this context kin collectivities take a place similar to that of "society," that is, they appear to impose group rule at the expense of the individual, as if kin/society and individual are two distinct and oppositional categories. Even Bourdieu, who clearly situates subjects within the context of habitus and not against it, does not examine the productive aspects of groups such as kin collectivities.

The ability of such collectivities to produce particular subject positions comes not just from their disciplinary power to "shape" (that is, constrain and control) children/kin, but from their power to provide identity, purpose, satisfaction, and reward, in short, to embed people in a nexus of social relations within which they find solidarity, support, and the means to accomplish some of their own goals. Such collectivities are almost completely powerless in the white middle-class United States, where individual men are situated as heads of family and empowered to create serial families over a lifetime. Black working-class families in the

United States, in contrast, show the ability of kin groups to create strong ties, although I am not thereby equating class with the relative strength of kin collectivities (such as poor families, strong ties).[6] I simply use this concept as another way to grasp the complicated relation between tombois and their kin groups. These collectivities provide a context that encourages loyalty and cooperation as well as strategic compromise, but they do not thereby override critical reflection or self-understanding.

Versions of Femininity in Community Space

Tombois' performance of femininity extends to their immediate surroundings, the community or neighborhood space I describe in chapter 4. Community space is interspersed with kin and long-time acquaintances who knew tombois when they were growing up and attending school in girls' uniforms. Although, as mentioned above, Tommi divides the world into two spaces, home and outside the home, where different behaviors are performed, not all public spaces outside the home are the same. Community space is distinguished by the extension of kin networks and their social and material support into public domains. As in household spaces, tombois present a complex positionality in community spaces that both calls on their masculinity and recalls their female bodies.

Dedi is friends with many of the men who come to the family business where s/he and other family members work. S/he talks to them easily and at length, unlike h/er unmarried sister, who is polite and courteous to men customers but spends little time in conversation with them. When asked why s/he has more freedom than women, Dedi said, "If a woman hangs out with guys, people will say she is bad, but for tombois, they understand. They say it's natural—of course a tomboi has men friends. Nobody is bothered by that." According to Dedi, even the wives of married men are unconcerned about their husbands spending time with a tomboi, the implication being that because s/he is a tomboi, wives do not perceive h/er as a potential threat to their marriage in the way that they would if s/he were a woman. Dedi said that many of the men confide (*curhat*) in h/er. "They even ask me about their problems with girlfriends—what do I think about this or that girl. Because, you know, I'm a female too, so of course I would know more about women." During this conversation Dedi asserts the naturalness of h/er interactions with other men, which is corroborated by others around h/er. Yet Dedi suggests at the same time that s/he has a better understanding of women than men do, which s/he attributes to h/er female body and h/er consequent knowledge of what girls are like. Here Dedi recalls h/er female body as part of h/erself, giving voice to a cultural expectation that female bodies produce female ways of knowing. Having a female body, then, is not seen as a contradiction of her masculinity but as part of h/erself, h/er experiences, and h/er understanding of the world.

Tombois constantly manage community space in ways that maintain their masculinity yet adhere to certain norms of femininity. When I visited Tommi's café one evening with Dedi, Robi, and Noni, I was surprised because Dedi would not smoke, although Robi was smoking. When I asked Dedi why s/he would not smoke, s/he only said, "*Segan.*" *Segan* refers to a feeling of reluctance to do something that is not quite proper or that others might criticize (Echols and Shadily 1989). In this instance we were in a café run by Tommi, Dedi's close friend, but two of Tommi's siblings, who also knew Dedi, were working there as well. While Dedi had told me that tombois can smoke because it is what men do, s/he was not operating under that standard in this space. Instead s/he felt *segan*; s/he was reluctant to be seen smoking in a place where people knew h/er and might report back to Dedi's family about h/er smoking. According to Dedi, "My family has never seen me smoke." H/er reluctance in this space is due to extensive kin and community networks that make it likely someone s/he knows will see h/er. Unlike Dedi, Robi was smoking because h/er family lives on the other side of the city and were not likely to show up there. When Dedi did finally take a drag on a cigarette, s/he looked extremely uncomfortable doing so and was very careful to hide the cigarette under the table. Dedi told me later that s/he was being clever (*berpandai-pandai*), h/er word for a strategic assessment of the situation. By being *segan* in this context, s/he avoids behavior that might cause h/er family shame despite h/er ready acknowledgement, to me, that it is acceptable for tombois to smoke. Whether s/he smokes or not depends on the context and the chances of h/er family finding out.

Not only do tombois consciously avoid masculine behaviors, like smoking, in certain contexts within household and community spaces, they also permit themselves to be read as women through others' use of female forms of address for them. Terms of address used in conversation in Indonesia are based on the age, sex, and status of both speakers, which effectively slot people into gendered categories. People tend to employ gender-marked kin terms when addressing acquaintances or close friends, bringing an idiom of siblingship and seniority into their interactions (J. Errington 1998). Robi mentioned to me that s/he is called aunt by h/er younger kin. Dedi is called Aunt Di (*tante* Di) by younger kin and "older sister" (*uni*, Minangkabau) by customers at h/er family business. Tommi is called "Uni" at work. Since some family members use h/er nickname, Tomboi, or call h/er "older brother" (*uda*, M.), I asked h/er why s/he was addressed like that at work. S/he said simply, "Because it's the workplace." By calling her Uni, the employee marked Tommi as a woman, which s/he did not contest, despite the fact that as a manager, Tommi could have been addressed by yet other terms. These gendered terms of address mark tombois as women and tip off casual bystanders who hear them being addressed that way.

Within community space where interactions with kin and close acquaintances are frequent, tombois are likely to be called on as kins*women*, marking not only their gender but also their sex, according to Indonesian understandings of sex/gender as a unitary construct. Because of the presence of kin and acquaintances in this space, tombois are unwilling to demand terms of address for men; in fact, they do not find it important to do so. Robi shrugged off the apparent inconsistency by saying, "It doesn't matter. At home we have to follow the rules." For Tommi, being called Uni is expected and unproblematic at work. Similarly, one of the *calalai* Davies interviewed said "it is not really important" whether s/he is called Miss or Mister (2007a, 59). In everyday practice terms of address invoke ties of kinship based on the cultural nexus between sex and gender, thus reminding tombois of their female bodies. Those terms are considered unproblematic because they reflect and substantiate one's kinship and solidarity with family and community, a position that produces a sense of well-being through relationality. The reminder of their female bodies is also a reminder of the security kinship offers.

Modeling Gender Plurality

Tombois' contextual performance of femininity would seem to contradict the perverse gender of the "woman who acts like a man," but may find resonance in a broader cultural discourse of transgender identities, particularly as expressed by waria. Historically associated with theater and dance, waria have moved seamlessly to television, where they are cast as entertaining drag queens who "pretend" to be women but always reveal their male bodies. In Padang, people know of and patronize waria hairdressers; in rural villages waria are hired as wedding planners. According to Dedi, part of society already accepts their existence.

Tombois express a certain affinity with waria through terms such as *satu bangsa* and *senasib*. Tommi said, "I like to hang out with waria. We are one people (*satu bangsa*), after all. They are a different sex, but the same as us otherwise." Danny used the term *senasib* (sharing the same fate or destiny) to describe h/er connection with waria. S/he said, "I consider them a part of our group because they share the same fate as we do." Robi expressed a similar opinion, adding, "I feel compatible (*merasa cocok*) with them." Waria, like tombois, express a gender that is at odds with the gender socially ascribed to their bodies. The phrases tombois use when talking about waria express a sense that they are both people who share the same destiny or lot in life. By articulating a commonality with waria, tombois are not suggesting that they are the same as waria, but that waria occupy an analogous position outside normative gender categories.

I asked several lesbi if waria are women and received a variety of answers. Lina was willing to say that, yes, waria are women. She reasoned that because they feel that they are women, then they must be women. Her sentiment corresponds with her view of Tommi as a man and supports Tommi's sense of h/erself as a man. Three tombois, however, said that while waria are like women, they are still men. Tommi said, "You can always tell. Even if a waria is very pretty, very sweet, the way they talk and the way they act gives them away." Robi said, "You can tell they are not women. It's the way they act; it's more than what women do, for instance, tossing their hair back. Women don't do that." Dedi said at first that, yes, they are women. "In fact, they are more feminine than women (*lebih perempuan*). But they can also be men, when they want to be, because they will fight back when they are threatened or angry about something."

Their descriptions of waria suggest that tombois see waria as a mixture of feminine and masculine, physically and emotionally. Their confidence that they "can always tell" indicates that they do not see waria simply as women but as individuals who mix feminine with masculine behaviors. In this way waria are models for expressing both femininity and masculinity. In fact the term "waria," chosen by waria to replace other derogatory terms, is a combination of the words *wanita*, woman, and *pria*, man. It signifies their sense of themselves as both women and men (Oetomo 1996). If waria, who share the same "fate" as tombois, are more than and less than women, then tombois find themselves in these descriptions as well. Waria masculinity and femininity helps tombois make sense of the multiplicitous ways they move in the world, as masculine females who also perform versions of femininity. Both are present; neither is erased.

Colluding with Misreadings

While tombois' positionality as masculine females within community spaces may call for certain compromises in forms of address, it also enables tombois to carry on relationships with women that are invisible to others. By colluding with others' assumptions about their positionality as women, tombois can, in some contexts, move in spaces that other men cannot. Sinnott calls this a "silent complicity" that allows *tom*s and *dee*s in Thailand "a level of social maneuverability in which they can construct their own social world" (2004, 145, 146). In colluding with certain misreadings, tombois are not necessarily performing femininity but are making use of others' readings of them as "women" to engage in practices that would otherwise be unacceptable for men.

I asked Dedi if there are things s/he can do that men cannot. S/he said, "I can live with a woman, or two women, whereas a man cannot properly live with a woman before they are married." Two or three "women" living together is permissible and will not cause problems, because, according to Dedi, "society considers tombois to be women." Further, in Indonesia as elsewhere in Southeast Asia, it is typical for girls and unmarried women to sleep together; no one thinks anything of it, because having someone to sleep with (of the same sex) is considered preferable to sleeping alone.[7] Tommi is accepted as a part of h/er girlfriend's family and frequently spends the night with Lina. Staying at Lina's house, however, is dependent on Tommi's being taken as a woman. No family would ever knowingly allow a man to stay overnight in the house with their unmarried daughter (Bennett 2005). According to Tommi, "I can stay overnight with my girlfriend, but if I was a guy, I would be thrown out (*diusir*) of the house." Similarly, Davies (2007b) notes that a *calalai* can enter the house of h/er girlfriend, even when no men are present, something that other men cannot do. In this way, she argues, *calalai* have more freedom to be with their partners than men do.

In Padang this freedom to move under the radar, so to speak, enabled Robi and Noni to live together in a small apartment because the landlady thought that they were both women and so did not question the arrangement. Not wanting to disturb the landlady's assumption, Robi did not allow Noni to call h/er "papi" at their apartment except when the two of them were alone together at night. In this way tombois make use of cultural norms of same-sex friendship and sociality to create a space for their relationships. Collusion in such instances creates tensions over the possibility of being found out, confronted, or gossiped about, but it also offers tombois the opportunity to live with their partners.

Being read as women also means that tombois, like women, are not seen as having sexual desires. As discussed in chapter 5, women are not thought to have any sexual desire "independent of the desire for children" (Bennett 2005, 31). Given this dominant construction of womanhood and desire in Indonesia, it is not surprising that among the general populace the term "tomboi," although associated with masculine gender behavior, does not connote sexuality or same-sex desire. People in general do not imagine that tombois have sexual relations with women, an assumption that tombois do not contradict verbally. Oetomo (1996) notes that the same is true for the term *banci*, which he states is generally associated with a feminine gender identity and not sexual behavior.[8] In Thailand as well, people do not assume that two women together are lovers because women are not thought to have sexual desires (Sinnott 2004). Tombois' collusion with assumptions about women's desires makes their own desires invisible, but this invisibility provides the space for tombois and their partners to create and maintain long-term relationships (see also Saskia Wieringa 2007).

Tombois' collusion with misreadings about their sexual relationships is a strategic practice that expresses both family loyalty and, importantly, a sense of masculinity. Kin do sometimes become suspicious of a tomboi's girlfriend, but such suspicions are always met with absolute denial, after which kin tend to leave the couple alone. Part of the reason for denying such accusations, according to Tommi, is to protect h/er family and h/er girlfriend. Tommi said that taking such a stance "makes me feel good because I don't want to make life difficult for my parents or cause problems for my girlfriend." Denial in this case maintains family honor and the honor of the girlfriend. Tommi's desire to protect h/er girlfriend situates Tommi's behavior within the corpus of masculinity. In h/er view honorable men should protect their girlfriends' reputations by ensuring that no gossip circulates about them. Interestingly, Sinnott (2007) argues that *tom* caretaking of their girlfriends reflects a *feminine* gender norm, rather than masculinity, because in Thailand, putting a woman first would not be considered a masculine trait. For Tommi, the sense of feeling good about h/er actions speaks to a body knowledge that moves h/er to take up a complex set of positions: denying their relationship to protect h/er girlfriend while at the same time showing respect to h/er family by not embarrassing them. Thus, colluding with misreadings of oneself as a woman and engaging in complex practices of femininity and masculinity enable tombois to preserve and benefit from the social relations within which they and their girlfriends live.

Vulnerability in Public Spaces

In the anonymity of public spaces tombois are usually read as men and move untroubled in men's spaces. As noted in chapter 4, when Robi goes shopping in the market, s/he is frequently addressed as "older brother" by market women. However, being tombois in public spaces is an uncertain proposition if others do not read them as men. Tombois have no guarantee they will be recognized and acknowledged as men in their everyday encounters with others outside their family and community. Tommi told me that many times s/he is asked if s/he is a man or a woman. When I asked how s/he replies, she said, "I don't say anything. If I talk, they will hear my voice and know that I am female, but everything else about me is male (*lelaki*), my clothes, and my character." Nonresponse is a typical Indonesian tactic to avoid causing embarrassment if the response might offend or upset the person asking the question. It also defends against tombois' inability to control others' perceptions of them. By not responding, Tommi avoids any further questions or unpleasantness that could arise. While the uncertainty may not be resolved for the curious, Tommi lets h/er presentation and dress as a man do the talking for h/er.

The uncertainty about how they are perceived provides further grounds for maintaining a consistent masculine demeanor in public. In the case mentioned in chapter 4, in which Tommi was harassed in public by a young man who took h/er for a woman, Tommi chose not to ignore the misperception and countered it with an aggressive response, challenging the other man to a fight. The challenge was so effective that the other man backed down. By acting more aggressively than other men, tombois are able to reset gender misperceptions in line with their own self-positioning. As Noni commented, "They act so tough, other guys are afraid of them." In fact none of the tombois had ever been attacked or harassed because they were tombois. In everyday encounters with men who do not know them, tombois manage the uncertainties of their gender by being as masculine as or more masculine than men. By looking and acting like other men, tombois ensure that others recognize and respond to them as men.

Double Entendres: Boys in the Girls' Room

While tombois see themselves as men, the complexities of their self-positioning come into high relief in public restrooms, where their bodies draw them back into the female world. In everyday life within their own communities and family spaces, tombois rarely have to deal with this issue because bathroom spaces are generally unmarked for gender. In commercial or public spaces, however, where restrooms are separated into men's and women's rooms, tombois are faced with a dilemma. During an interview I conducted with Tommi at the hotel where I was staying, we took a break so s/he could go to the restroom. Since we were not near my room, I took h/er to the public restroom. I asked h/er which one s/he wanted to use, and s/he said, the women's restroom. When I asked why, s/he said, "I don't want any trouble in the men's restroom." When Tommi returned, s/he said s/he had been harassed by a woman who told h/er s/he was in the wrong restroom. Restrooms pose difficult choices for tombois. Tommi clearly was not willing to use the men's restroom, perhaps feeling at greater risk if a man confronted h/er than if a woman did. Despite being read as a man in the women's restroom, s/he felt more confident that a woman would not be as difficult to deal with as a man.

Robi recounted with much laughter the time s/he was at an airport and went into the women's bathroom.

> An older woman (*amak*, M.) looked at me and yelled, "Hey man, what are you doing? You can't just come in anywhere you want!" I acted like nothing was the matter, and when I came back out of the stall, she figured it out and said, "Eh, you're a woman (*padusi*, M.)! I thought you were a guy!" I was kind of embarrassed but what can you do?

In this case Robi is met with considerable opposition by this older woman, who is not under the same constraints as younger women to act modestly, but s/he ignores her in order to avoid further embarrassment, letting the woman decide for herself who this person is. The interaction is somewhat unnerving for Robi, but, like Tommi, s/he does not consider using the men's room.

The self-assurance of being just like men falls apart at the restroom door, when normative gender's material consequences force tombois to use strictly women's spaces (restrooms, sex-segregated spaces in mosques). Restrooms recall tombois' female designation and offer an unsettling moment in which the coherence of their self-positioning falters. Robi's laughter expresses both embarrassment and amusement at being read properly as a man but having to reveal that h/er body is designated female. In this moment and in this public space s/he becomes visible as someone who does not fit normative codes. H/er inability to make masculinity fit in a public context, where such revelations are unseemly, temporarily disturbs both the social order and h/er own sense of security.

Playing with Positionality: Tomboi "Camp"

As tombois move across spaces, they take up different subject positions, enacting versions of masculinity and femininity. Although they see themselves as men, their bodies do not correspond with normative manhood in the deterministic way of the sex/gender system, thus making them vulnerable to being read as what they are not. Dedi had told me that s/he is a "woman at home," which to h/er means enacting a proper femininity in a particular context to maintain family relations. Yet on another day as Sri and I were sitting with Dedi and Tommi in Robi and Noni's apartment, something different happened.

Dedi joked that s/he was a "woman (*wanita*) for a day." S/he had just gotten h/er menstrual period, s/he said. S/he started acting coyly, tilting h/er head to the side, and sitting in a typically feminine position with h/er legs bent to the side, hands folded neatly in h/er lap. Tommi joked that Dedi was feeling more sensitive today. Sri said, "If you're femme, then help clean up the dirty dishes." Dedi laughed and in mock protest complained, "Why is it always me? I've been washing dishes since early morning!" As quickly as s/he had started it, Dedi then changed h/er demeanor and pretended to be very mannish. Rather than sitting cross-legged in the way men do, and as s/he normally sits, s/he sat with legs askew, started speaking in a deeper voice and in a coarse manner.

This parody of femininity and masculinity in turn recalls the use of camp in gay men's culture in the United States, but with a twist. In this instance a tomboi, who identifies as a man, parodies femininity by exaggerating feminine behavior. H/er audience jumps right into the act, saying how sensitive s/he is being, a reference to women's supposedly more delicate nature. Sri reminds Dedi of h/er duties as a woman, so Dedi complains about how overworked s/he is. But the parody does not end there. Dedi follows it with a brief performance of an exaggerated masculinity, that of the street toughs (*préman*) with whom some tombois hang out.

I witnessed a couple instances of camp behavior only on my return trip to Padang in 2004, attesting perhaps to the tombois' greater comfort with me and to the security of having a safe space in Robi and Noni's apartment. Alternatively, these performances may be related to their own comfort with themselves as men or to a growing awareness of their interstitial position as men who are not physically men (in the culturally prescribed manner), a double vision that lends itself to camp humor.

"Camp" is a term originating in gay men's subcultures in the United States to refer to humorous performances that parody gender normativity. Arguments about whether camp is only applicable to gay men or is only a parody of femininity have absorbed U.S. feminist and queer scholars, but with the appearance of drag kings in the early 1990s, it became clear that camp was not just the realm of gay men (see Halberstam 1998).[9] Given all the debates about the meaning of camp, I prefer to rely on Newton's *Mother Camp* for the clarity of her ethnographic analysis. Newton states that "camp usually depends on the perception or creation of incongruous juxtapositions" (1972, 106). In Newton's analysis gay camp means intentionally and humorously pointing to the violations of normative categories of manhood—of the way that "homosexuals" impersonate men— and of marking the distance between themselves and normative ("straight") men.

What marks camp humor in the female impersonators that Newton studied, and has been consistently misread by some feminist critics, is not a consistent and exaggerated portrayal of femininity but a constant switching among different registers of masculinity and femininity, with each change bringing renewed laughter from the audience. By manipulating gender, putting it "on and off again at will," camp and drag point to the superficiality of all gender (Newton 1972), a point elaborated by Butler:

> In imitating gender, drag implicitly reveals the imitative structure of gender itself—as well as its contingency. Indeed, part of the pleasure, the giddiness of the performance is in the recognition of a radical contingency in the relation between sex and gender in the face of cultural configurations of causal unities that are regularly assumed to be natural and necessary (1990, 175).

Moe Meyer's (1994) efforts to revitalize camp as a queer cultural critique in *The Politics and Poetics of Camp* returns camp to its place of honor, not as imitation, irony, or usurpation, but as a recognizable political statement that denaturalizes gender categories, creating the radical contingency that Butler speaks of. In the same work Cynthia Morrill's (1994) refiguring of camp comes closest to tombois' own experiences; camp marks the aftermath of the shattering that occurs when the queer subject recognizes the impossibility of representing his or her desires within normative parameters.

Camp and drag have an uneasy relationship with transgender communities in the United States because performers are rarely understood as trans. In addition their own subject positions are generally muted in favor of the act (see Halberstam 2005). Camp as performed by Dedi, however, is a parody of something s/he is not. In this regard the kind of "camp" one does depends on the gendered perspective of the performer, a point that is often neglected when scholars speak of being lesbian or gay as a form of camp. Newton's (1996) description of a butch lesbian performing as a drag queen comes closest to Dedi's own camp performance of femininity.

Dedi's camp behavior appears to be a critique of normative gender categories. But by parodying versions of both femininity and masculinity, where does Dedi situate h/erself? What is s/he saying about gender? Dedi's parody makes fun of and thereby identifies those things that s/he is not—coy, flirtatious, beset with domestic chores, and alternatively, extremely rude and coarse—thus differentiating h/er own sense of masculinity from both the femininity of women and the macho toughness of street thugs. This play on gender may be interpreted as a way to negotiate and express the distance between and h/er difference from femininity and a particular form of hypermasculinity. It draws attention to the gender binary in which s/he is situated and h/er lack of representation in that binary. Dedi's parody speaks to h/er own excesses, which sidestep, go beyond, and thereby belie and critique normative sex/gender.

Dedi's camp parody was not the only instance in which tombois played with categories of sex/gender. In other instances Tommi's and Dedi's clowning played on the tensions between their masculinity and their female bodies. The first instance happened at the outing we took to a nearby river.

> I was sitting on a rock by the river, watching everyone splash around, when Tommi came out of the water. S/he was dripping wet, and h/er baggy shorts were clinging to h/er body. Grinning, s/he stuck h/er hand down h/er shorts and extended one finger, so that it looked like the water dripping off her shorts was actually the act of peeing with a penis. Then s/he laughed and went to dry h/erself.

On another occasion when Dedi came to visit me at Sri's house, s/he arrived by motorcycle in a downpour. As we sat down on the porch to talk, I commiserated with h/er because s/he was soaked through. S/he said, "I'm cold," and then, covering her pubic area with her hands, said teasingly "the little one (*nan ketek*, M.) is cold too." I had not heard that expression before but took it to mean a reference to a little penis, not a clitoris.

Tombois situate themselves as men, but that does not keep them from playfully pointing out the incongruity between their bodies and those of "real" men. Humorously claiming a "little one" may signify a desire for male genitalia, but at the same time it acknowledges a female body. Such behavior falls in line with the bawdy nature of waria entertainers, who accentuate their "breasts" in a play on their own male bodies. In Indonesia the form of drag found in transvestite performances in various theatrical venues and television shows are enjoyed by mainstream audiences, who relish the opposition created between masculine and feminine (see Peacock 1978). Since both performer and audience "know" that breasts do not belong on male bodies, this performance of incongruity is funny.

By pointing to an absence, are tombois also hinting at the pain of that absence, evidenced in their belief that femmes want sex with a "real" man who has a penis, or in their willingness to give up their girlfriends to "real" men who can give them children? As I noted in chapter 4, tombois do not all agree that they are just the same as men. Tommi said the only difference was physical, while Robi declared that there was no difference, although Robi had at one point desired sex reassignment surgery. When I asked about the possibility of surgery, which they had heard about through the media, neither Dedi nor Tommi expressed an interest in it. Tommi said, "I don't want to burden my parents. Besides, when I die, people would be confused about who I really am." When I asked Dedi if s/he would have surgery if s/he could, s/he said s/he would have to think about that. Then s/he said, "Probably not, because of money and my family. It would be too hard on my family if I did that. They would be embarrassed. I was born female and that's that." But when Sri asked Dedi if s/he were born again, what would s/he want to be, s/he said emphatically and without hesitation, "A man (*laki-laki*), of course!" and raised her arm bent at the elbow, fist high, the sign of the "muscle man."

These comments suggest that physically changing their bodies is not something that seems sensible to tombois. They have their families to think about. "People would be confused," Tommi said, meaning that others know s/he is "really" a female and it does not make sense to change that. Camp behavior, then, is a way to play out the tension of being men and yet not quite men, pointing out the socially inscribed contradictions between their bodies and men's bodies, and thus marking their difference from sex/gender normativity. James Peacock claims that Javanese delight in transvestite performances because "they break taboos, release tensions, and permit the disorderly mixing of normally segregated categories" (1978, 218). If his assessment is pertinent not only for Java but across Indonesia, where similar examples of such oppositional blendings and transvestite practices can be found (discussed in chapter 2), then tombois' parodies, in the Indonesian context, are neither wishful thinking nor bitter pathos. As Newton notes, "Camp humor is a system of laughing at one's incongruous position instead of crying. That is, the humor does not cover up, it transforms" (1972, 109). Camp humor transforms the situation into something funny and at the same time creates a positive identity, according to Newton. One of Newton's interviewees explained, "A camp is a flip person who has declared emotional freedom. She is going to say to the world, 'I'm queer' " (Newton 1972, 110). Tombois do not make open declarations of their difference, but their ability to camp about their ambiguous position is similarly an act of defiance. Some Indonesians may view this defiance as foolhardy but many also find it intriguing and even admirable.[10]

Tombois, Trans-Identities, and Contingent Masculinities

The awareness of tombois' female bodies that is shared by their kin and community carries with it certain consequences for tombois. Within household and community spaces tombois' female bodies are called upon by family members and recalled by tombois. Despite positioning themselves as men, tombois manifest particular practices congruent with those spaces and accede to certain interpretations and cultural expectations that are attached to female bodies. The femininity a tomboi invokes at home and in community spaces suggests that tomboi masculinity is a contingent masculinity that takes into account the culturally dictated positioning attached to female bodies and the material effects of that positioning.

In this sense tomboi subjectivity aligns closely with Halberstam's (1998) notion of female masculinity, a term she uses to open up exploration of masculinities across female bodies, in particular the performance of masculinities by butch lesbians. Her attempt to separate masculinity from men by examining female masculinities has been criticized by trans theorist Jean Bobby Noble (2006) for aligning it with lesbian masculinity and female bodies. Halberstam, for her part, was trying to shake lose the claims of lesbian writers that masculine women such as Anne Lister were lesbians who had no other way to express their desires for women than by being mannish, a claim that situated masculine behavior as pretense. Halberstam's vision of gender is worth quoting at length.

> ... sexual and gender identities involve some degree of movement (not free-flowing but very scripted) between bodies, desires, transgressions, and conformities; we do not necessarily shuttle back and forth between sexual roles and practices at will, but we do tend to adjust, accommodate, change, reverse, slide, and move in general between moods and modes of desire (1998, 147).

Halberstam here refuses the progressive narrative that sees butch becoming stone butch becoming female-to-male; she emphasizes instead the contingencies of gender without resorting to notions of fluid or free-flowing gender. By not fixing a position called transsexual or transgender or butch lesbian, she offers a way to think about female masculinities that can incorporate differing versions of masculinities, such as those found in Southeast Asia and elsewhere.[11] If female masculinity is about culturally defined "women," however, then tombois exceed Halberstam's taxonomy because they acknowledge the cultural expectations attached to female bodies even as they see themselves as men.

At the same time tombois' positionalities resonate with trans-identities articulated by trans theorists in the United States. The literature on trans-identities offers several useful models for thinking about transmasculinities. Jason Cromwell, an anthropologist and trans theorist, argues that transgender and transsexual are "genders that exist outside the binary of two" (1999, 127). He suggests that gender-variant, gender-blending transmen are not like other men because they have different histories, bodies, identities, and sexualities than nontransgendered men, thus positioning transmen at somewhat of a distance from nontransgendered men. In his autobiographical monograph Jamison Green makes a slightly different point, stating that "transsexual men may appear feminine, androgynous or masculine," as *any man* might, thereby insisting on the right to call himself a man while at the same time raising the possibility that there are no authentic claims to masculinity (2004, 506). Zachary Nataf points out that transgendered people "feel varying degrees of identification and belonging to another gender category" (2006, 447).

The differences in emphasis among these three theorists attest to the variability of trans-identities, and the need, as Sandy Stone (1993) originally suggested, to expand the bounds of culturally intelligible gender. Nataf's point, in particular, that transgendered people do not fit neatly into one gender category or another, resonates with my analysis of tomboi subjectivities. Tombois' abilities to move back and forth across the ideological boundaries of a normative sex/gender system underscore the challenge to fixed identities and binary gender categories offered by these trans theorists. In addition, my approach to gendered subjectivities offers another tool to understand transgender processes and variability. By defining masculinity as contingent, I give priority to social interactions and cultural contexts in the production of gender, rather than focus on differences from and variability within normatively defined categories of gender.

Tombois I interviewed demonstrate their masculinity through everyday practices, as well as in their dress, appearance, posture, and language, but in certain contexts they perform a version of femininity when expectations of filial duty and proper womanhood are unavoidable. Not only do tombois consciously hide certain masculine behaviors, such as smoking, to avoid bringing shame to their families, they also permit themselves to be read as women within household and community spaces. Actions within family and community spaces point to the context-specificity of tomboi praxis. Although tombois see themselves "the same as men," thereby defining themselves in accordance with dominant gender norms, family and community spaces require other practices that express femininity as well as masculinity. Social relations of kinship and family connect tombois with discourses of femininity that are strategically incorporated into tomboi praxis. Because subjects are embedded in multiple social relations, I account for the efficacy of kin and family relations in tombois' lives through the "sense of reality" as well as the social and material rewards of belonging, identity, and solidarity that tombois gain as members of kin collectivities.[12]

By identifying tombois' masculinity as contingent masculinity, I am not suggesting that it is a partial masculinity or an intermediate gender identity. Tombois' masculinity is one of many versions of masculinity in Southeast Asia that transgresses normative categories of "woman" and "man," in this case through an explicit referral to and performance of feminine and masculine behaviors. Tombois also strategically manipulate cultural gender codes of femininity to create space for themselves and their partners. Tombois speak of having female bodies and doing feminine things, while at the same time they declare that they are the "same as" or "just like" men. By situating tombois' masculinity as contingent, I offer a concept of trans-identities that takes into account the social relations and cultural frameworks within which people live and make sense of themselves.

At this point I return to queers of color theorists to use the lens of multiracial, multiethnic belonging to further address the apparent conundrum of contingent masculinities. Anzaldúa's skillful analysis of "mestiza consciousness," which has become a foundational work in theories by queers of color, offers another way to make sense of tomboi subjectivity, a connection first noted by Cromwell, who recognized the similarities to trans-identities in Anzaldúa's recitation of her queerness.[13] Recollecting both her shame and exhilaration at hearing border music (*corridos*), Anzaldúa came to understand these doubled and contradictory feelings as part of her dual ethnic identity, which was neither completely Mexican nor American, but a synergy of both. In a similar manner, tombois express a sense of self that is both masculine and feminine, depending on the context, a product of social relations and cultural practices that are valued and necessary to their sense of well-being. Where Anzaldúa saw a cultural collision at the point of contact between two (or more) cultures with incompatible frames of reference, tombois' experience is not so much collision as a moving back and forth between different ideologies and meanings, between the world of kin and community and the lesbi world, a movement that produces different but equally valued feelings.

Anzaldúa's response to living in the borderlands was not simply to balance two opposing forces. She recognized that there were multiple forces at work within overlapping structures and so learned to tolerate and sustain contradiction and ambiguity. According to Anzaldúa, "[The new mestiza] has a plural personality, she operates in a pluralistic mode—nothing is thrust out, the good the bad and the ugly, nothing rejected, nothing abandoned" (1987, 79). Applying this sense of plurality, of sustaining ambiguity, to tombois' way of being in the world helps to situate tombois as cultural operators in a particular historical and social context. As with Anzaldúa's mestiza, tombois embody seemingly conflicting feelings—of being men, loving women, and being loyal to their kin—without negating any of those feelings.

In line with Anzaldúa's theory, a theory of contingent masculinities takes into account the multiple allegiances as well as anxieties that produce rich and complicated subjectivities. Tombois in Padang take up and embody sometimes contrastive subject positions in different contexts. Their positionality may differ from other men, but at the same time it does not mean that their expression of masculinity is less masculine or manly. For tombois, as for all genders, the boundaries are blurred. There is no "real" man or "real" woman, as Butler (1990) cogently argued, that tombois mimic or reject, but something much more complex. Recognizing the complexity and contingency of tombois' subject positions, or to paraphrase Quiroga (2000), its inherent messiness, extends the possibilities of trans-subjectivities beyond gender polarity to incorporate multiple and disparate individuals and communities.

Translocal Queer Connections

> *To prescribe an exclusive identification for multiply-constituted*
> *subjects, as every subject is, is to enforce a reduction and paralysis.*
>
> —JUDITH BUTLER

LOCATED IN A REGIONAL METROPOLIS, tombois and their girlfriends participate in and reflect the hegemonic Indonesian ideology of sex/gender. This ideology is crosscut by a number of discourses, but the focus in this chapter is on national and transnational queer discourses with their progressive narrative of the development of modern sexual identities. Activist lesbian discourse in particular holds the expectation that modern lesbian subjects will express a self-consciousness or awareness of sexual identity as "lesbians" and "women." The intersections of global, activist discourses with localized and translocal meanings, however, produce much more complex and layered subjectivities than a narrative of 'sexual identity' suggests.

In Padang, tombois and their girlfriends access global circuits of queer knowledge and see themselves as part of a global community, but differentiate themselves from the identities promoted and encouraged by activist lesbian organizations in Indonesia. In this chapter I examine the ways lesbi activists in Jakarta and tombois and girlfriends in Padang intercept and selectively appropriate circuits of queer knowledge. I attend to the specificities of location by analyzing the circulation and use of particular linguistic terms, phrases, and strategies. Then I illustrate the uneven circulation and reception of queer knowledge by exploring the friction created as identitarian positions bump up against each other within and across communities. I demonstrate that asymmetries of reception result not in hierarchies of identities, but in a multiplicity of queer subjectivities that are all part of the global queer ecumene.

The queer discourses that I investigate come from two intersecting spheres: international lesbian and gay, or more recently LGBT, organizations, which are oriented to Western queer knowledge and the queer political movements of the United States and Europe, and activist networks and identity-based communities and organizations in Indonesia. These discourses are not separate and distinct, but intersect in many intriguing and contradictory ways. They produce a transnational queer discourse that is multiple and disparate, shaped by asymmetries of race, class, and gender, and reconstituted into particular subjectivities that do not fit neatly into Western-defined identity categories.

Circulation of Queer Knowledge

To the extent that lesbian women are the dominant *female* figure in transnational queer space, it is accomplished by relegating masculine or trans-identified females to the status of premodern or protolesbian. In fact, as I noted in chapter 1, queer masculinities have troubled feminist and lesbian narratives since at least the 1970s in the United States. As the meaning of "lesbian" shifted to "woman-loving-woman," butch-femme identities fell into disfavor, a position most strongly associated with lesbian feminist thinking of the time.[1] Despite later efforts by some theorists to establish connections among lesbian, butch, and FTM transgender, the dismissal of masculine females from the category of lesbian extended to international lesbian organizations.[2] Bacchetta relates how lesbian international nongovernmental organizations (INGOs) in the 1990s, despite internal debates, were generally oriented toward issues pertaining to "out" lesbians and ignored other forms of queer female subjectivities that did not conform closely to "dominant-sector European ideals of lesbian identity" (2002, 950). King (2002) points out how lesbian feminist definitions were taken on by international lesbian activists, as exemplified in Moniker Reinfelder's (1996) book *Amazon to Zami*. According to King (2002), the claim that "lesbians don't ape heterosexuals" attained a global coherence that delegitimized butch-femme pairings and distanced framings of lesbian identity from "local" versions of that pairing.

In addition the ubiquitous "LGBT" of Western gay discourse provides a fixed set of categories and the assurance of familiar definitions in which, if slippage within categories is recognized, slippage across them is not. In this more expansive version of "Lesbian" and "Gay," the "T" in LGBT works to resolve the messy categories of identity politics, creating a distinct boundary between lesbian/gay and transgender.[3] "T" refers to and incorporates, among others, masculine females and transgendered men, who are thereby set apart from butch lesbians, although transgendered individuals express a range of sexual orientations including lesbian.

"LGBT" circulates globally, particularly in the activities and Web sites of international sexual rights organizations and conferences.[4] The use of the term LGBT by these organizations is not necessarily meant to promote or claim particular identities. In regionally focused pages of their Web sites, more specific or "local" terms may be used, as well as such phrases as "gender and sexual diversity."[5] In fact the use of LGBT may be more closely related to efforts to create a broad appeal across diverse international communities (Dohrman 2007). Nevertheless Western labels have a certain cachet that offers users a "modern" or urban sensibility and connection to a larger international community (see Vanita 2002). This cachet works to promote "LGBT" as an originary ideal equated with fixed and stable identities within which all sexual diversity can be slotted. These identities are variously taken up by activists and nonactivists alike in their efforts to secure a stake in the global LGBT community.

Although tombois and their girlfriends place themselves at opposite ends of a gender spectrum, they see themselves at the same time as part of a lesbi world (*dunia lesbi*) that intersects in varying ways and to varying degrees with national and transnational queer discourses and movements. The means by which these discourses circulate globally are quite varied, although Western queer studies tend to privilege activist movements and the Internet as primary sites of knowledge transmission. Other forms of media carry queer knowledge, including mainstream newspapers, magazines, and films, albeit typically couched in negative terms, but these media still offer the possibility of imagining difference. As noted in chapter 2, mainstream media constitute one site through which queer knowledge and discourse circulate in Indonesia.

Other key sites of knowledge transmission in Indonesia are the small urban communities and networks of lesbi, gay, and waria, each with their own particular knowledges and their different connections to global queer discourses (see also Alison Murray 1999, Saskia Wieringa 1999). Activist groups within these urban communities model themselves after and gain resources from international lesbian and gay organizations. These groups work to promote a broader understanding about and acceptance of lesbi and gay individuals as well as provide support for and connections among their lesbi or gay members.

While waria have been acknowledged and visible in Indonesia for many decades, the early 1980s saw the appearance (and disappearance) of several small organizations, primarily on the island of Java, formed by individuals who identified as gay or lesbi.[6] One of the longest lasting groups, GAYa Nusantara, which is primarily a gay group but has included a few lesbi and waria, was organized in the mid-1980s. The first lesbian group, PERLESIN (Persatuan Lesbian Indonesia), was organized and disbanded in the early 1980s.[7] PERLESIN was founded by individuals who saw themselves as masculine lesbians (Saskia Wieringa 1999). Because the femme partners were not thought to suffer from the same societal pressures, the butches expressed some resistance to the inclusion of femmes in the organization.

Since 1998 two activist lesbian organizations, the Internet-based lesbian group in Jakarta, Swara Srikandi, and Sector 15 of the Indonesian Women's Coalition (Koalisi Perempuan Indonesia, KPI), developed a significant presence in Indonesia. The Indonesian Women's Coalition was established to support women's issues and defend women's rights. It has actively pushed to insert human rights, women's rights, and minority sexual rights into the Indonesian constitution. Within this group Sector 15 was created as the "minority sexual orientation group," which includes lesbians, bisexuals, and transgender individuals.[8] These organizations, usually spearheaded by well-educated, well-traveled, English-speaking activists from the upper echelons of Indonesian society, have looked to the lesbian and gay movements and literature of Europe and North America for models and resources but have also created their own Indonesian understanding of queer identities.

The circuits of knowledge these organizations access connect to differing global and regional locations. Both gay and lesbi organizations publish newsletters and Web sites that contain, for instance, translations or English-text articles of academic and political treatises on sexual orientation and sexual rights, as well as reviews of gay and lesbian literature, news of gay rights marches, and listings of movies with gay or lesbian content. GAYa Nusantara's international connections are more heavily invested in and through HIV/AIDS organizations as well as LGBT groups that are dominated by gay men. Lesbian activist organizations in Jakarta, since the late 1990s, have been assisted by Western lesbian academics and/or have received funding from international lesbian and women's organizations, such as Astraea and Global Fund for Women. Although Swara Srikandi started without any external support, international funding has allowed for expanded services and travel to national and international queer Asian conferences, where they have been able to plug into global networks of queer organizations that have some lesbian representation.[9] Leaders of Sector 15 of KPI in Jakarta have attended international queer conferences and taken advanced international academic training in sexuality studies. According to one KPI member, "The strategy for Sector 15 is to publicize our existence by getting info about lesbians into the media. Almost nothing is known or written about lesbi in Indonesia, just about homo men."

Waria individuals and organizations are another conduit of queer information and discourse. While some activist groups may contain a mix of gay and waria, many waria groups are organized specifically around waria interests and concerns, which are not always the same as those of activist gay or lesbi groups. Many waria have traveled and worked in cities throughout Indonesia and neighboring countries. In cities including Padang waria have their own organizations and occasionally put on balls and beauty contests that draw on and attend to national and international fashion and global drag performances. In Padang waria work as hairdressers, wedding planners, part-time dancers, and also dance instructors. As noted in chapter 1, a waria provided my initial contact with lesbi in Padang. S/he had worked for several years as a cook in a city on the island of Java and claimed to know how to cook European, Korean, and Indonesian foods. H/er knowledge of global queer circuits was evident in h/er awareness of an annual gay event in Bandung, on the island of Java, and of Sydney, Australia's annual gay parade. H/er access to queer circuits is limited by h/er modest income but reflects the sorts of information that circulate by word of mouth in queer communities in Indonesia.

Queer discourses that circulate through these groups are accessed in uneven ways in rural and cosmopolitan spaces, producing different readings in different locations. Where activist knowledge circulates in Indonesia primarily through newsletters and Internet Web sites, these circuits are unavailable to the lower-middle and working-class lesbi in Padang I interviewed, who do not have the computer knowledge or disposable income to be able to routinely access the Internet and are fearful of receiving or possessing written publications that might identify them as lesbi. For those not linked directly to international lesbian and gay organizations, and not actively participating in or seeking information from national activist groups, access to queer discourses comes primarily through their interactions with waria individuals and organizations and through the travel of tombois between Padang and other metropolitan communities of Indonesia, primarily Jakarta and Medan. During the 1980s and 1990s, this information traveled to West Sumatra by word of mouth as tombois visited or lived for brief periods of time in Jakarta and elsewhere in Indonesia. Thus queer knowledge circulates unevenly in Indonesia; in some places it is less dependent on institutional spaces or publications than on the everyday interactions and travels of lesbi, gay, and waria individuals.

Travel is important, as Grewal and Kaplan note, because it is "part of the knowledge production through which subjects are constituted" (2001, 671). The contours of travel for lesbi I interviewed are limited by available income, resources, and gendered expectations. The primary means of travel for lower-middle and working-class lesbi consist of the small and large public buses and ferries that travel across and between the islands of Indonesia. Viable destinations are only those places where relatives can be found to provide a place to sleep; hotels and even hostels are unaffordable. Further, although most lesbi I interviewed have traveled within Sumatra and beyond, they travel in decidedly gendered ways. Women's travels are more closely monitored by family. I asked Danny's girlfriend, Epi, who has been to Jakarta on trips with family members, if she had ever been to a gay meeting place or bar in Jakarta. She responded in the negative. She is unable to move outside the circle of family, relatives, or business contacts in Jakarta without raising suspicion or censure for her actions. She maintains her respectability by remaining within proper spaces. Jeni said that she had never met any lesbians outside of Padang, and in fact her only interactions with other lesbi were limited to her immediate group of friends.

Because tombois travel more widely and with less supervision than their girlfriends, much of the queer knowledge that circulates among their networks comes through tombois' interactions with lesbi, gay, and waria in other cities. Such interactions occur primarily in working-class contexts and public spaces (see Alison Murray 1999). Jakarta is one of the global queer spaces known for its gay cruising areas and particular locales in malls or nightclubs where lesbi, gay, or waria meet each other.[10] One tomboi, who lived with h/er relatives in Jakarta off and on for two years in the 1990s, went to some of the bars and hangouts in Jakarta where gay or lesbi congregated. Another tomboi from Padang living in Jakarta returns home only occasionally with the latest conversations about lesbi subjectivities that circulate in h/er space in Jakarta. Tombois' movements between urban areas and other locales in Indonesia expose them to urban queer discourses that they bring back to Padang to be remarked on with others, re-worked, and then updated with each new trip to the metropole (Oetomo 1996).

Queer Vernacular as Community Marker

One of the best ways to illustrate the uneven circulation and reception of queer knowledge is to track the movement of particular linguistic terms and phrases. In this section I examine the terms and phrases that tombois and their girlfriends use to describe themselves and what these say about their self-understanding, their sense of community with individuals like themselves, and their relation to the label "lesbi."

The terms "lesbi," "lesbian," and "gay" were taken up by lesbi and gay groups in Jakarta as their identifiers in the early 1980s, despite media-influenced associations with deviance, crime, and illness (see Gayatri 1993). These terms circulated not only in the media but on the streets and among the social networks of those in same-sex relationships (Alison Murray 1999; Saskia Wieringa 1999).[11] For instance, PERLESIN used the word "lesbian" in its title (Saskia Wieringa 1999). The founder of GAYa Nusantara, the Cornell-educated linguist Dédé Oetomo, established a direct link between Western gay discourse and his own activist efforts in Indonesia. Oetomo states that his use of the terms "gay" and "lesbian" in Indonesian follows the terms as used in (1980s) gay America (Oetomo 1996). GAYa Nusantara adopted a triangle, within which are the letters G-A-Y, as the symbol for the organization. In the first edition of the GAYa Nusantara newsletter Oetomo defines "gay" and "lesbian" as people who are attracted to the same sex, that is, a woman to a woman and a man to a man (Oetomo 1987, 10). KPI's Sector 15, reflecting the 1990s international sexual rights discourse, uses the phrase "minority sexual orientation" to define its members. Swara Srikandi defines "lesbian" as a "woman who is sexually oriented to other women" (Wina 2003). In appropriating Western labels, these groups lay claim to certain meanings attached to those labels, but by taking up the labels they are not simply imitating Western identities. Rather, activists tend to rely on those terms and definitions as a way to validate their own existence and connect with a global movement.

For their part tombois and their girlfriends grew up knowing the word "lesbi." Tommi said s/he had heard it in elementary school, which s/he started in 1980. As indicated in chapter 5, some were taunted with the word when schoolmates suspected they were too intimate with another girl. Tommi's one boyfriend, whom s/he dated for a short time while s/he was in junior high school, called h/er a "lesbi" when s/he refused to kiss him. The term "lesbi" was taken on as an identifying label at some point by both tombois and their girlfriends, but they maintain an uneasy relationship to it. Tombois who travel to Jakarta, like Tommi, hear the word "lesbi" used by others like themselves in places where lesbi and gay congregate. The prevalence of "butch" lesbians in working-class contexts substantiate and accord with tombois' views that lesbi are like men (see Gayatri 1994, Alison Murray 1999).

As I tried to make sense of the meaning of "lesbi" as used in Padang, Tommi explained to me, "A lesbi is a woman with a woman. But tombois are included as well." Tommi gave the definition endorsed and promoted by activist organizations, but by adding tombois to the definition, s/he included them under the label "lesbi" as well, even though s/he sees h/erself as a man. Most girlfriends also include themselves under the label "lesbi" because they are involved with tombois, although, as noted in chapter 5, taking on that label may depend on how long they have been with a tomboi partner. Although girlfriends state that their attraction to tombois is consonant with their attraction to men in general, and makes them the same as other (heterosexual) women, they claim the label "lesbi" as well.

At the same time that they stand under the label "lesbi," tombois and girlfriends in Padang shift its meaning. Explaining who is included in the category of lesbi, Robi said, "Lesbi includes those who are masculine and feminine."[12] Because their partners are differently gendered, a "lesbi" in their understanding of the term is not a *woman* attracted to other *women*, but a *female* who is attracted to the other gender. "Lesbi" in this sense refers to partners who are female-bodied, but at the same time it serves as an umbrella term that incorporates their different subjectivities. For tombois and girlfriends, the label "lesbi" includes individuals with different histories and different routes into the lesbi world. "Lesbi," then, signifies a group that occupies a space distinct from the rest of the world. Consequently, "lesbi" as a circulating category is not a stable term throughout Indonesia but is appropriated and reconstituted to fit particular meanings.

Waria/Gay and Lesbi Vernacular

Although "lesbi" cannot be said in public spaces, tombois and femmes have a rich vocabulary of terms they use in their conversations with each other. Through their interactions with waria, they have access to waria experiences and views of the world, as well as waria vernacular. I use "vernacular" here instead of "language," even though it is spoken of by Indonesian scholars as "waria language" (*bahasa waria*), because it is primarily a distinctive vocabulary or lexicon in which new terms are created by adding certain syllables.[13] Boellstorff (2004) refers to this vernacular as *bahasa gay*, that is, a language created and spoken by gay men, while Oetomo (1989) calls this vernacular "bahasa gay/waria." Given the greater visibility and longer presence of waria in Indonesia, it would seem to suggest that waria linguistic practices are a primary source for gay vernacular. Oetomo (1989) notes that the boundaries between the two communities are not distinct since the two groups socialize together, suggesting that they both use the same words. I privilege the waria connection due to the close friendship between some of the tombois and waria in Padang, but it would be incorrect to assume waria are the only source, since tombois' travels in Jakarta and elsewhere bring them in contact not only with waria, but with gay and other lesbi. Because their communities are interconnected, expressions and practices quickly disseminate across all groups. It remains a question, however, whether there is a specifically lesbi vernacular spoken only among lesbi or if lesbi have contributed to the corpus of gay/waria vernacular.

A study of waria vernacular in Yogyakarta, Java, found that new terms are created by adding certain syllables, typically "ong" or "es," to word stems and by switching initial vowel to "e." This practice is apparent in the following derivations: *laki-laki* (man) becomes *lekong* or *lekes*, *homo* becomes *hemong* or *hemes*, and *perempuan* (woman, female) becomes *pewong* or *pewes* (Koeswinarno 1999; see also Oetomo 2001). *Lesbong*, the word for lesbian, comes from adding "ong" to the stem of "lesbi." When I asked Robi when s/he first became aware she was "like this," s/he filled in with *lesbong*. The term *lesbong*, however, which specifically recalls the term lesbi, is not frequently used by tombois and femmes in Padang in everyday speech and may be dropping out of use, for I did not hear it in 2004. Tombois in Padang prefer the term *lekong* (man) for themselves, but its pair, *pewong*, is not used for femmes. Another term, *binong*, which refers to femmes, is also not used by the lesbi I talked to in Padang. Tombois call their girlfriends *mawar*, which is not a word combination but an Indonesian word meaning rose, or *peré*, which comes from the word *perempuan*. For instance, Sri asked Robi about a woman she had met recently. Sri asked, "Is she *lekong*?" "No, *peré*," Robi replied, making *lekong/peré* a pair. Because waria use the term *peré* for their boyfriends as well, it appears that the term signifies the gender normative partner for both waria and tombois.

In addition to *lesbong*, a popular word used particularly in public spaces to replace the stigmatized term "lesbi" is *lines*. *Lines* (pronounced lee-ness in U.S. English) is the most frequently used term for "lesbi" in Padang, one that began to fill my field notes as I incorporated their terms into my vocabulary. For instance, when asked how she identifies, Epi said, "I consider myself *lines*, certainly, but I would go back to a guy if Danny broke up with me." This conversation occurred in my hotel room, yet Epi used *lines* rather than "lesbi," suggesting that the term has become so commonplace that it is used regardless of the location. Further, the consistency of usage of this term among lesbi in Padang, even in more private spaces, indicates that it is their preferred identifier. Among the *calalai* whom Davies (2007a) studied, *lines* is used for the femmes only, but in Padang both tombois and femmes use it to refer to themselves. Its popularity may be due to the fact that it provides no clue to outsiders as to its meaning.

Over time the origins of *lines* have become somewhat muddled. One Jakartan lesbian activist told me *lines* is derived from Lisa Bonet, the actor who played one of the Huxtable daughters on *The Cosby Show*, a popular American television show that ran from 1984–1992. Alison Murray (1999) mentions that the slang term for lesbian used in Jakarta was *Lisa Bonet* or *lisbon*. *Lines* is used without comment as a synonym for lesbi in the second issue of *GAYa Nusantara* (1988, 22), suggesting that it was already in common usage in 1988. Oetomo's "Gay/ waria Indonesian dictionary," first published in *GAYa Nusantara* no. 9 (1989, also Oetomo 2001) states that *lines* is derived from infixing "in" in the following manner: lesbi > *linesbini* > *lines*. Whatever the derivation of the term, it circulated through the waria, gay, and lesbi communities in Jakarta and was picked up by traveling waria, calalai, and tombois to disseminate across Indonesia.

In addition to alternative words for lesbi, Robi mentioned that there are a number of other code words that they use in conversation. The ones s/he readily recalled were those that may be used to negotiate sleeping over or talking about sex.[14] Lesbi in Padang use these terms as a way to keep naïve bystanders unawares. Their conversations can be carried on in public spaces without any hesitation because anyone who may overhear them will not know the actual meaning of the words. As Cromwell (1995) noted in his study of speech practices by transgendered individuals, coded speech works creatively to avoid exposure and exclude outsiders. At the same time it marks behaviors that are negatively valued outside such speech communities. In this case what is negatively valued coalesces around non-normative sexuality. Being able to use these terms also signifies one's insider status, a point I develop below.

Other terms that circulate among tombois and their girlfriends are indicative of specifically lesbi circuits of knowledge. These include a set of terms originating, according to Gayatri (1993), in lesbian circles in Medan, Sumatra: *sentul* (tomboi) and *kantil* (femme), which are slang words for the masculine and feminine partners.[15] Several tombois in Padang, who had traveled to Medan and had met other lesbi there, knew of the terms, but I never heard them used in any consistent manner. Lesbi in Padang are also familiar with the English words "butch" and "femme," which they encounter via tomboi connections with lesbi individuals or communities in Jakarta. Lesbi in Padang do not incorporate the two terms into their everyday speech, preferring to use the Indonesian terms *cowok* and *cewek* (guy/girl) or other waria vernacular.[16] Importantly, however, they believe that "butch" and "femme" are cognates of *cowok* and *cewek*. Knowledge of the English words and their imagined association with the Indonesian words creates a sense of connection with lesbian communities far beyond West Sumatra and Indonesia. These particular words also facilitate a sense that individuals in these communities share the same gendered desires and meanings, creating a world in which everyone is positioned as either tomboi or femme.

Idioms that circulate in lesbi and gay circles in Jakarta and travel to West Sumatra to become part of tomboi and femme speech provide a way to understand their sense of self and community. Gay men in Jakarta use the phrase "falling into the gay world" (*terjun ke dunia gay*) to describe becoming involved with another man (Howard 1996). Howard states that these men describe a homosexuality that is contingent on spatial and temporal contexts, taking place in "a gay world" and not outside of it. Similarly, the phrase "the lesbi world," which appeared in various newsletters published by lesbi organizations in the 1990s and 2000s and in a "lesbian" section of *GAYa Nusantara*, employs the same concept of a separate world but in this case for lesbi. This phrase traveled to Padang via tombois such as Tommi, who had spent nearly two years in Jakarta and used the phrase the most often, but others, both tombois and their girlfriends, were also familiar with the expression and used it occasionally. This phrase contains the word "lesbi," which I heard used only in the private space of interviews in my hotel room. In public spaces "lesbi" was dropped from the phrase, which then became "that world" or "our world." Consider the following uses of the phrase among lesbi in Padang:

"[X] had just fallen into the lesbian world (*terjun ke dunia lesbi*) that year," used by Tommi to describe a woman who had become involved with her first tomboi.

Lina, one of the femmes, said, "I fell into that world (*dunia itu*) when I started dating Tommi."

Robi: "[My first lover] taught me about life in the lesbian world, including sleeping together."

Dedi asked, "Why is [she] interested in knowing about our world (*dunia kami*)," distinguishing h/er world from the world occupied by a heterosexual, married woman.

Dunia lesbi is a place shared by both tombois and their girlfriends. This phrase signifies movement from the everyday world of family and kin into a new world populated by others like themselves, lesbi. Girlfriends are seen as "falling into" the lesbi world, while their tomboi partners seem always to have been there. *Dunia lesbi* is not the world of tombois, nor of waria and gay, but the world of lesbi couples, both tombois and their girlfriends. Tombois and their partners participate in the lesbi world and see it as a shared space, a separate space where only people like themselves exist. It conveys a sense of solidarity and belonging among those who share a certain kind of love. Individuals in this world share a special vernacular; their knowledge and use of these words and the phrase *dunia lesbi* indicate their familiarity with and membership in such a world.

Thus *dunia lesbi* is not localized but incorporates a lesbian world populated by global others. These others are read as sharing the same understanding of lesbi as those in Padang. As noted in chapter 5, photos I brought with me of my lesbian friends in the United States were pored over to ascertain who were the tombois and who were the femmes. Famous lesbians such as Martina Navratilova and Melissa Etheridge, whose stories of betrayal by "femme" lovers are well known in Indonesia, secure a strong connection between lesbi in Padang and a global *dunia lesbi*. Both women are read as butches and their girlfriends as femmes who, unsurprisingly to tombois in Padang, left their partners for men. Thus while the circulation of terms such as "lesbi," "butch," and "femme," as well as images of famous lesbians, connect tombois and their girlfriends to a global lesbian world, these terms and images are read in a way that supports a gendered construction of sexuality. In the circulation of queer knowledge, lesbi in Padang use their own culturally available models to interpret global queer discourses and arrive at meanings that make sense to them, creating their own particular version of *dunia lesbi*.

Contradiction in Terms

While appropriating and employing a rich and diverse vocabulary that signifies a particular vision of the world, tombois and their girlfriends are at the same time confronted with contradictory discourses and linguistic practices that have the potential to disrupt the sense of difference that their relationships are based on. As discussed in chapter 2, print media representations of lesbi couples as differently gendered partners have provided one resource for understanding themselves as tombois and femmes. Tombois' travels to Jakarta also connect them with lesbi who fit with and confirm tombois' masculine gender expression. However, terms that appear regularly in Indonesian newspapers, including *biseks* and *sesama jenis*, complicate these gendered understandings.

According to an article in *Kompas*, a well-known mainstream newspaper available throughout Indonesia, *biseks* (Indonesian, derived from the English word "bisexual") is used for individuals "who have sex with the same sex (*sesama jenis*) as well as with the other sex (*lain jenis*)" (*Kompas Cybermedia* 2003). *Biseks* is another term, like *lesbi* and *gay*, that has been adapted by Indonesians from European and U.S. scholarly discourses on sexuality. This particular newspaper article presents Alfred Kinsey's work as the authoritative source on bisexuality. *Biseks*, however, muddies the waters of a gender binary in which opposites attract because it offers the possibility that a person may desire and have sex with both women and men.

Biseks introduces a different understanding of sexuality than the one that operates in the lesbi world, at least for the individuals I interviewed. Most of the lesbi I interviewed were not familiar with the term *biseks* in 2001 and did not use it. When I explained it to femmes, they said simply that they are attracted to tombois, who they see as men, and so do not see themselves as *biseks*. As Nila and Jeni were careful to point out, they are "normal" women attracted to men, which includes ordinary men and tombois. Tombois do not consider themselves bisexual because they have sex with women only. Both tombois and femmes are attracted to their opposites, an understanding that they carefully maintain, as noted in chapter 4, by guarding the borders of masculinity and femininity.

Among the tombois who are familiar with the term, it is not used in a consistent manner, suggesting that it is not a well-recognized or accepted concept among lesbi in Padang. Robi said one of h/er ex-girlfriends was *biseks* because she had tomboi lovers but also was interested in a feminine woman. Robi used the term *biseks* creatively to refer to a person who was attracted to different genders, tombois and women, thereby equating tombois with men and asserting a crucial difference between tombois and women. In contrast, Andri used the term *biseks* in relation to married heterosexual women who have sex with tombois on the side. Regarding bisexual women, Andri said, "They only want to be pleasured and not give pleasure to their partners," an assessment that seems to come from h/er statement to me that married women who are unhappy with their husbands sometimes turn to tombois, but they may not be invested in their tomboi lovers. In this case *biseks* is used to refer to a woman who is attracted to tombois and men, which then places tombois in a different category than men. Andri did not, however, use the term *biseks* to refer to h/er own girlfriend, who had also dated other men. In contrast, in a conversation in 2004 about a former girlfriend who likes men and tombois, Tommi said, "She's *biseks*." When I asked why s/he used that term, Tommi said, "I read about it, but I had to explain it to my girlfriend because she didn't understand."

As used in print media, *biseks* refers to sexual attraction for the same and the opposite sex. When applied to femmes, it imposes a cultural framework at odds with femme desires for the opposite sex, men and tombois, by repositioning tombois as same sex, that is, women. If some tombois are beginning to apply the term *biseks* to their (ex-) girlfriends, it suggests that the term is making inroads in the way tomboi and femme couples think about gender and sexual attraction.

By making tombois and men different, it threatens to destabilize tombois' sense of themselves as men.

While *biseks* has had minimal resonance with lesbi in Padang, the term *sesama jenis*, which means "of the same kind" and is used to refer to people in same-sex relationships, is more readily used as a term to describe one's partner. This term has greater potential for troubling the understandings of gender and sexuality on which tombois and their partners rely. *Jenis kelamin* is the Indonesian expression used to refer to one's "sex." *Jenis* means type or kind and *kelamin* is typically translated as sex or gender, so *jenis kelamin* means type of (physical) sex. Again following English-speaking nations (United States/Australia/United Kingdom), Indonesians translate "opposite sex" as *lawan jenis*, the opposite kind, and "same sex" as *sesama jenis*, the same kind (also *sejenis*, of one kind). These phrases, which have become shorthand for the longer phrase *sesama jenis kelamin* (same-sex), are used in popular print media and in publications by lesbi and gay activists. For instance, an article in *Kompas* defines homosexuals as "people who are sexually attracted to others who have the same sex [*jenis kelamin sama*]" (Ma'shum and Tyas 2004). From its earliest issues *GAYa Nusantara* defined lesbi and gay people as those whose orientation or attraction is toward the same sex (*sesama jenis kelaminnya*) (Oetomo 1987, 10). In *Lembar Swara*, the newsletter of Swara Srikandi, "lesbian" is defined as a woman who loves "those of the same kind (that is, women) [*sesama jenisnya (yaitu perempuan)*]" (Wina 2003, 8). Although the *Lembar Swara* author clarifies that the "same kind" refers to women, the phrase *sesama jenis* appears to stand on its own colloquially as a reference to "lesbi" (or gay), while in the earlier *GAYa Nusantara* definition, it is accompanied by the word *kelamin*. Thus lesbi and gay individuals have come to be referred to as those who are attracted to "the same sex" (*sesama jenis*).

The circulation of this term, *sesama jenis*, through mainstream media and activist circles underscores its acceptance as a descriptor of lesbi and gay desire. Given the assumption of sameness between partners, which is coded in the phrase *sesama jenis*, I was surprised to hear two femmes use the term *sesama jenis* to describe their desires for tombois. Epi explained her situation by saying: "I am attracted to the same sex (*sesama jenis*)." Jeni likewise said, "As for other people, they are attracted to the opposite sex (*lawan jenis*), but I'm attracted to the same sex (*sesama jenis*). It's the same with waria. They are men (*laki-laki*) who are attracted to men (*laki-laki*)." By comparing herself to waria, whom she defines as men or males attracted to men, is Jeni saying that she is a woman attracted to other women, the same sex (*sesama jenis*)? By using this term she seems to espouse sameness between herself and her partner, as two "women," which she had otherwise never articulated. As noted in chapter 4, tombois and femmes position themselves as opposites; it is the difference between them that creates the attraction. For Jeni in particular, she is adamant that her attraction to Andri is the same as her attraction to other men, that is, an attraction to the opposite sex. Thus the two concepts, stated in different contexts and at different times, appear not to overlap in her mind or to trouble her understanding of her desires. It is as if the concept *sesama jenis* comes from a different domain that does not interfere with her self-positioning as a femme attracted to men.

Sesama jenis, which defines lesbi and gay as those who are interested in others like themselves, puts tombois and their girlfriends in the same category. But in the context of their relationships tombois situate themselves differently from their women partners, ignoring the culturally ascribed femaleness of their bodies to position themselves as men. If *sesama jenis* insists that both partners in a lesbi couple are women, then in their own and others' eyes, how viable is tombois' self-positioning as men? In Indonesia, the concepts of sex and gender are used interchangeably in the popular press. For example, a psychologist who writes health columns for *Kompas*, translated *identitas jenis kelamin*, literally "sex identity," as "gender identity" (Sadarjoen 2005), a move that reinforces the connection between gender and sexed bodies; it claims that the truth of one's sex (*jenis kelamin*) is irrevocably the same as one's gender.

If the phrase *sesama jenis* insists on a lesbi sexuality that is attracted to "the same kind," then it raises troubling questions for thinking about tomboi masculinity. To the extent that the term *sesama jenis* has become common parlance, it brings the tomboi position closer to "women," making tombois *the same as* girlfriends. Consequently it threatens to shift the grounds of lesbi relationships from one of difference to one of sameness, a shift that some girlfriends, such as Noni (mentioned in chapter 5), seem willing to take on because it makes sense of her attraction to female bodies and her lack of desire for men's bodies. However, this term could potentially destabilize tombois' own sense of self by its refusal to see them as other than "women" because of their female bodies and, as when they were in school, bring renewed attention to their cultural embodiment as females. Or it may cause tombois greater anxiety about how they are perceived by others, creating a situation in which their masculinity must be ever more defiantly or openly expressed.

The potential for popular terminology and discourses of lesbi identity to disrupt relationships was apparent in the troubles that Tommi experienced with a recent girlfriend, Asnita, the one whom Tommi called *biseks*. Asnita seemed to view their relationship differently than Tommi did. Tommi dated Asnita when she was in high school. When they broke up, Asnita started seeing Tommi's younger brother. They renewed their relationship later, when Asnita was in college, but it only lasted a few months. When Sri and I visited Tommi one evening at h/er business, I asked about h/er girlfriend. S/he told me that Asnita was mad at h/er and relayed the following story:

> Last week I nearly got burnt when I tried to light the gas burner at work. I only singed my face and hair a bit, but because of that my hair is really short in the front. Now Asnita is mad at me and won't talk to me because she doesn't like how short my hair is. Well, it's not that she doesn't like it; she just doesn't want me to be so obvious. She also doesn't want me to wear my ball cap, so when she comes around, I take it off [said with rakish grin].

Tommi later asked Sri, half pleading and half joking, "Help me find another girlfriend, one who is loyal and understands my situation!" According to Tommi, Asnita is not happy with Tommi's overly short hair and ball cap, which signal that Tommi is different, a tomboi. Her efforts to change Tommi's looks suggest that she thinks Tommi should try to be more feminine. To what end is not clear.[17] Is Asnita uncomfortable being seen with someone who looks so masculine? Does she think of Tommi as a woman and want h/er to look more like one? Tommi sees their relationship in terms of difference, like husband and wife, not like two women. In asking Sri for help, Tommi reveals how troubled s/he is by Asnita's demands. Tommi wants someone who will love h/er for h/er masculinity, not someone who wants h/er to look more feminine.

The discord in their relationship suggests that each one is drawing on different discourses and circuits of knowledge about gender and sexuality. Although Tommi said s/he has always been a tomboi and is acknowledged as one by h/er family and friends, who call her "tomboi," the efforts of this younger, college-educated girlfriend to change Tommi point to a growing friction as competing discourses become more prevalent both within and outside lesbi groups. As activists become more visible and vocal in Indonesia, *sesama jenis* has the potential to develop into the definitive version of lesbi and gay "identities" in Indonesia. To the extent that more conservative religious and state discourses prevail in Indonesia, or are enacted in law (see Blackwood 2007), they may undermine tombois' subject position by making it less comprehensible.

Circuits of Knowledge and the Contentious "New" Lesbi

While none of the tombois in the group had a university education, two of the girlfriends, including Asnita, were currently attending university and had access to other queer discourses via the Internet or English-language texts. As noted earlier, these discourses insistently define lesbians as women-loving-women. In Indonesian activist and middle-class lesbi circles this definition has produced a new lesbi subjectivity, *andro*, a person who identifies as neither too masculine nor too feminine. *Andro*, a shortened form of the English word "androgyne," developed not only in conjunction with the international discourse of lesbian identity, but in response and resistance to the categories of tomboi and femme.

While masculine-identified tombois were some of the early leaders of lesbian organizations in the 1980s, activists in the 1990s involved with the short-lived group Chandra Kirana were leery of including them because of their assumed identification with men. Gayatri (1994), a university-educated, lesbian feminist activist who had traveled extensively overseas and who spearheaded Chandra Kirana, claimed that masculine-acting tombois were predominantly from the working class and were not like lesbians of the middle and upper-middle classes. Gayatri (1993) specifically excluded "female-transvestites" (her translation), as she called them then, from her research on lesbians in Indonesia because she felt that their identification as men separated them from lesbians. Her position reflects the global queer discourse of modernity that assumes modern lesbian and gay couples should reflect gender sameness not gender difference. In the emerging lesbian activist movement in the 1990s tombois were perceived as imitating men and hence in need of modernization and education (see also Alison Murray 1999, Saskia Wieringa 1999). Gayatri has softened her stance over time and has come to include "butch-femme roles" ("butch" here is equated with tombois) within the category of "lesbians" (see Gayatri 1996).

In 2004 I met with several members of KPI's Sector 15 in Jakarta. One woman, Lin, who is university-educated and in her mid-thirties, said, "I identify as 'no label' or *andro* because I don't feel either too masculine or too feminine. I'm a woman who loves a woman [*perempuan cinta perempuan*]." This interpretation of lesbi identity distinguishes itself from tomboi and femme by refusing the grammar of difference. Andro and "no label," as the terms suggest, do not connote gender differences, but, in line with international lesbian activist discourse, speak only of desire for someone who is also "woman." "Woman" here is not defined, however, as a normative, heterosexual woman. The andro woman is neither too masculine nor too feminine, but somewhere in the middle. These lesbi *women* see themselves as resisting binary gender as well as gender-based coupling by desiring other women, not men or tombois. (See figure 7.1.)

That same year I met a woman in Padang who had only recently started socializing with members of the group of lesbi I interviewed. Gia, who was attending university, came from a fairly well-off family of government administrators.

FIGURE 7.1. Drawing of a lesbi couple. *Semai*, a KPI publication, September 2001.

With a good command of English, she had been surfing the Internet since high school. Gia, who identified herself as andro, caused quite a bit of controversy through her interactions with the tombois and femmes. Gia's story points to some of the emergent tensions:

> I was tomboi-ish when I was growing up. I always wore what my brother did and wanted the same things he did. In high school I was with my first girlfriend for a year and a half. My parents never suspected anything, but after I came out to them, I came under greater surveillance. They always ask me where I'm going, who with, when I'm coming back, which they never did before. They won't let my girlfriends sleep over.

[I asked Gia how she identifies.] If you want to use a label, then andro, but I don't like to be put in a box; I don't like labels. Lesbi here [in Padang] don't understand that term, so I tell them I'm femme, because I'm more like that right now. But tombois have too many rules about how their girlfriends should act. If they ask what andro is, I explain that andro is between butch and femme. You might have a butch lover or a femme lover, it depends on the person. They still ask me which I like, *peré* or tomboi. I don't know. What's important is how I feel about someone. I don't care whether they're tomboi or *peré*. I've given the women here stuff to read, but they still don't get it. They're just afraid I'm going to take their lovers—of either persuasion.

From the time she was in junior high Gia said she found information about lesbi on the Internet and in books; it was through those searches that she came in contact with Swara Srikandi's Web site. In addition she had been able to purchase a number of European and U.S. lesbian-themed videos and novels.[18] For her, being lesbi is not about how a person looks, tomboi or femme, but about how she feels about that person. Gia's access to particular circuits of knowledge create a different understanding of lesbi for her, in part because she values international queer knowledge and its categories of meaning, and in part because of her education and her family background. Gia dislikes the restraints imposed by tomboi and femme categories, so being andro makes sense to her. "I enjoy different qualities in different lovers. If a lover spoils me, I like to spoil her in return," she told me. Given her expectation of and desire for equality and sameness, the idea of being attracted to only tombois or femmes does not fit with her image of herself or of lesbi desire.

Gia's refusal to be labeled proved contentious for the tombois and femmes she knew in Padang. They were confused by her and unsure how to read her. Lina, Tommi's girlfriend, told me about the first time she met Gia.

It wasn't clear to me from Gia's style of behavior what she was because she smokes and has short hair. So I asked her straight out, "What role (*posisi*) do you take?" Gia replied, "Right now, I am feminine because my lover is a tomboi." So then once that was clear, I felt more comfortable with her sitting close to me and touching me in a casual way. It was okay because she's another woman, not a tomboi. But if she was a tomboi, then I wouldn't want to be so close to her [because Lina has a tomboi partner].

Other members of the group expressed similar concerns about Gia.

197

When a conversation turned to the fact that Gia is andro, Noni said in frustration, "If she's with *lekong*, then she's *peré*. If she's with a *peré*, then she's *lekong*!"

Danny replied, "Ya, that's weird [*aneh*]."

Noni continued, "Ya, if she's *peré*, then I can sit by her, and we're comfortable next to each other. But I'm not sure what she is, so I have to be careful around her."

For Noni it is important to know what a person is, tomboi or *peré*, because then she knows how to respond to and interact with that person. If Gia were in fact a tomboi, then for Noni to be close with her would be construed as flirting and could get Noni in trouble with her tomboi partner.

Their unresolved questions about Gia's positioning as a lesbi makes interactions with her uncomfortable because in their understanding of the lesbi world, there are only tombois and femmes. Gia herself commented, "Everyone in the group is either tomboi or *peré*. Because I'm different, they accuse me of breaking up the group. So I keep my distance." Gia's self-positioning is problematic not only because they cannot figure out how to interact with her, but because she threatens the stability of known and secure positions, the opposites of tomboi and femme. Her explanations make no sense to them, nor do her efforts to situate herself at least temporarily within their categories ("I tell them I'm femme right now") help to appease them. In their world tombois and femmes do not switch between categories. Their consternation underlines the importance of gender difference in their understanding of the lesbi world and the threat posed by a new lesbi who does not recognize or value difference in relationships.

Marking Transgender, Displacing Tombois

During a trip to Jakarta in 2004, I visited the office of KPI's Sector 15 in a neighborhood in south Jakarta. The office consisted of a long open space with tables, desks, and bookcases stacked with piles of papers, several computers and monitors in various stages of use and disuse, posters hung on the walls, and bulletin boards cluttered with flyers and announcements. I talked briefly with Lin, one of the members who identifies as andro whom I mentioned earlier. Lin had short hair and was dressed in casual clothes, including a polo shirt and trousers. Although she speaks English, she was more comfortable speaking to me in Indonesian.

I asked Lin if she thought there was a difference between lesbi and tomboi, so she explained, "There are lesbi who are butchie or femme, but the primary thing is they feel like women. Even some "no label" can look somewhat like tombois, like I do, but it's not complete." I had started the conversation by asking about tombois, but as we talked Lin inserted the word "transgender." She continued,

> Transgender is someone who doesn't want h/er body touched. That person would not be considered under the umbrella of lesbi. Lesbi pleasure each other, but a transgender person doesn't enjoy being touched, s/he is the one doing the touching (*actif*). When I first came out in high school, I thought I had to be a tomboi, so I acted more like that. But I've read lots since then and decided I could be a woman and love another woman, so I changed how I think about myself.

Lin's story speaks to shifts in her own self-perception as she acquires certain knowledge, through reading, about lesbian identity. She does not attribute her knowledge directly to Western lesbian discourse, but her statements echo a particular historical version of that discourse, with its notions of coming out, woman-loving-woman, and mutual sexual pleasuring that at the same time rejects too-masculine women (see King 2002). While the term "lesbi" in her mind is somewhat fluid, containing butchie, femme, andro, and no label, which are the terms used in Indonesian, it excludes tombois because they are thought to be like men. As I discuss in this section, her narrative reveals the operation and reception of a global queer discourse whose appeal as an originary model underwrites an idealized lesbian identity of woman-loving-woman that is refigured into Indonesian categories by lesbian activists.

The category "transgender" made its appearance on the global stage in the 1990s and was taken up by activist lesbian groups in Jakarta as a way to distinguish male-identified individuals from lesbians. Prior to that time the reception of waria and tombois within the growing gay and lesbian movements in Indonesia had been inconsistent at best, reflecting earlier trends in global queer discourse.[19] Tombois continued to be a troubling issue for activist lesbian and feminist groups in the 1990s, who could not reconcile tombois with their own definition of lesbians and who tended to see tombois as old-fashioned, patriarchal, and oppressive to their girlfriends (see Saskia Wieringa 2007).

By the early 2000s lesbian activist organizations began to consolidate the term "lesbian" around the "originary" ideal of Euro-American lesbianism by defining lesbians as "women-loving-women," while using the term "transgender" for those tombois who identify as men. While working to find a space for masculine-identified tombois, Sector 15 as well as Swara Srikandi advocated models of sexual identity and visibility in line with certain Western and feminist models of sexuality and sexual rights, models that contested the subjectivities and relationships of tombois and their girlfriends. I recount here efforts to recategorize Indonesian subjectivities in the 2000s as new Western terms entered the Indonesian activist lexicon and the resulting tensions that these efforts produced. My discussion focuses on efforts by lesbian activists to affix labels, not on the sexual identities of the activists themselves. Even among activists, the subjectivities they take up are more complex and diverse than the labels they endorse, as Lin's narrative suggests. My discussion of these labels is not meant to suggest that lesbi activists in Jakarta blindly endorse transnational queer discourse, nor does their claim to those labels reflect an elitist stance (see also Vanita 2002).

As with tombois' reception of transnational queer discourse, activists make sense of proffered sexual identities within the context of their particular location. The women in these Jakarta-based organizations generally, but not always, have university educations, professional jobs, and various levels of proficiency in English. In addition they rely on the Internet for information and connections with other lesbi in Jakarta and globally. My information on activist organizations came from participation in their meetings and informal discussions with members and leaders of these organizations in 2001 and 2004 as well as from their literature, Web sites and listservs. My discussions with them focused on the strategies, goals, and constituents of the organizations themselves, not on the individual members or how they identified, although this was sometimes brought up in conversation.

The repositioning of masculine-identified tombois by lesbi activists was articulated clearly by Wina in the first issue of Swara Srikandi's monthly newsletter, *Lembar Swara*, which began publication in May 2003. Wina (her self-chosen pseudonym used on-line and in written work) is one of the founders and leaders of Swara Srikandi. Her article, titled "Terms/Expressions of the LGBT World," offers an unambiguous set of definitions for the terms "lesbian," "gay," "bisexual," and "transgender" (LGBT).[20] According to Wina, she wrote the article in hopes of resolving any confusion for her readers about the meanings of these terms. Wina, a thirty-something professional woman who wears feminine attire to work (skirt, blouse, dress jacket, and low heels), converses easily in English. She defines herself as andro, neither butch nor femme, and is apparently comfortable in both her work attire and her more casual jeans.

In her article Wina distinguishes between "butch" lesbians and "FTM transgender," the terms she uses. She defines butch as: "a lesbian who in appearance is a tomboi (*berpenampilan tomboi*), is masculine (*kelaki-lakian*), and prefers men's clothes (men's shirts, long pants, very short hair), however, DON'T FORGET that while a butch is a tomboi, she (*dia*) considers herself a woman and doesn't have a problem being a women or hate her body" (2003, 8, capitalization in the original). Wina defines "FTM transgender" as a "female who feels that she is a man and frequently thinks about becoming a man." She then explains the difference between the two terms: A "butch" dresses and acts like a man "but still considers herself to be a woman (*perempuan*) and does not hate her female body," while "transgender (FTM) is a foreign term for a woman who feels that s/he is a man" and "feels trapped in a female body that s/he does not like" (Wina 2003, 8–9). To make sure that readers understand, Wina capitalizes the following text: "TRANSGENDER FTM IS NOT A LESBIAN." Wina goes on to note that people in general often confuse the two "because a transgender FTM person does not dress any differently than a butch lesbian." However, she hopes that readers "will finally understand and make the distinction that a butch is not transgender, as long as she feels strongly that she is a woman" (2003, 9). In her narrative, "FTM transgender" is the only term said to be "foreign," while "lesbian," "gay," "bisexual," and "butch" are unmarked, indicating their longer history of usage in Indonesia and in the activist movement itself. Her article points to the recent acquisition of "transgender" from international LGBT discourse and its acceptance as a relevant term for Indonesian identities despite its "foreign" origin.

"Transgender" as a global term is being used here to resolve a perceived conflict between the meanings of "lesbi" and "tomboi." With the arrival of the term "transgender," and the authoritative weight that it carries as an originary term of the global gay movement, Wina argues for a distinction that divides tombois into FTM transgender and butch lesbians based on the way that they think about their bodies. According to Wina, to be a lesbi, a tomboi must consider herself a woman. If she considers herself a man, then she is not a lesbian, or a butch, but an FTM transgender. Yet in Wina's discussion, "butch lesbians" and "FTM transgender" are quite similar in appearance and dress. Her insistence on distinguishing between them evinces the discomfort felt by activist women for whom "tomboi" is a troubling and ambiguous category. Despite her desire to use gender difference as an authoritative way of managing this uncertainty, Wina's comment that people cannot really tell the difference between a butch lesbian (tomboi) and an FTM transgender person by looking at them points to the ambiguity of the category tomboi. Following the publication of Wina's article, Swara Srikandi reorganized their Web site to serve the needs of "lesbians" and "bisexual" women only, while excluding FTM transgender.

The other lesbian activist group, Sector 15, does not exclude FTM transgender individuals from its group, but it, too, defines "transgender" as something very different from "lesbi." As Lin recounted earlier, the category of tomboi is replaced by butchie *lesbians* and transgendered people. Lesbians are *women*, transgendered people (FTMs) are not. Further distinctions are made on the basis of their sexual practices. According to Lin, FTMs are like men because they are the active partner in sexuality ("the one doing the touching") rather than the coparticipant ("pleasuring each other"). Lin's own description of becoming a lesbian situates her tomboi-ness as pre-lesbi; tomboi was the identity she took on before she "knew" more about lesbians through reading. The circuits of knowledge she accesses through reading are predominately English-language books, articles, and Web sites on lesbian/gay identity and lesbian/gay issues; such literature is generally unavailable in the Indonesian language. In line with global LGBT discourse the "tomboi" comes to occupy the space of premodernity, the space before this new knowledge took hold.[21] This activist discourse seeks to speak for all Indonesian lesbians at the same time that it distances itself from FTM transgendered people and tombois.

Queer Knowledge, Multiple Receptions

While queer knowledge circulated unevenly among lesbi across Indonesia in the 1980s and 1990s, by the early 2000s this circulation had begun to change form and intensify, as international funding allowed activist lesbian organizations to develop broader connections beyond the island of Java. KPI, in particular, initiated contact with lesbi on other islands through meetings and the establishment of branch organizations, including one located in Padang. The resultant shift in knowledge transmission put Padang lesbi into direct contact with these groups and their discourse of sexual identity and rights. The following exchange provides further insights into the selective reception of queer knowledge and the diversity of lesbi, gay, and waria subjectivities in Indonesia.

Leaders of the Padang branch of Sector 15 were invited to attend the national KPI conference in Jakarta in early 2004.[22] After receiving funds to help cover the costs, Dedi, who was a high school graduate, nearing thirty, decided to make the trip as a representative of the new branch. During this conference a conversation between Dedi and one of the activists took place that revealed some of the tensions and asymmetries in queer knowledge. The lesbian activist, one of the leaders of Sector 15 in Jakarta, had some fluency in English and training from a university overseas. Dedi was eager to make connections with other lesbi beyond Padang and was willing to risk being known as a lesbi, at least among women at the conference in Jakarta. A brief exchange between Dedi and a lesbian activist was witnessed by my research associate:

Activist: What do you consider yourself to be, a man or a woman?
Dedi: I'm like a man.
A: That means you're not a lesbian. You're transgender.

On recounting the story to me later that year, Dedi said, "I didn't say anything then [in response]. I didn't understand 'transgender.' I'd never heard of it before. But it doesn't matter, I know how I feel." Curious about h/er impressions of the lesbi she met in Jakarta, I asked Dedi if s/he noticed a difference between lesbi in Jakarta and lesbi in Padang. Dedi said:

No, they're the same as in Padang, femmes and tombois. You can see it in their appearance. The only difference is the femmes in Jakarta can smoke, but in Padang they're not allowed to. When I first met Lin, I had a hard time distinguishing between her and her partner, which one was femme (*peré*) and which one tomboi, because Lin smokes and carries herself like a tomboi. I had to ask [another activist who had moved to Jakarta from Padang], then I knew.

In the initial conversation, the activist tries to re-situate Dedi within national/global understandings of gender and sexuality, but without success. Dedi is oblivious to the term "transgender" and appears to be unconcerned that s/he is expected to identify as "transgender." Despite being introduced to the term and encouraged to think of herself as "transgender," Dedi returns to Padang with h/er own categories intact. On being asked to reflect about what s/he saw in Jakarta, she reveals that s/he did not see any difference. According to Dedi, Jakarta lesbi "are the same as" Padang lesbi.

At the same time that lesbian activists in Jakarta are inserting masculine-identified tombois into the category "transgender," lesbi in West Sumatra find this recategorization unintelligible. The lack of reception of activist discourse here is striking. Dedi admits of no difference, even though in the beginning s/he had trouble fitting the activist lesbi into h/er own binary categories. The Padang lesbi from whom s/he asked for clarification confirmed what s/he thought s/he knew, that is, that there are only femmes and tombois. Although s/he had trouble at first identifying Lin as femme because Lin smoked, she was able to make sense of Lin's position because Dedi knew that h/er female (and heterosexual) cousins in Jakarta had taken up smoking. As a global metropolis, Jakarta is seen as the space of "modernity," different from places on other islands, which are viewed by Java-centric people as being somewhat more conservative. Thus, femmes in Jakarta may smoke, whereas those in Padang "are not allowed to smoke" because it would be deemed improper for a woman to do so, yet they are both still recognizably femme in Dedi's eyes. Even though Lin sees herself as andro, as far as Dedi is concerned, Lin is femme.

Dedi's inability to see "difference," in this case between h/erself and lesbi in Jakarta who identify as *andro* or "no label," hints at the vulnerability of h/er own position both in Padang and in the face of better-educated and better-traveled urban activists. By seeing only sameness, Dedi assures h/erself of h/er own familiar position in the lesbi world. Being the same admits no other way of being, no exceptions, and no deviation in the face of a repositioning, as "transgender," that would otherwise raise some deeply troubling questions for h/er: If I'm transgender, what is my partner? Is she lesbi? Am I not lesbi? If lesbi are two "women," where does that leave me? Do I not belong to the lesbi community? In fact in a 2004 article in *Lembar Swara*, the author claimed that masculine-identified females are "trannie" (transgender) and their women partners are heterosexual or bisexual, thus excluding both from the term "lesbi" (MilaBlü 2004). The meanings and experiences that signify being "lesbi" may differ for tombois and their girlfriends, but they consider each other to be part of the lesbi world. By shifting the definition of lesbi to exclude tombois who are like men, activists call into question tombois' understandings of their own relationships as well as the comfort and security they feel in their lives as tombois. Tombois' lack of reception of LGBT discourse in the form of the term "transgender" is not due to a lack of understanding of the term, however, but to their own particular understandings of the lesbi world.

Identities or subject positions that are culturally available in particular localities serve as the basis for negotiating with global gay discourse. Jakartan lesbian activists orient their subject positions to the "originary" (Euro-American) lesbian ideals defining lesbians as "women who love women." In Padang, tombois and their partners lay claim to the label "lesbi," used across Indonesia and derived from the globalized label "lesbian," as a signifier for their relationships and community while rejecting the term "transgender" that has been proffered to them. Their use of the label "lesbi" belies originary models because it encompasses both tombois and their girlfriends. Despite activists' efforts to resituate them, tombois and girlfriends do not fit neatly within the sexual categories of "LGBT" claimed by national activist groups. In this instance the friction produced between these two positions leads to a stalemate, as neither side is convinced of the other's rightness. In the many possible responses to the friction of global encounters, Tsing (2005) suggests that the affluent may fashion themselves in relation to an imagined worldliness. Tombois do not fashion themselves in relation to the global gay ecumene, but they imagine themselves as part of it in a way that fits their reception and understanding of the world.

For most of the tombois and their partners, the potential shifts in meaning do not seem to trouble their self-positionings, particularly for those couples who have been in long-term relationships. Although the term *sesama jenis* has been taken on by the lesbi I interviewed in Padang as a referent to their relationships, it would seem that it does not threaten their gender differences. Other than Asnita, no one expressed discomfort with the masculine or feminine characteristics of their partners. Rather, as noted in chapter 4, they were more likely to extol just those characteristics as reasons for their attraction and proof of their own gendered position. These individuals see the lesbi world as populated by two different types of people, tombois and femmes. Those who do not see it that way, like Gia, remain on the margins of social networks populated by tombois and femmes. At the same time terms such as "same sex," "transgender," and "bisexual," as well as activist discourses, subtly and persistently offer a different way of thinking about lesbi relationships that over time may increase friction in the lesbi world in Padang, possibly creating new divisions or exclusions among its members.

Asymmetries of Queer Knowledge

In the complexity of cultural production, global flows, and transnational practices, queer discourses circulate unevenly and are accessed by lesbi in Padang in ways particular to their location. Until recently, their sexual subjectivities were not directly informed by the growing lesbian/gay movement in Indonesia or by the Internet, which have been viewed as some of the primary vehicles producing new sexual subjectivities. Even direct contact with activist lesbi in Jakarta did not alter at least one tomboi's particular self-understanding as a lesbi. Because lesbi intercept queer knowledge in class- and gender-delimited ways, their subjectivities reflect the particularities of place and the particular circuits they access. Boellstorff's (2005b) analysis of gay and lesbi in Indonesia provides a useful way to think about national gay citizenship, but it does not attend to the multiplicity of lesbi and gay subjectivities in Indonesia. Through selective reception of transnational queer knowledge, lesbi in Padang produce subjectivities that differ from those claimed by national activist groups as well as from middle-class, educated, and urban lesbi. By exploring lesbi lives in a regional metropolis and working-class context, this book demonstrates the importance of specific circuits of knowledge in the production of queer subjectivities.

Despite their inability to access new technologies and print media published by national and international lesbian and gay activist organizations, lesbi in Padang are not isolated from global networks; rather they access these networks, and the queer knowledge they produce, through different means. They rely on word-of-mouth communication as they travel across Indonesia and meet other lesbi, gay, and waria in other regional and global metropolises. Much of their media access to queer knowledge comes from mainstream media, whether television, movies, or print media, with their contradictory messages about desire and deviance, their obsession with stories about lesbian/gay and transgender celebrities, and their reports on the Indonesian state's response to international sexual rights movements. As lesbi subjectivities in Padang demonstrate, global processes are not unidirectional, moving toward "modern" understandings, but are constituted at multiple points of reception to produce particular meanings. Lesbian activists as well as tombois and femmes each reflect the particularities and asymmetries of class, gender, and ethnicity in Indonesia, as they intersect with transnational queer discourses.

While their subjectivities may be imagined in Western queer discourse as premodern or lacking in modern sexual knowledge, the difference that tombois and their girlfriends represent is not the difference of outmoded gender-based sexualities. Their particular reception of queer discourse points to the asymmetries of knowledge production across gender and class. I use the term "asymmetries" here, following Ann Stoler (1997), because it does not infer lack or absence, which would suggest the existence of some correct form of LGBT discourse or knowledge correctly received. "Asymmetries" point to differences in reception and the consequent multiplicity of structures, discourses, and experiences that produce desires and subjectivities. These asymmetries disturb any claims about proper or even "modern" forms of same-sex desire. The versions of masculinity and femininity represented in this study demonstrate how processes of asymmetrical reception of global and national discourses produce sexual and gender subjectivities that exceed any single or binary categorization.

Queer studies research that attends to the contentious issue of globalized sexualities suggests a complicated process at the intersection of global and local characterized by hybridity or syncretization (see Altman 2001; Manderson and Jolly 1997; Povinelli and Chauncey 1999). Manalansan's (2003) work on Filipino gay men in the United States demonstrates how these men negotiate Filipino and U.S. American sexual and gender ideologies by taking into account both *bakla* and gay meanings in their self-constructions. According to Manalansan, the term *bakla* "encompasses homosexuality, hermaphroditism, cross-dressing and effeminacy," thus raising the possibility that these diverse subjectivities "are not moored to any fixed category" (2003, ix). Sinnott's use of hybridity to characterize the processes of *tom* and *dee* subject formation in Thailand also takes an important step that moves beyond notions of hybrid blendings. She argues that hybridity reflects "the process whereby nodes of masculinity and femininity are created and consequently contested, manipulated and transformed" (2004, 39), pointing to an ongoing process of intense cultural interaction and exchange. Similarly, the subjectivities of lesbi activists, tombois, and femmes demonstrate the disparate ways that global queer discourses are accessed, addressed, and exchanged in ways that refuse any self-evident or stable categories. Both tombois and femmes are already part of and crucially interconnected with a global queer community, suggesting that subjectivities are not created in a singular or even hybrid fashion at some meeting point between the global and local but through many different intersections within and between regions and nations.

Reflections

Tombois and their partners challenge the coherence of both lesbian and transgender identities as they have been represented in global LGBT discourse. The complexities of their subject positions make it impossible to align them with either global LGBT discourse or Indonesian activist-defined categories of "lesbian" or "transgendered," pointing to the need to dismantle fixed gender and sexual categories that limit identities to LGBT. At the same time, the asymmetries of reception and importance of ethnicity, class, and gender to the production of particular gendered and sexual subjectivities demonstrate that there is neither a homogeneous global, nor a national queer identity. Thus, strategies to address sexual rights must be sensitive to the differences within and across groups, nations, and regions of the world.

The critique of queer studies offered by queers of color theorists in the United States, and their recognition that family and community are as important as queerness, is another critical analytic for globalized sexualities. Anzaldúa's work and that of other queers of color theorists discussed in chapter 6 point to the synergy of multiple allegiances and multiple subjectivities through which ambiguities of ethnic and sexual identities or, in this case, of femininity and masculinity, are strategically maintained. By highlighting the contingency of subjectivities, this analytic recognizes multiple paths and processes in the production of queer subjectivities, without interrupting the links with family and community where these may be important (see Quiroga 2000). As a way to understand tomboi masculinity, in particular, and globalized sexualities more broadly, it demonstrates the value of sustaining ambiguity both as a means of resistance and as a way to produce a sense of well-being and wholeness.

In talking about the possible return of gender to queer studies, Robyn Wiegman (2007) suggests that gender functions as a powerful interpretive force, compelling its subjects to understand identity and erotic practice within its terms. The intervention I make into gender theory—at the everyday practice of gender where performance meets norm—is to assert that gender's *force* and its undoing lie in its normativity. Gender is no more than a norm; it is the acceptance of a category of difference based on bodies. Thus, normative gender, deeply rooted in the habitus of shared meaning, may compel initially (in childhood) or at length (through adulthood), but it also compels and produces its opposite, Foucault's perverse proliferation in, for instance, "the woman who acts like a man." And yet it also creates the possibility to exceed those binary oppositions because of the "truth" that lies at the heart of gender, that norms are fixed in both senses of the word; they are extremely rigid and they are unequally defined.

The ability to navigate multiple subject positions comes in part from the recognition at some level of the arbitrariness of these norms. In the same way that Anzaldúa came to understand the incompatibilities of her Mexican and American identities, or subjected groups the mismeasure of their personhood or citizenship, so tombois and femmes realize the impossibility of representing their desires within normative parameters. Recognizing this impossibility, they make certain compromises and forego other accommodations in the process of creating new subjectivities that sustain contradiction and ambiguity. For example, femmes may disavow the culturally ascribed femaleness of their partners' bodies to claim a heteronormative subject position. Or, in desiring a long-term relationship with a tomboi, some femmes may come to redefine the meaning of womanhood. Tombois may believe that femmes want sex with a "real" man who has a penis, and thus are willing to give up their girlfriends to men who can give them children, but they can also parody the practical sense of a world in which men are men and women are women. Through camp behavior they point out the socially inscribed contradictions between their bodies and men's bodies and thus mark their difference from sex/gender normativity. Tombois' interpretation of masculinity reads against the grain, shifting masculinity to their female bodies in a move that exposes the fallacy of the norm. Through their everyday practices, tombois and femmes substantiate Butler's theory that gender is artificial—lacking an original—and thus find a space to reimagine it.

Tombois and femmes do not produce themselves just as they see fit, however. Within their particular field of practice, to return to Bourdieu, they integrate multiple forms of knowledge to take up intelligible subject positions and yet at the same time creatively respond to and manipulate the structures of knowledge. The language of the acting subject in this book may seem to suggest that tombois and femmes are purposeful agents who knowingly take up particular positions to create their own sense of self. But in representing them as subjects and actors, and addressing processes of self-formation, I situate that active process within structures of knowledge and not outside of them. If my language implies conscious (yet not autonomous) actions, my emphasis on embodied practices, narratives of enactment, and performance of gender underscores the way such positions are actually taken up, not necessarily through conscious decision but in the processes and social interactions of everyday life. At the point at which tombois shift meanings of sex/gender, and lesbi relationships convey rewards despite their marginalized position, tombois and femmes gain critical perspective on normative categories, at least momentarily, to imagine and create other futures together.

The tombois and femmes I interviewed do not participate in any mode of resistance expected or encouraged by national and international queer activists, but by avoiding direct conflict they create a space for themselves—in collaboration with their families and kin—that moves back and forth across normative boundaries. These crossings are not without their dangers, including the threat or actuality of state oppression and assault by religious fanatics, which activists so rightly warn about. Since the year 2000, Indonesian state officials have made efforts to institute stricter laws around sexuality and marriage (see Blackwood 2007). The passage of the antipornography bill in 2008 does not bode well for greater tolerance. Clearly, lesbi and gay activism is essential to the struggle for tolerance and sexual rights, just as understanding difference is important for the security of all those queer subjects who in their own ways risk the displeasures of the dominant society. Deterioration in the political or religious climate may threaten the level of acceptance that tombois have, resulting in possible loss of kin and community or denial of their personhood. But the response to such threats cannot be to "prescribe an exclusive identification for multiply-constituted subjects" (Butler 1993, 116). Rather it requires recognition of the complexity of sexual and transgender subjects and the knowledge they offer about self, contingency, community, and agency in a globalized world.

Notes

Chapter 1: Gender, Sexuality, and Queer Desires

Epigraph. Butler 1993, 231.

1. When referring to tombois, I use the pronominal constructions "s/he" and "h/er" as a way to disrupt the binary genders of the English language. This point is discussed more fully later in the chapter.
2. To protect their identities, I use fictitious names for all the individuals mentioned in this book. In addition, life history details are altered or purposely left imprecise to some extent to maintain anonymity of the individuals.
3. See also Boellstorff 2005b; Mark Johnson 2005; Wilson 2004.
4. See also definitions offered by Bornstein 1994; Wilchins 1997.
5. *Lesbi* and *gay* are Indonesian words derived from the English terms "lesbian" and "gay," but they do not have the same meanings as their cognates. *Gay* is used in Indonesia to refer to gay men only.
6. For critiques of anthropological ethnocartography, see Boellstorff 2002; Weston 1993.
7. *Waria* is one of the Indonesian terms for male-bodied individuals who dress and act in a manner similar to normatively gendered women and take men as lovers. For *gay*, see note 5.
8. For lengthier discussions of issues related to research on lesbians, see Blackwood 2002; Sinnott 2009; Saskia Wieringa and Blackwood 1999. For discussion of problems related to historical research on lesbians, see Vicinus 1993.
9. See Blackwood 1995a, 1998, for a more detailed discussion of these individuals' lives.
10. I use the pronominal construction "s/he" for waria as well as for tombois. See note 1.
11. Most people in West Sumatra speak two languages, Indonesian, the national language, and Minangkabau, the first language for most people born in West Sumatra. I usually conducted interviews together with my research associate, who is a native speaker of Minangkabau. Since most of my interviewees spoke Minangkabau as their first language and were more comfortable in that language, Sri took the lead in the interviews, asking questions in Minangkabau; I would follow up with some questions in Indonesian. Our conversations outside of formal interviews were a mix of Minangkabau and Indonesian.

12. See Kennedy and Davis 1993 on a butch-femme community in the 1930s–1960s in New York State. See Nestle 1992a, 1992b; Stein 1997, regarding the rejection of butches and femmes by lesbian feminists in the 1970s.

13. For a detailed history of the region, see Abdullah 1972; Dobbin 1983; Drakard 1990.

14. Based on shipping data from 2001–2005, http://www.telukbayurport.com, accessed September 30, 2006.

15. Based on economic factors such as facilities and services provided, Rutz (1987, 208) lists Padang as a "higher order center with partial functions of a regional metropolis"; it falls just below six major urban centers in Indonesia labeled as "regional metropolises" and the one Indonesian city Rutz labels a metropolis, Jakarta.

16. Exact figures are not available because state census statistics do not identify inhabitants by ethnicity.

17. See Blackwood 2000; Sanday 2002.

18. The New Order refers to the regime of General Suharto, who became acting head of state in 1966 and remained president up until 1998.

19. I also heard stories of several wealthy married women who had been involved with tombois, but I was unable to meet any of these women.

20. See Dick 1985; Robison 1982, 1996; Tanter and Young 1990.

21. The ranking of Minangkabau clans is based on the origins of the clan members. Those who first settled the village became the elite or high-ranking lineages. Later arrivals ("newcomers") attached themselves to the high-ranking lineages to become the middle rank or client lineages. The low rank was composed of descendants of slaves, or servant kin, who served elite families and were subordinate to them. See Blackwood 2000.

22. See Boellstorff 2005a for a discussion of gay Muslims in Indonesia.

23. Of the four lesbi I met in 1990, the three tombois were at that time all in their late twenties to early thirties; the one woman involved with a tomboi was in her early fifties.

24. Her story is presented in chapter 5.

25. These migrants came primarily from the northern and coastal districts of West Sumatra, including Pasaman and Padang Pariaman, and the southern district of Pesisir Selatan.

26. See also Manalansan 1997, 2003, which call for recognition of multiple localized articulations of sexualities.

27. This problem, of course, is not just true of queer studies but has been a founding assumption in Western scholarship, as a number of feminists and other scholars have pointed out. See for example, Collier and Yanagisako 1987; Mohanty 1991.

28. In fact tracing queer globalization may unintentionally highlight European and American origins. See, for instance, Puar's (2001) identification of queer globalization processes in Trinidad with the multiple circuits of gay tourism, postcolonial

gay identities, global gay cities, international HIV/AIDS activism, and global drag performances.

29. See also Gopinath 2007; Nast 2002; Sinnott 2009.

30. See further Blackwood 2002.

31. Other analyses of queer female subjectivities in Southeast Asia and in diasporic South Asian texts include Gopinath 2005; Sinnott 2004; Wilson 2004.

32. See Boellstorff 2005b; Howard 1996.

33. Regarding *hijra*, see Nanda 1990; Reddy 2005.

34. For Asia, see Sinnott 2004; Saskia Wieringa, Blackwood and Bhaiya 2007; Wilson 2004; for Africa, see Morgan and Wieringa 2005.

35. See in particular, Alarcón 1990; E. Patrick Johnson 2005; Moya 1997; Quiroga 2000; Sandoval 2000.

36. For more on this topic, see Biehl, Good, and Kleinman 2007; Hall 1996; Ortner 2006.

37. For more in-depth discussion of this topic, see Dirks, Eley, and Ortner 1994; Mahmood 2005; Moore 1994.

38. For more discussion of the problem of categories in sexuality studies, see Elliston 1995; Mohanty 1991; Saskia Wieringa and Blackwood 1999.

39. Note on pronunciation: "c" in Indonesian is pronounced like "ch" in "church, "e" is pronounced "ay" (ā), "k" in this instance is a glottal stop. Thus *cewek* is pronounced "chayway' " for speakers of U.S. English.

40. Davies (2007a, 2007b) also uses s/he and hir for *calalai* (male-identified females) and *calabai* (female-identified males) in Sulawesi.

41. See also Besnier 1993; Elliston 1999; Kulick 1998 regarding their takes on gender/pronoun usage.

42. Thanks to Jeffrey Dickemann for pointing this out to me.

43. See, for instance, Volcano and Dahl 2008; also the Femme Collective at http://www.femmecollective.com, accessed December 24, 2008.

44. See also Towle and Morgan 2002.

45. Literature on the butch/FTM border wars includes Halberstam 1994, 1998; Halberstam and Hale 1998; Rubin 1992. See also Cromwell 1999.

46. A good example of such a conference was the 1st International Conference of Asian Queer Studies held in Bangkok, Thailand, July 2005 and sponsored by the AsiaPacifiQueer Network of Sydney, Australia.

Chapter 2: Shifting Discourses of Gender and Desire

Epigraph. Stoler 1995, 166.

1. See Foucault 1978, 1980.

2. See, among many others, Ramazanoğlu 1993; Hartsock 1990; Sawicki 1991.

3. See, for example, Abrams 2002.
4. See, in particular, Manderson and Jolly 1997.
5. See Blackwood 2005a; Peletz 2006, 2009.
6. See Andaya 2000; Boellstorff 2005b; Duff-Cooper 1985; Mark Johnson 1997; Karsch-Haack 1911; van der Kroef 1954; Peletz 1997, 2002, 2006; Sinnott 2004 (esp. chap. 2); Yengoyan 1983.
7. See Blackwood 2005a regarding the disappearance of female ritual transvestites. Peletz 2006 provides a rich history of the decline of male ritual transvestites across Southeast Asia. Andaya 2000 shows that male-bodied *bissu*, ritual transvestites in Muslim South Sulawesi, continued to practice until well into the twentieth century despite conversion to Islam. Davies 2007a (chap. 6) documents contemporary *bissu*, who perform for ordinary people as well as nobility.
8. See Blackwood 2005a; Atkinson 1990; Davies 2007a for more details.
9. Many thanks to Tom Boellstorff for sharing this account with me.
10. Similarly Sinnott recounts an older style of female masculinity in Thailand, before the word *tom* was coined, in which a masculine woman was said to be "like a man" or referred to as "the woman who was like a man" (2004, 53–56).
11. The history of women's efforts to gain political power in Indonesia documents some of the ways these gender ideologies were refined. See Hadler 2008; Sears 1996; Saskia Wieringa 1992, 2002.
12. The five principles of the *Pancasila* are: (1) belief in one God, (2) just and civilized humanitarianism, (3) Indonesian unity/nationalism, (4) democracy led by wisdom born of consultation, and (5) social justice for the Indonesian people (Morfit 1986).
13. The one exception was a married woman who was born in 1964 and did not self-identify as a lesbi, despite being involved with a tomboi.
14. This discussion bypasses a long-simmering debate in Western gender theory about the relation between "sex" and "gender" and whether they should be conceptually distinguished or not.
15. See Blackburn 2004; Robinson 1989; Sullivan 1994.
16. The substantial literature on the state ideology of women as wives and mothers includes Bennett 2005; Blackburn 2004; Brenner 1998; Djajadiningrat-Nieuwenhuis 1987; Sears 1996; Sullivan 1994; Suryakusuma 1996; Saskia Wieringa 1992. See also Boellstorff 2005b; Howard 1996 regarding men and the Indonesian state's family imperative (*azas kekeluargaan*).
17. See also Gouda 1995.
18. But see Bowen 1993; Hefner 2000; and particularly van Doorn-Harder 2006.
19. NU is considered more traditionalist and Muhammadiyah reformist or modernist. These two organizations claim a total membership of 70 million (van Doorn-Harder 2006; Hooker and Lindsey 2003).
20. Wahid is a highly respected Muslim cleric who was the third president of Indonesia (1999–2001).

21. With the end of Indonesian state control of television in the mid-1990s and the increase in foreign television series and movies, the range of women characters has increased dramatically.

22. See Hatley 1990; Hughes-Freeland 1995; Keeler 1987; Pausacker 1991; Peacock 1968; Saskia Wieringa 2000.

23. The two stories appeared in *Tempo*, April 23 and 30, 1981.

24. See also Boellstorff 2005b.

25. See also Alison Murray 1999; Oetomo 1996.

26. The Minangkabau terms can be translated "mother cow" and "calf" (connotation unknown). My consultant explained that the two men become sweethearts (*jadi gula-gula*). Aceh had a similar tradition, called *seudati* or *sadati*, of young men performers who played women's roles and had men lovers (Dr. Herwandi, Department of Literature, Andalas University, personal communication, July 7, 2004; see also Hurgronje 1906; Oetomo 1987, 2001).

27. See also Pauka 1998.

28. Folktales have been standardized and published by the Indonesian and Regional Literature Project of the Indonesian State Department of Education and Culture.

29. One of the earliest appears to be a novel by the Chinese Indonesian writer Lie Kim Hok written in 1884, which is itself based on an older epic Malay folktale, Syair Abdul Muluk. Lie's novel recounts the exploits of Siti Raffiah, second wife of Abdul Muluk, who dresses as a man in order to rescue her kidnapped husband and along the way kills seven men and is married to the younger daughter of the sultan as a reward for bringing peace to his land (Zaini-LaJoubert 1996). Other Minangkabau stories that draw from this genre include *Siti Baheram* and *Sabai nan Aluih*. Many thanks to Matthew Cohen for bringing this literature to my attention.

30. My synopsis is based on the preface and summary in the book, which is written in Indonesian. The tale is written in Minangkabau.

31. Elements of this text that are incongruent with Minangkabau matrilineal practices suggest it originated with Chinese and Malay storytellers. For instance, Nafis (n.d.) notes that the father has a lead role, whereas in many Minangkabau tales the uncle plays a lead role. In still others, the senior woman or mother has the lead role (see Johns 1958). At story's end Gadih Ranti moves with her children to her husband's kingdom, whereas according to Minangkabau matrilocal practice, her husband would remain with her.

32. The chapter is titled "Gadih Ranti bajalan panjang" (M.) (Gadih Ranti's distant travels).

33. Jennifer Fraser, e-mail to author dated July 21, 2004. Thanks to Jennifer, who recorded this performance, for bringing it to my attention.

34. Further, as I argued in Blackwood 2000, despite the dominant ideology of womanhood, rural Minangkabau women in Taram construct their own understandings of motherhood and wifedom that incorporate their ownership, control, and/or labor in the rice fields.

215

35. For other expressions of gender nonconformity in Indonesia, see Alison Murray 1999; Sears 1996; Saskia Wieringa 2002.
36. The relevant chapter in Oetomo 2001 is "Homoseksualitas di Indonesia," originally published in 1991.
37. See also Jackson 1997.
38. A young tomboi from South Sumatra said the term s/he knew was *jantan tino*, which means male-female or effeminate male. *Jantan* means male, *tino* is short for *batino* (*betina*, Indonesian), which means female or woman in South Sumatra (Stevens and Schmidgall-Tellings 2004).
39. See Robinson 2001 for further discussion of the relation between *adat* and Islam.
40. Article 292 of the State Penal Code.
41. See Alexander 1991; Alexander and Mohanty 1997; Puar 2001.
42. Regarding Dutch treatment of homosexuality and transgender behavior historically, see Crompton 1981; Dekker and van der Pol 1989; van der Meer 1991.
43. For further discussion of these changing discourses, see Blackwood 2007.
44. See Dwyer 2002 for more on the complexity of processes between the nation and everyday life.

Chapter 3: Learning to Be Boys and Girls

1. For overviews of the anthropological literature on childhood, see Bluebond-Langner and Korbin 2007; Hirschfeld 2002.
2. For examples of feminist anthropological studies that address girlhood, see Abu-Lughod 1993; Callaway 1987; Watson 1986.
3. See also Mageo 1991.
4. See also Benedict 1939; Munroe, Whiting, and Hally 1969.
5. See, for example, Besnier 1993; Elliston 1999; Herdt 1993; Jacobs, Thomas, and Lang 1997; Mark Johnson 1997; Manalansan 2003.
6. Adolescence for girls in the United States disrupts that truth as their tomboyish behavior, which had previously been accepted as a phase of childhood, is now met with a blanket refusal by others to relate to or see them as tomboys or to treat them as anything other than feminine women. See Elise 1999; Halberstam 1999.
7. See Bowen 1991; George 1996; Junus 1994; Steedly 1993; Tambiah 1985.
8. I assume that any harrowing or abusive events experienced by tombois at the hands of their parents or other kin would have been mentioned to me.
9. See Lancaster 2003 on the prevalence of biological views in U.S. media accounts of homosexuality.
10. See further Shelly Errington 1983; Keeler 1987 regarding Indonesian selves.
11. Like any folk theory, this one works when it works. Other tombois did not grow up surrounded by brothers or other men but had both brothers and sisters, and, in one case, all sisters.

Chapter 4: Doing Gender

Epigraph. Butler 1990, 174.

1. The social history of this dichotomy is quite extensive; Eley 1994 provides a good introduction to its use from the French Revolution through Habermas that includes various feminist critiques. See also Gal 2002; Landes 1998; Yanagisako and Collier 1987.

2. See, for example, Mary Weismantel's discussion (2001) of the blurring of domestic/public space by Andean market women.

3. See Phillips et al. 2000; Gill Valentine 2002.

4. For works that attend to relations between queer and non-queer family and kin, see Manalansan 2003; Quiroga 2000; Wekker 2006. Other relevant work queering non-white/non-U.S. intimate domestic space includes Gopinath 1998; Patel 2004.

5. From the *Oxford English Dictionary* 1989, accessed on-line Sept. 30, 2008.

6. See also Kulick (2000); Livia and Hall (1997).

7. This speech practice may vary within and across locales in West Sumatra and may also depend on the relative status of speakers.

8. According to J. Errington (1998), *mami*, *papi*, *tante*, and *om*, which are Dutch cognates, are commonly used among educated urban speakers and are considered typical of Jakartan lingo. Use of these terms in Padang demonstrates their movement beyond Jakarta. However, unlike Errington's Javanese speakers, who use *mami* and *papi* to refer to parents, lesbi couples in Padang use the terms for each other.

9. See also Kulick 1998.

10. As I discuss in chapter 6, however, some public spaces do carry risks for tombois. Their unwillingness to use men's restrooms speaks to a concern about the possible risks present in such an intimate, yet public, men's space.

Chapter 5: Desire and Difference

1. "Coming out" takes many different forms, but see Stanley and Wolf 1980; Zimmerman 2000.

2. Upik and Jon's relationship also seems to bear some similarity to the much-debated woman-marriages in Africa, although in this case neither partner had any money to begin with.

3. Some of the tombois may prefer not to be touched sexually, although I did not ask any of the tombois I interviewed about that. Sinnott 2004 mentions the practice of untouchability among *tom*s in Thailand. Some masculine females in the United States who engage in a similar practice are called stone butch. See Faderman 1991; Feinberg 1993; Kennedy and Davis 1993.

4. See Bennett 2005; Blackwood 1995b, 1998; Howard 1996.

5. See also Boellstorff 2005b; Howard 1996.

6. As with gender, the mechanisms that regulate sexuality are a product of the synthesis of customary practices (*adat*) and Islamic law. See Robinson 2001.

7. Schein's 2000 discussion of shifts in Miao identity offers a similar example, although the potential consequences are not as severe.

Chapter 6: Ambiguities in Family, Community, and Public Spaces

Epigraph. Mohanty 1991, 11.

1. See Boellstorff 2005b; Howard 1996.
2. See Blackwood 2000; Kipp 1993.
3. See Geertz 1984; Kipp 1993.
4. See also Bennett 2005; Howard 1996.
5. In contrast, see David Murray, who counterpoises Martinique *gai* men's concerns to maintain family respectability with their desires to escape to places where "same-sex desire and sociality may be freely expressed" (2000, 268).
6. See Stack 1974; also Blackwood 2005b. For literature on Afro-Caribbean extended families, see, for instance, Mohammed 1986; Monagan 1985; Olwig 1981.
7. See also Sinnott 2004.
8. The term *banci* is considered somewhat derogatory and was replaced by the neologism "waria."
9. See Butler 1999; Case 1993; Davy 1994; Meyer 1994; Sarah Murray 1994; Tyler 1991. Davy 1994, for instance, argues that camp does not work for lesbian theatrical endeavors in the way that it does for gay men.
10. However, even during the time Peacock conducted his research in the 1960s, reformist Muslims were attempting to discourage transvestite performances. Such opposition has seen a resurgence since the fall of Suharto in 1998. Radical Islamicist groups in Indonesia have attacked waria groups, including one attempt to stop a waria beauty contest in 2005. At the same time waria/transvestite entertainers seem to be even more popular in Indonesian television and movies. See BBC News 2005.
11. See also Morgan and Wieringa 2005.
12. See further Moore 1994.
13. Anzaldúa 1987; Cromwell 1999. For other theorists who have developed this line of thinking, see also Alarcón 1990; Ferguson 2004; E. Patrick Johnson 2005; Muñoz 1999; Quiroga 2000; Sandoval 2000.

Chapter 7: Translocal Queer Connections

Epigraph. Butler 1993, 116.

1. Some of the literature and debates about butch-femme identities includes Case 1993; Faderman 1991; Lyon and Martin 1972; Nestle 1992b; Radicalesbians 1997; Stein 1997.

2. Among those theorists building bridges across categories of lesbian, butch, and FTM, see Rubin 1992; Halberstam 1998.

3. The "B," or Bisexual, tends to receive much less attention in activist discourse, while Lesbian and Gay are privileged.

4. LGBT is prominently used on the Web sites of, among many others, the International Lesbian and Gay Association (ILGA), http://www.ilga.org/index.asp, and the International Gay and Lesbian Human Rights Commission, http://www.iglhrc.org/site/iglhrc/, both accessed April 23, 2007.

5. See, for example, "Third ILGA-Asia regional conference," which states that ILGA "recognizes the diverse ways by which genders and sexualities are experienced and defined in Asia," at http://asia.ilga.org/3rd_ilga_asia_regional_conference_chiang_mai_thailand_24_27_january_2008/about_the_conference, accessed December 10, 2007.

6. For histories of these organizations, see Boellstorff 2005b; Howard 1996; Oetomo 2001; Saskia Wieringa 1999.

7. See Saskia Wieringa 1999, regarding the development of PERLESIN.

8. The terms "minority sexual orientation" and "lesbian" are used by Sector 15 in their English-language writings.

9. Some of the travel facilitated by external funding for members of Swara Srikandi in the early 2000s included attendance at an Al-Fatiha (LGBTQ Muslim) conference in the United States, an International Lesbian and Gay Association—Asia (ILGA-Asia) conference, and a Sydney (Australia) Gay Games and Global Rights conference.

10. Early issues of *GAYa Nusantara* contain long lists of places where gay men or waria hang out (*tempat ngeber*), but none are mentioned for lesbi. See also Boellstorff 2005b; Oetomo 1996.

11. Regarding their circulation among gay organizations, see Boellstorff 2005b; Howard 1996.

12. Actually Robi said *lines* (see derivation in text) rather than "lesbi."

13. See also Kulick's (1999) caution concerning the identification of language with particular identity groups.

14. This list, provided in 2001, included the following words: *cium* (kiss) > *cumi*; *pegang* (hold, touch) > *peges*; *tidur* (sleep) > *tinjau*; *payudara* (female breast) > *tetong*; *pantat* (buttocks) > *pastra*.

15. These two terms are now identified as Javanese. See Webster 2008.

16. English words are appropriated in some cases in tattoos, such as "Love Hate" on one tomboi's foot, or nicknames, such as the one the children of a femme lover used for her tomboi partner: Loy, standing for "Love-Only-You." These words are not used to articulate desire in the way that they are for gays in the southern Philippines, as is suggested by Mark Johnson (1997), which may indicate a potential class difference across regions.

17. Asnita, who did not socialize with the other femmes and tombois that Tommi knew,

had already distanced herself from Tommi when I arrived in 2004, so I was unable to interview her.

18. Some of the videos she had seen included *If these walls could talk 2*, *Bound*, *Aimee and Jaguar*, and *Kissing Jessica Stein*.

19. See also Saskia Wieringa 2007, which addresses the situation for a generation of Jakarta butches and femmes in their forties through sixties.

20. Translations of Indonesian are mine. The spellings of LGBT in the original are "lesbian," "gay," "biseksual," and "transgender."

21. For an interesting comparison, see Lorway 2008, which suggests that lesbian activists in Namibia enable and support the expression of female gender transgression.

22. This branch was established after I left West Sumatra in 2001 and was comprised of several of the individuals who had participated in my research and whom I had connected with lesbi activists in Jakarta.

Bibliography

Abdullah, Taufik. 1972. "Modernization in the Minangkabau World: West Sumatra in the Early Decades of the Twentieth Century." In *Culture and Politics in Indonesia*, ed. Claire Holt, pp. 179–245. Ithaca, NY: Cornell University Press.

Abrams, Lynne. 2002. *The Making of Modern Woman: Europe, 1789–1918*. New York: Longman.

Abu-Lughod, Lila. 1993. *Writing Women's Worlds: Bedouin Stories*. Berkeley: University of California Press.

Alarcón, Norma. 1990. "The Theoretical Subject(s) of *This Bridge Called My Back* and Anglo-American Feminism." In *Making Face, Making Soul: Creative and Critical Perspectives by Feminists of Color*, ed. Gloria Anzaldúa, pp. 356–369. San Francisco: Aunt Lute Books.

Alcoff, Linda. 1994. "Cultural Feminism versus Post-structuralism: The Identity Crisis in Feminist Theory." In *Culture/Power/History: A Reader in Contemporary Social Theory*, ed. Nicholas B. Dirks, Geoff Eley, and Sherry B. Ortner, pp. 96–122. Princeton, NJ: Princeton University Press.

Alexander, M. Jacqui. 1991. "Redrafting Morality: The Postcolonial State and the Sexual Offences Bill of Trinidad and Tobago." In *Third World Women and the Politics of Feminism*, ed. Chandra T. Mohanty, Ann Russo, and Lourdes Torres, pp. 133–152. Bloomington: Indiana University Press.

———, M. Jacqui, and Chandra T. Mohanty, eds. 1997. *Feminist Genealogies, Colonial Legacies, Democratic Futures*. New York: Routledge.

Alhamidy, Li. 1951. *Islam dan perkawinan* (Islam and marriage). Jakarta: Penerbit al Ma'arif.

Altman, Dennis. 1996. "Rupture or Continuity? The Internationalization of Gay Identities." *Social Text* 48:77–94.

———. 2001. *Global Sex*. Chicago: University of Chicago Press.

Andaya, Leonard. 2000. "The Bissu: Study of a Third Gender in Indonesia." In *Other Pasts: Women, Gender and History in Early Modern Southeast Asia*, ed. Barbara Watson Andaya, pp. 27–46. Honolulu: University of Hawai'i Press.

Anderson, Benedict R. O'G. 1990. *Language and Power: Exploring Political Cultures in Indonesia*. Ithaca, NY: Cornell University Press.

Anzaldúa, Gloria. 1987. *Borderlands/La Frontera: The New Mestiza*. San Francisco: Aunt Lute Books.

Appadurai, Arjun. 1996. *Modernity at Large: Cultural Dimensions of Globalization*. Minneapolis: University of Minnesota Press.

Aripurnami, Sita. 1996. "A Feminist Comment on the Sinetron Presentation of Indonesian Women." In *Fantasizing the Feminine in Indonesia*, ed. Laurie Sears, pp. 249–258. Durham, NC: Duke University Press.

Armstrong, Elizabeth A. 2002. *Forging Gay Identities: Organizing Sexuality in San Francisco, 1950–1994*. Chicago: University of Chicago Press.

Atkinson, Jane Monnig. 1990. "How Gender Makes a Difference in Wana Society." In *Power and Difference: Gender in Island Southeast Asia*, ed. Jane Monnig Atkinson and Shelly Errington, pp. 59–93. Stanford, CA: Stanford University Press.

Bacchetta, Paola. 1999. "When the (Hindu) Nation Exiles Its Queers." *Social Text* 61 (Winter): 141–166.

———. 2002. "Rescaling Transnational 'Queerdom': Lesbian and 'Lesbian' Identitary-Positionalities in Delhi in the 1980s." *Antipode: A Radical Journal of Geography* 34 (5): 947–973.

Badan Pusat Statistik Propinsi SumBar. 2000. *Sumatera Barat dalam angka* (West Sumatra in numbers). Padang.

BBC News. 2005. "Row over Indonesia Transvestite Show." June 27. Available at http://news.bbc.co.uk/2/hi/asia-pacific/4626167.stm (accessed October 31, 2008).

Benedict, Ruth. 1939. "Sex in Primitive Society." *American Journal of Orthopsychiatry* 9:570–573.

Bennett, Linda Rae. 2005. *Women, Islam and Modernity: Single Women, Sexuality and Reproductive Health in Contemporary Indonesia*. New York: RoutledgeCurzon.

Besnier, Niko. 1993. "Polynesian Gender Liminality through Time and Space." In *Third Sex, Third Gender: Beyond Sexual Dimorphism in Culture and History*, ed. Gilbert Herdt, pp. 285–328. New York: Zone Books.

Biehl, João, Byron Good, and Arthur Kleinman. 2007. *Subjectivity: Ethnographic Investigations*. Berkeley: University of California Press.

Binnie, Jon. 2004. *The Globalization of Sexuality*. London: Sage Publications.

Blackburn, Susan. 2004. *Women and the State in Modern Indonesia*. Cambridge: Cambridge University Press.

Blackwood, Evelyn. 1995a. "Falling in Love with an-Other Lesbian: Reflections on Identity in Fieldwork." In *Taboo: Sex, Identity and Erotic Subjectivity in Anthropological Fieldwork*, ed. Don Kulick and Margaret Willson, pp. 51–75. New York: Routledge Press.

———. 1995b. "Senior Women, Model Mothers and Dutiful Wives: Managing Gender Contradictions in a Minangkabau village." In *Bewitching Women, Pious Men: Gender and Body Politics in Southeast Asia*, ed. Aihwa Ong and Michael Peletz, pp. 124–158. Berkeley: University of California Press.

———. 1998. "*Tombois* in West Sumatra: Constructing Masculinity and Erotic Desire." *Cultural Anthropology* 13 (4):491–521.

———. 2000. *Webs of Power: Women, Kin and Community in a Sumatran Village*. Lanham, MD: Rowman and Littlefield.

———. 2001. "Representing Women: The Politics of Minangkabau Adat Writing." *Journal of Asian Studies* 60 (1):125–149.

———. 2002. "Reading Sexuality across Cultures: Anthropology and Theories of Sexuality." In *Out in Theory: The Emergence of Lesbian and Gay Anthropology*, ed. Ellen Lewin and William Leap, pp. 69–92. Urbana: University of Illinois Press.

———. 2005a. "Gender Transgression in Colonial and Post-colonial Indonesia." *Journal of Asian Studies* 64 (4):849–879.

———. 2005b. "Wedding Bell Blues: Marriage, Missing Men, and Matrifocal Follies." *American Ethnologist* 32 (1):3–19.

———. 2007. "Regulation of Sexuality in Indonesian Discourse: Normative Gender, Criminal Law and Shifting Strategies of Control." *Culture, Health and Sexuality* 9 (3):293–307.

———, and Saskia E. Wieringa, eds. 1999. *Female Desires: Same-Sex Relations and Transgender Practices Across Cultures*. New York: Columbia University Press.

———, and Saskia E. Wieringa. 2007. "Globalization, Sexuality and Silences: Women's Sexualities and Masculinities in an Asian Context." In *Women's Sexualities and Masculinities in a Globalizing Asia*, ed. Saskia E. Wieringa, Evelyn Blackwood, and Abha Bhaiya, pp. 1–20. New York: Palgrave Macmillan.

Bluebond-Langner, Myra, and Jill E. Korbin. 2007. "Challenges and Opportunities in the Anthropology of Childhoods: An Introduction to 'Children, Childhoods, and Childhood Studies.'" *American Anthropologist* 109 (2):241–246.

Boellstorff, Thomas. 1999. "The Perfect Path: Gay Men, Marriage, Indonesia." *GLQ: Journal of Lesbian and Gay Studies* 5 (4):475–510.

———. 2002. "Ethnolocality." *The Asia Pacific Journal of Anthropology* 3 (1):24–48.

———. 2004. " 'Authentic, of Course!': *Gay* Language in Indonesia and Cultures of Belonging." In *Speaking in Queer Tongues: Globalization and Gay Language*, ed. William L. Leap and Tom Boellstorff, pp. 181–201. Urbana: University of Illinois Press.

———. 2005a. "Between Religion and Desire: Being Muslim and *Gay* in Indonesia." *American Anthropologist* 107 (4):575–585.

———. 2005b. *The Gay Archipelago: Sexuality and Nation in Indonesia*. Princeton, NJ: Princeton University Press.

Bornstein, Kate. 1994. *Gender Outlaw: On Men, Women and the Rest of Us*. New York: Vintage Books.

Bourdieu, Pierre. 1990. *The Logic of Practice*. Richard Nice, trans. Stanford, CA: Stanford University Press.

———. 1998. *Masculine Domination*. Richard Nice, trans. Stanford, CA: Stanford University Press.

Bowen, John R. 1991. *Sumatran Politics and Poetics: Gayo History, 1900–1989.* New Haven, CT: Yale University Press.

———. 1993. *Muslims through Discourse: Religion and Ritual in Gayo Society.* Princeton, NJ: Princeton University Press.

———. 2003. *Islam, Law and Equality in Indonesia: An Anthropology of Public Reasoning.* Cambridge: Cambridge University Press.

Brenner, Suzanne A. 1998. *The Domestication of Desire: Women, Wealth and Modernity in Java.* Princeton, NJ: Princeton University Press.

———. 1999. "On the Public Intimacy of the New Order: Images of Women in the Popular Indonesian Print Media." *Indonesia* 67:13–37.

Budiman, Leila. 2004. "Perkawinan Lesbian" (Lesbian marriage). *Kompas Cybermedia*, December 22. Available at http://www.kompas.com/kesehatan/news/0412/22/144308 .htm (accessed April 14, 2006).

Butler, Judith. 1990/1999. *Gender Trouble: Feminism and the Subversion of Identity.* New York: Routledge.

———. 1993. *Bodies that Matter: On the Discursive Limits of "Sex."* New York: Routledge.

———. 2001. "Doing Justice to Someone: Sex Reassignment and Allegories of Transsexuality." *GLQ: Journal of Lesbian and Gay Studies* 7 (4):621–636.

Callaway, Barbara J. 1987. *Muslim Hausa Women in Nigeria.* Syracuse, NY: Syracuse University Press.

Cameron, Deborah, and Don Kulick. 2003. *Language and Sexuality.* Cambridge: Cambridge University Press.

Case, Sue-Ellen. 1993. "Toward a Butch-femme Aesthetic." In *The Lesbian and Gay Studies Reader*, ed. Henry Abelove, Michèle Aina Barale, and David Halperin, pp. 294–306. New York: Routledge.

Chabot, H. Th. 1960. *Kinship, Status and Sex in the South Celebes.* Richard Neuse, trans. New Haven, CT: Human Relations Area Files.

Chauncey, George. 1994. *Gay New York: Gender, Urban Culture, and the Making of the Gay Male World, 1890–1940.* New York: Basic Books.

Collier, Jane Fishburne, and Sylvia Junko Yanagisako, eds. 1987. *Gender and Kinship: Essays toward a Unified Analysis.* Stanford, CA: Stanford University Press.

Collins, Elizabeth Fuller, and Ernaldi Bahar. 2000. "To Know Shame: *Malu* and Its Uses in Malay Societies." *Crossroads: An Interdisciplinary Journal of Southeast Asian Studies* 14 (1):35–69.

Crompton, Louis. 1981. "The Myth of Lesbian Impunity: Capital Laws from 1270 to 1791." *Journal of Homosexuality* 6 (1/2):11–25.

Cromwell, Jason. 1995. "Talking about without Talking about: The Use of Protective Language among Transvestites and Transsexuals." In *Beyond the Lavender Lexicon: Authenticity, Imagination, and Appropriation in Lesbian and Gay Languages*, ed. William L. Leap, pp. 267–295. Amsterdam: Gordon and Breach Publishers.

———. 1999. *Transmen and FTMs: Identities, Bodies, Genders and Sexualities.* Urbana: University of Illinois Press.

Cruz-Malavé, Arnaldo, and Martin F. Manalansan IV. 2002. "Introduction: Dissident Sexualities/Alternative Globalisms." In *Queer Globalizations: Citizenship and the Afterlife of Colonialism*, ed. Arnaldo Cruz-Malavé and Martin F. Manalansan IV, pp. 1–10. New York: New York University Press.

Davies, Sharon Graham. 2007a. *Challenging Gender Norms: Five Genders among the Bugis in Indonesia*. Belmont, CA: Thomson Wadsworth.

———. 2007b. "Hunting Down Love: Female Masculinities in Bugis South Sulawesi." In *Women's Sexualities and Masculinities in a Globalizing Asia*, ed. Saskia E. Wieringa, Evelyn Blackwood, and Abha Bhaiya, pp. 139–157. New York: Palgrave Macmillan.

Davy, Kate. 1994. "Fe/male Impersonation: The Discourse of Camp." In *The Politics and Poetics of Camp*, ed. Moe Meyer, pp. 130–148. New York: Routledge.

Dekker, Rudolf M., and Lotte C. van de Pol. 1989. *The Tradition of Female Transvestism in Early Modern Europe*. New York: St. Martin's Press.

Devereux, George. 1937. "Institutionalized Homosexuality of the Mohave Indians." *Human Biology* 9 (4):498–527.

Dick, H. W. 1985. "The Rise of a Middle Class and the Changing Concept of Equity in Indonesia: An Interpretation." *Indonesia* 39:71–92.

Dirks, Nicholas B., Geoff Eley, and Sherry B. Ortner. 1994. "Introduction." In *Culture/Power/History: A Reader in Contemporary Social Theory*, ed. Nicholas B. Dirks, Geoff Eley, and Sherry B. Ortner, pp. 3–45. Princeton, NJ: Princeton University Press.

Djajadiningrat-Nieuwenhuis, Madelon. 1987. "Ibuism and Priyayization: Path to Power?" In *Indonesian Women in Focus: Past and Present Notions*, ed. E. Locher-Scholten and A. Niehof, pp. 43–51. Dordrecht: Foris Publications.

Dobbin, Christine. 1983. *Islamic Revivalism in a Changing Peasant Economy: Central Sumatra, 1784–1847*. Scandinavian Institute of Asian Studies Monograph Series no. 47. London: Curzon Press.

Dohrman, Rebecca. 2009. "Strategic Ambiguity at Work: A Thematic Analysis of Strategic Ambiguity in International Sexuality-based Organizations' Websites." Paper presented at the International Communication Conference, May.

Drakard, Jane. 1990. *A Malay Frontier: Unity and Duality in a Sumatran Kingdom*. Ithaca, NY: Cornell University Press.

Duff-Cooper, Andrew. 1985. "Notes about Some Balinese Ideas and Practices Connected with Sex from Western Lombok." *Anthropos* 80:403–419.

Durkheim, Émile. 1984 [1933]. *The Division of Labor in Society*. W. D. Halls, trans. New York: The Free Press.

Dwyer, Leslie K. 2000. "Spectacular Sexuality: Nationalism, Development and the Politics of Family Planning in Indonesia." In *Gender Ironies of Nationalism: Sexing the Nation*, ed. Tamar Mayer, pp. 25–62. London: Routledge.

Echols, John M., and Hassan Shadily. 1989. *Kamus Indonesia Inggris: An Indonesian-English Dictionary*. Jakarta: PT Gramedia.

Eley, Geoff. 1994. "Nations, Publics, and Political Cultures: Placing Habermas in the Nineteenth Century." In *Culture/Power/History: A Reader in Contemporary Social Theory*, ed. Nicholas B. Dirks, Geoff Eley, and Sherry B. Ortner, pp. 297–335. Princeton, NJ: Princeton University Press.

Elise, Dianne. 1999. "Tomboys and Cowgirls: The Girl's Disidentification from the Mother." In *Sissies and Tomboys: Gender Nonconformity and Homosexual Childhood*, ed. Matthew Rottnek, pp. 140–152. New York: New York University Press.

Elliston, Deborah. 1995. "Erotic Anthropology: 'Ritualized Homosexuality' in Melanesia and Beyond." *American Ethnologist* 22 (4):848–867.

———. 1999. "Negotiating Transnational Sexual Economies: Female Māhū and Same-sex Sexuality in 'Tahiti and Her Islands.' " In *Female Desires: Same-sex Relations and Transgender Practices across Cultures*, ed. Evelyn Blackwood and Saskia E. Wieringa, pp. 232–252. New York: Columbia University Press.

Errington, J. Joseph. 1998. *Shifting Languages: Interaction and Identity in Javanese Indonesian*. Cambridge: Cambridge University Press.

Errington, Shelly. 1983. "Embodied Sumange' in Luwu." *Journal of Asian Studies* 43 (3):545–570.

———. 1990. "Recasting Sex, Gender, and Power: A Theoretical and Regional Overview." In *Power and Difference: Gender in Island Southeast Asia*, ed. Jane Monnig Atkinson and Shelly Errington, pp. 1–58. Stanford, CA: Stanford University Press.

Faderman, Lillian. 1991. *Odd Girls and Twilight Lovers: A History of Lesbian Life in Twentieth-Century America*. New York: Penguin.

Feinberg, Leslie. 1993. *Stone Butch Blues: A Novel*. Ithaca, NY: Firebrand Books.

Ferguson, Roderick A. 2004. *Aberrations in Black: Toward a Queer of Color Critique*. Minneapolis: University of Minnesota Press.

Foucault, Michel. 1978. *The History of Sexuality*. Vol. 1: An Introduction. New York: Vintage.

———. 1980. *Power/Knowledge: Selected Interviews and Other Writings, 1972–1977*, ed. Colin Gordon. New York: Pantheon Books.

Fraser, Jennifer Anne. 1998. "Queer as Theory: Reading Music Queerly across Cultures." Master's thesis, Brown University.

———. 2007. "Packaging Ethnicity: State Institutions, Cultural Entrepreneurs, and the Professionalization of Minangkabau Music in Indonesia." PhD dissertation, University of Illinois, Urbana-Champaign.

Gal, Susan. 2002. "A Semiotics of the Public/Private Distinction." *differences: A Journal of Feminist Cultural Studies* 13 (1):77–95.

Gayatri, B. J. D. 1993. "Coming Out but Remaining Hidden: A Portrait of Lesbians in Java." Paper presented at the International Congress of Anthropological and Ethnological Sciences, Mexico City, Mexico.

———. 1994. "Sentul-kantil, Not Just Another Term: Kekayaan relasi gender female-homosexual kontemporer di Jawa" (Female-homosexual gender relations in contemporary Java). Ms.

———. 1996. "Indonesian Lesbians Writing Their Own Script: Issues of Feminism and Sexuality." In *Amazon to Zami: Towards a Global Lesbian Feminism*, ed. Moniker Reinfelder, pp. 86–97. London: Cassell.

Geertz, Clifford. 1984. " 'From the Native's Point of View': On the Nature of Anthropological Understanding." In *Culture Theory: Essays on Mind, Self, and Emotion*, ed. R. A. Shweder and R. A. LeVine, pp. 123–136. Cambridge: Cambridge University Press.

George, Kenneth M. 1996. *Showing Signs of Violence: The Cultural Politics of a Twentieth-century Headhunting Ritual.* Berkeley: University of California Press.

Gopinath, Gayatri. 1998. "Homo-economics: Queer Sexualities in a Transnational Frame." In *Burning Down the House: Recycling Domesticity*, ed. Rosemary Marangoly George, pp. 102–124. Boulder, CO: Westview Press.

———. 2002. "Local Site/Global Contexts: The Transnational Trajectories of Deepa Mehta's *Fire.*" In *Queer Globalizations: Citizenship and the Afterlife of Colonialism*, ed. Arnaldo Cruz-Malavé and Martin F. Manalansan IV, pp. 149–161. New York: New York University Press.

———. 2005. *Impossible Desires: Queer Diasporas and South Asian Public Cultures.* Durham, NC: Duke University Press.

———. 2007. "Queer Regions: Locating Lesbians in *Sancharram.*" In *A Companion to Lesbian, Gay, Bisexual, Transgender, and Queer Studies*, ed. George Haggerty and Molly McGarry, pp. 341–354. New York: Blackwell Publishers.

Gouda, Frances. 1995. *Dutch Culture Overseas: Colonial Practice in the Netherlands Indies, 1900–1942.* Amsterdam: Amsterdam University Press.

Green, Jamison. 2004. *Becoming a Visible Man.* Nashville, TN: Vanderbilt University Press.

Grewal, Inderpal, and Caren Kaplan. 1994. "Introduction: Transnational Feminist Practices and Questions of Postmodernity." In *Scattered Hegemonies: Postmodernity and Transnational Feminist Practices*, ed. Inderpal Grewal and Caren Kaplan, pp. 1–33. Minneapolis: University of Minnesota Press.

———. 2001. "Global Identities: Theorizing Transnational Studies of Sexuality." *GLQ: Journal of Lesbian and Gay Studies* 7 (4):663–679.

Hadler, Jeffrey. 2008. *Muslims and Matriarchs: Cultural Resilience in Indonesia through Jihad and Colonialism.* Ithaca, NY: Cornell University Press.

Halberstam, Judith. 1994. "F2M: The Making of Female Masculinity." In *The Lesbian Postmodern*, ed. Laura Doan, pp. 210–228. New York: Columbia University Press.

———. 1998. *Female Masculinities.* Durham, NC: Duke University Press.

———. 1999. "Oh Bondage, Up Yours! Female Masculinity and the Tomboy." In *Sissies and Tomboys: Gender Nonconformity and Homosexual Childhood*, ed. Matthew Rottnek, pp. 153–179. New York: New York University Press.

———. 2005. *In a Queer Time and Place: Transgender Bodies, Subcultural Lives.* New York: New York University Press.

————, and C. Jacob Hale. 1998. "Transgender Butch: Butch/FTM Border Wars and the Masculine Continuum." *GLQ: A Journal of Lesbian and Gay Studies* 4 (2):287–310.

Hall, Stuart. 1996. "Introduction: Who Needs Identity?" In *Questions of Cultural Identity*, ed. Stuart Hall and Paul du Gay, pp. 1–17. London: Sage Publications.

Hannerz, Ulf. 1996. *Transnational Connections: Culture, People, Places*. New York: Routledge.

Hartsock, Nancy. 1990. "Foucault on Power: A Theory for Women?" In *Feminism/Postmodernism*, ed. Linda J. Nicholson, pp. 157–175. New York: Routledge.

Hasyim, Syafiz. 2006. *Understanding Women in Islam: An Indonesian Perspective*. Jakarta: Solstice Publishing.

Hatley, Barbara. 1990. "Theatrical Imagery and Gender Ideology in Java." In *Power and Difference: Gender in Island Southeast Asia*, ed. Jane Monnig Atkinson and Shelly Errington, pp. 177–207. Stanford, CA: Stanford University Press.

Hefner, Robert W. 1997. "Islamization and Democratization in Indonesia." In *Islam in an Era of Nation-States: Politics and Religious Renewal in Muslim Southeast Asia*, ed. Robert W. Hefner and Patricia Horvatich, pp. 75–127. Honolulu: University of Hawai'i Press.

————. 2000. *Civil Islam: Muslims and Democratization in Indonesia*. Princeton, NJ: Princeton University Press.

————, and Patricia Horvatich, eds. 1997. *Islam in an Era of Nation-states: Politics and Religious Renewal in Muslim Southeast Asia*. Honolulu: University of Hawai'i Press.

Herdt, Gilbert, ed. 1993. *Third Sex, Third Gender: Beyond Sexual Dimorphism in Culture and History*. New York: Zone Books.

Hirschfeld, Lawrence A. 2002. "Why Don't Anthropologists like Children?" *American Anthropologist* 104 (2):611–627.

Hoebel, E. A. 1949. *Man in the Primitive World*. New York: McGraw-Hill.

Holland, Dorothy, and Jean Lave. 2001. "History in Person: An Introduction." In *History in Person: Enduring Struggles, Contentious Practice, Intimate Identities*, ed. Dorothy Holland and Jean Lave, pp. 3–33. Santa Fe, NM: School of American Research.

Honigmann, John J. 1954. *The Kaska Indians: An Ethnographic Reconstruction*. New Haven, CT: Yale University Press.

Hooker, M. B. 2003. *Indonesian Islam: Social Change through Contemporary Fatāwā*. Honolulu: University of Hawai'i Press.

————, and Tim Lindsey. 2003. "Public Faces of Shari'ah in Contemporary Indonesia: Towards a National Madhhab." *Studia Islamika* 10 (1):23–64.

hooks, bell. 1990. Yearning: Race, Gender, and Cultural Politics. Boston, MA: South End Press.

Howard, Richard Stephen. 1996. "Falling into the Gay World: Manhood, Marriage, and Family in Indonesia." PhD dissertation, University of Illinois, Urbana.

Hughes-Freeland, Felicia. 1995. "Performance and Gender in Javanese Palace Tradition." In *"Male" and "Female" in Developing Southeast Asia*, ed. Wazir Jahan Karim, pp. 181–206. Washington, DC: Berg Publishers.

Hurgronje, C. Snouck. 1906. *The Achehnese.* A. W. S. O'Sullivan, trans. Leiden: E. J. Brill.

Jackson, Peter. 1997. "Kathoey><Gay><Man: The Historical Emergence of Gay Male Identity in Thailand." In *Sites of Desire, Economies of Pleasure: Sexualities in Asia and the Pacific,* ed. Lenore Manderson and Margaret Jolly, pp. 166–190. Chicago: University of Chicago Press.

Jacobs, Sue-Ellen, Wesley Thomas, and Sabine Lang, ed. 1997. *Two-spirit People: Native American Gender Identity, Sexuality and Spirituality.* Urbana-Champaign: University of Illinois Press.

Jagose, Annamarie. 1997. *Queer Theory: An Introduction.* New York: New York University Press.

Johns, Anthony H. 1958. *Rantjak Dilabueh: A Minangkabau Kaba.* Ithaca, NY: Cornell University Department of Far Eastern Studies.

Johnson, E. Patrick. 2005. " 'Quare' Studies, or (Almost) Everything I Know about Queer Studies I Learned from My Grandmother." In *Black Queer Studies: A Critical Anthology,* ed. E. Patrick Johnson and Mae G. Henderson, pp. 124–157. Durham, NC: Duke University Press.

Johnson, Mark. 1997. *Beauty and Power: Transgendering and Cultural Transformation in the Southern Philippines.* Oxford: Berg Publishers.

———. 2005. "Living like Men, Loving like Women: *Tomboi* in the Southern Philippines." In *Changing Sex and Bending Gender,* ed. Alison Shaw and Shirley Ardener, pp. 85–102. Oxford: Bergahn Books.

———, Peter Jackson, and Gilbert Herdt. 2000. "Critical Regionalities and the Study of Gender and Sexual Diversity in South East and East Asia." *Culture, Health and Sexuality* 2 (4):361–375.

Junus, Umar. 1994. "Kaba: An Unfinished (His-) Story." *Southeast Asian Studies* 32 (3):399–415.

Kahn, Joel S. 1993. *Constituting the Minangkabau: Peasants, Culture and Modernity in Colonial Indonesia.* Providence, RI: Berg Publishers.

Karsch-Haack, Ferdinand. 1911. *Das Gleichgechlechtlige Leben der Naturvolker.* Munich: Reinhardt.

Kartini. 1984. "About Homosexuals." In *Gays in Indonesia: Selected Articles from Print Media,* ed. Translation Group, p. 48. Fitzroy, Victoria: Sybylla Press.

Kay, Jackie. 2000. *Trumpet: A Novel.* New York: Vintage Books.

Keeler, Ward. 1987. *Javanese Shadow Plays, Javanese Selves.* Princeton, NJ: Princeton University Press.

Kellar, Natalie. 2004. "Beyond New Order Gender Politics: Case Studies of Female Performers of the Classical Balinese Dance-drama *Arja.*" *Intersections* 10. http://wwwsshe .murdoch.edu.au/intersections/issue10/kellar.html (accessed March 17, 2006).

Kennedy, Elizabeth, and Madeline Davis. 1993. *Boots of Leather, Slippers of Gold: The History of a Lesbian Community.* New York: Penguin Books.

King, Katie. 2002. "There Are No Lesbians Here: Lesbianisms, Feminisms, and Global Gay Formations." In *Queer Globalizations: Citizenship and the Afterlife of Colonialism*, ed. Arnaldo Cruz-Malavé and Martin F. Manalansan IV, pp. 33–45. New York: New York University Press.

Kipp, Rita Smith. 1993. *Dissociated Identities: Ethnicity, Religion, and Class in an Indonesian Society*. Ann Arbor: University of Michigan Press.

Knappert, Jan. 1999. *Mythology and Folklore of South-East Asia*. Oxford: Oxford University Press.

Koeswinarno. 1999. "Sex, Language and Identity: A Study about "Being *Waria*" in the Yogyakarta World of *Waria*." *Jurnal Antropologi* 2 (3):83–111.

Kompas Cybermedia. 2003. "Homoseksual!" December 4. Available at http://www.kompas.com/kesehatan/news/0312/04/064545.htm (accessed June 9, 2005).

Kroeber, Alfred L. 1940. "Psychosis or Social Sanction." *Character and Personality* 8 (3):204–215.

Kulick, Don. 1998. *Travesti: Sex, Gender and Culture among Brazilian Transgendered Prostitutes*. Chicago: University of Chicago Press.

———. 1999. "Transgender and Language: A Review of the Literature and Suggestions for the Future." *GLQ: Journal of Lesbian and Gay Studies* 5 (4):605–522.

———. 2000. "Gay and Lesbian Language." *Annual Reviews in Anthropology* 29:243–285.

Lai, Franco. 2007. "Lesbian Masculinities: Identity and Body Construction among Tomboys in Hong Kong." In *Women's Sexualities and Masculinities in a Globalizing Asia*, ed. Saskia E. Wieringa, Evelyn Blackwood, and Abha Bhaiya, pp. 159–180. New York: Palgrave Macmillan.

Lancaster, Roger N. 2003. *The Trouble with Nature: Sex in Science and Popular Culture*. Berkeley: University of California Press.

Landes, Joan. 1998. "Introduction." *Feminism: The Public and the Private*, ed. Joan Landes, pp. 1–20. Oxford: Oxford University Press.

Leigh, Barbara. 1994. "Female Heroes in School Examinations: Traditions and Tensions in Creating a Gendered State." *Asian Studies Review* 17 (3):23–33.

Livia, Anna. 1997. "Disloyal to Masculinity: Linguistic Gender and Liminal Identity in French." In *Queerly Phrased: Language, Gender, and Sexuality*, ed. Anna Livia and Kira Hall, pp. 349–368. New York: Oxford University Press.

———, and Kira Hall. 1997. " 'It's a Girl!': Bringing Performativity Back to Linguistics." In *Queerly Phrased: Language, Gender, and Sexuality*, ed. Anna Livia and Kira Hall, pp. 3–18. New York: Oxford University Press.

Logsdon, Martha. 1985. "Gender Roles in Elementary School Texts in Indonesia." In *Women in Asia and the Pacific: Towards an East-West Dialogue*, ed. Madeleine J. Goodman, pp. 243–262. Honolulu: University of Hawai'i Press.

Lorway, Robert. 2008. "Defiant Desire in Namibia: Female Sexual-gender Transgression and the Making of Political Being." *American Ethnologist* 35 (1):20–33.

Lyon, Del, and Phyllis Martin. 1972. *Lesbian/Woman*. New York: Bantam Books.

Mageo, Jeannette Marie. 1991. "Samoan Moral Discourse and the *Loto*." *American Anthropologist* 93 (2): 405–420.

Mahmood, Saba. 2005. *Politics of Piety: The Islamic Revival and the Feminist Subject.* Princeton, NJ: Princeton University Press.

Manalansan, Martin F. IV. 1997. "In the Shadows of Stonewall: Examining Gay Transnational Politics and the Diasporic Dilemma." In *The Politics of Culture in the Shadow of Capital*, ed. Lisa Lowe and David Lloyd, pp. 485–505. Durham, NC: Duke University Press.

———. 2003. *Global Divas: Filipino Gay Men in the Diaspora.* Durham, NC: Duke University Press.

Manderson, Lenore, and Margaret Jolly, eds. 1997. *Sites of Desire, Economies of Pleasure: Sexualities in Asia and the Pacific.* Chicago: University of Chicago Press.

Manderson, Lenore, and Margaret Jolly. 1997. "Sites of Desire/Economies of Pleasure in Asia and the Pacific." In *Sites of Desire, Economies of Pleasure: Sexualities in Asia and the Pacific*, ed. Lenore Manderson and Margaret Jolly, pp. 1–26. Chicago: University of Chicago Press.

Ma'shum, Yahya, and Roellya Arrdhyaning Tyas. 2004. "Bedanya homoseks" (The difference of homosexuality). *Kompas Cybermedia*, December 24. Available at http://www.kompas.com/kesehatan/news/0412/24/062721.htm (accessed April 14, 2006).

Mas'udi, Masdar F. 1994. "Reinterpreting Islamic Teachings on Women." In *Islam and the Advancement of Women*, ed. Lily Zakiyah Munir, Abdul Mun'im D.Z., and Nani Soraya, pp. 15–31. Jakarta: CV. Tunas Pribumi.

McHugh, Ernestine. 2002. "Contingent Selves: Love and Death in a Buddhist Society in Nepal." *Cultural Anthropology* 17 (2):210–245.

McNaron, Toni A. H. 2002. "Coming Out Stories." In *glbtq: An Encyclopedia of Gay, Lesbian, Bisexual, Transgender, and Queer Culture.* Available at http://www.glbtq.com/literature/coming_out,2.html (accessed October 21, 2008).

Meyer, Moe. 1994. "Reclaiming the Discourse of Camp." In *The Politics and Poetics of Camp*, ed. Moe Meyer, pp. 1–22. New York: Routledge.

MilaBlü. 2004. "Lesbian dan transgender." *Lembar Swara* 9–10: 6–9.

Mohammed, Patricia. 1986. "The Caribbean Family Revisited." In *Gender in Caribbean Development*, ed. Patricia Mohammed and Catherine Shepherd, pp. 170–182. Mona, Jamaica: University of the West Indies.

Mohanty, Chandra T. 1991. "Cartographies of Struggle: Third World Women and the Politics of Feminism." In *Third World Women and the Politics of Feminism*, ed. Chandra T. Mohanty, Ann Russo, and Lourdes Torres, pp. 1–47. Bloomington: Indiana University Press.

Monagan, Alfrieta Parks. 1985. "Rethinking 'Matrifocality.'" *Phylon* 46:353–362.

Moore, Henrietta L. 1994. *A Passion for Difference: Essays in Anthropology and Gender.* Bloomington: University of Indiana Press.

Morfit, Michael. 1987. "Pancasila Orthodoxy." In *Central Government and Local Development in Indonesia*, ed. Colin MacAndrews, pp. 42–55. Singapore: Oxford University Press.

Morgan, Ruth, and Saskia E. Wieringa. 2005. *Tommy Boys, Lesbian Men and Ancestral Wives: Female Same-sex Practices in Africa*. Johannesburg: Jacana Media.

Morrill, Cynthia. 1994. "Revamping the Gay Sensibility: Queer Camp and *Dyke Noir*." In *The Politics and Poetics of Camp*, ed. Moe Meyer, pp. 110–129. New York: Routledge.

Moussay, Gérard. 1998. *Tata Bahasa Minangkabau* (Minangkabau grammar). Rahayu S. Hidayat, trans. Jakarta: Kepustakaan Populer Gramedia.

Moya, Paula M. L. 1997. "Postmodernism, 'Realism,' and the Politics of Identity: Cherríe Moraga and Chicana Feminism." In *Feminist Genealogies, Colonial Legacies, Democratic Futures*, ed. M. Jacqui Alexander and Chandra T. Mohanty, pp. 125–150. New York: Routledge.

Munir, Lily Zakiyah, Abdul Mun'im D.Z., and Nani Soraya, eds. 1994. *Islam and the Advancement of Women*. Jakarta: CV. Tunas Pribumi.

Muñoz, José Estaban. 1999. *Disidentifications: Queers of Color and the Performance of Politics*. Minneapolis: University of Minnesota Press.

Munroe, Robert L., John W. M. Whiting, and David J. Hally. 1969. "Institutionalized Male Transvestism and Sex Distinctions." *American Anthropologist* 71 (1):87–91.

Murray, Alison J. 1999. "Let Them Take Ecstasy: Class and Jakarta Lesbians." In *Female Desires: Same-sex Relations and Transgender Practices across Cultures*, ed. Evelyn Blackwood and Saskia E. Wieringa, pp. 139–156. New York: Columbia University Press.

Murray, David A. B. 2000. "Between a Rock and a Hard Place: The Power and Powerlessness of Transnational Narratives among Gay Martinican Men." *American Anthropologist* 102 (2):271–270.

Murray, Sarah E. 1994. "Dragon Ladies, Draggin' Men: Some Reflections on Gender, Drag and Homosexual Communities." *Public Culture* 6:343–363.

Nafis, Anas. n.d. "Randai pernah dinyatakan haram" (Randai was once forbidden). Ms.

Naim, Mochtar. 1971. "Merantau: Minangkabau Voluntary Migration." PhD dissertation, Australian National University.

Nanda, Serena. 1990. *Neither Man nor Woman: The Hijras of India*. Belmont, CA: Wadsworth.

Nast, Heidi J. 2002. "Queer Patriarchies, Queer Racisms, International." *Antipode: A Radical Journal of Geography* 34 (5):874–909.

Nataf, Zachary I. 2006. "Lesbians Talk Transgender." In *The Transgender Studies Reader*, ed. Susan Stryker and Stephen Whittle, pp. 439–448. New York: Routledge.

Nestle, Joan. 1992a. "The Femme Question." In *The Persistent Desire: A Femme-butch Reader*, ed. Joan Nestle, pp. 138–146. Boston: Alyson Publications.

———, ed. 1992b. *The Persistent Desire: A Femme-butch Reader*. Boston: Alyson Publications.

Newton, Esther. 1972. *Mother Camp: Female Impersonators in America*. Englewood Cliffs, NJ: Prentice-Hall.

———. 1996. "Dick(less) Tracy and the Homecoming Queen: Lesbian Power and Representation in Gay Male Cherry Grove." In *Inventing Lesbian Cultures*, ed. Ellen Lewin, pp. 162–193. Boston: Beacon Press.

Noble, Jean Bobby. 2006. *Sons of the Movement: FtMs Risking Incoherence on a Post-queer Cultural Landscape*. Toronto: Women's Press.

Norton, Jody. 1999. "The Boy Who Grew Up to Be a Woman." In *Sissies and Tomboys: Gender Nonconformity and Homosexual Childhood*, ed. Matthew Rottnek, pp. 263–273. New York: New York University Press.

Oetomo, Dede. 1987. "Homoseksualitas di Barat dan di Indonesia" (Homosexuality in the West and in Indonesia). *GAYa Nusantara* 1 (1):9–20.

———. 1989. "Kamus gay/waria Indonesia (1)" (Gay/waria Indonesian dictionary). *GAYa Nusantara* 9:39–42.

———. 1996. "Gender and Sexual Orientation in Indonesia." In *Fantasizing the Feminine in Indonesia*, ed. Laurie Sears, pp. 259–269. Durham, NC: Duke University Press.

———. 2001. *Memberi Suara pada yang Bisu* (Giving voice to the mute). Yogyakarta: Galang Press.

Olwig, Karen Fog. 1981. "Women, 'Matrifocality' and Systems of Exchange: An Ethnohistorical Study of the Afro-American Family on St. John, Danish West Indies." *Ethnohistory* 28 (1):59–78.

Ortner, Sherry B. 2006. *Anthropology and Social Theory: Culture, Power, and the Acting Subject*. Durham, NC: Duke University Press.

Pangkahila, Wimpie. 2003. "Seksologi: 'Apakah saya lesbian … ?' " (Sexology: "Am I a lesbian?"). *Kompas Cybermedia*, July 15. Available at http://www.kompas.com/ kesehatan/news/0307/15/104249.htm (accessed April 14, 2006).

Parker, Lynette. 1997. "Engendering School Children in Bali." *The Journal of the Royal Anthropological Institute* 3 (3):497–516.

———. 2009. "Religion, Class and Schooled Sexuality among Minangkabau Teenage Girls." *Bijdragen tot del Taal-, Land- en Volkenkunde* 165 (1):62–94.

Patel, Geeta. 2004. "Homely Housewives Run Amok: Lesbians in Marital Fixes." *Public Culture* 16 (1):131–158.

Pauka, Kirsten. 1998. *Theater and Martial Arts in West Sumatra: Randai and Silek of the Minangkabau*. Athens: Ohio University Center for International Studies.

Pausacker, Helen. 1991. "Srikandhi and Sumbadra: Stereotyped Role Models or Complex Personalities?" In *The Art and Culture of South-East Asia*, ed. Lokesh Chandra, pp. 271–297. New Delhi: International Academy of Indian Culture and Aditya Prakashan.

Peacock, James. 1968. *Rites of Modernization: Symbolic Aspects of Indonesian Proletarian Drama*. Chicago: University of Chicago Press.

———. 1978. "Symbolic Reversal and Social History: Transvestites and Clowns of Java." In *The Reversible World: Symbolic Inversion in Art and Society*, ed. Barbara Babcock, pp. 209–224. Ithaca, NY: Cornell University Press.

Peletz, Michael G. 1997. " 'Ordinary Muslims' and Muslim Resurgents in Contemporary

Malaysia: Notes on an Ambivalent Relationship." In *Islam in an Era of Nation-states: Politics and Religious Renewal in Muslim Southeast Asia*, ed. Robert W. Hefner and Patricia Horvatich, pp. 231–273. Honolulu: University of Hawai'i Press.

———. 2002. *Islamic Modern: Religious Courts and Cultural Politics in Malaysia*. Princeton, NJ: Princeton University Press.

———. 2006. "Transgenderism and Gender Pluralism in Southeast Asia since Early Modern Times." *Current Anthropology* 47:309–340.

———. 2009. *Gender Pluralism: Southeast Asia since Early Modern Times*. New York: Routledge.

Phillips, Richard, Diane Watt, and David Shuttleton, eds. 2000. *De-centring Sexualities: Politics and Representations beyond the Metropolis*. London: Routledge.

Pikiran Rakyat. 2002. "Kita teruskan semangat Ibu Kartini" (We carry on the spirit of Mother Kartini). Available at http://www.seasite.niu.edu/flin/kita_teruskan_semangat_ibu_kartini.htm (accessed November 3, 2006).

Plummer, Ken. 1992. "Speaking Its Name: Inventing a Lesbian and Gay Studies." In *Modern Homosexualities: Fragments of Lesbian and Gay Experience*, ed. Ken Plummer, pp. 3–25. London: Routledge.

Povinelli, Elizabeth A., and George Chauncey. 1999. "Thinking Sexuality Transnationally: An Introduction." *GLQ: Journal of Lesbian and Gay Studies* 5 (4):439–449.

Puar, Jasbir Kaur. 2001. "Global Circuits: Transnational Sexualities and Trinidad." *Signs: Journal of Women in Culture and Society* 26 (4):1039–1065.

Puteri. 1984. "For Mother." In *Gays in Indonesia: Selected Articles from Print Media*, ed. Translation Group, pp. 7–8. Fitzroy, Victoria: Sybylla Press.

Quiroga, José. 2000. *Tropics of Desire: Interventions from Queer Latino America*. New York: New York University Press.

Radicalesbians. 1997. "The Woman-identified Woman." In *The Second Wave: A Reader in Feminist Theory*, ed. Linda Nicholson, pp. 153–157. New York: Routledge.

Ramazanoğlu, Caroline, ed. 1993. *Up against Foucault: Explorations of Some Tensions between Foucault and Feminism*. New York: Routledge.

Raymond, Janice. 1979. *The Transsexual Empire: The Making of the She-male*. Boston: Beacon Press.

Reddy, Gayatri. 2005. *With Respect to Sex: Negotiating Hijra Identity in South India*. Chicago: University of Chicago Press.

Reinfelder, Moniker, ed. 1996. *Amazon to Zami: Towards a Global Lesbian Feminism*. London: Cassell.

Robinson, Kathryn. 1989. "Choosing Contraception: Cultural Change and the Indonesian Family Planning Programme." In *Creating Indonesian Cultures*, ed. Paul Alexander, pp. 21–38. Sydney: Oceania Publications.

———. 2001. "Gender, Islam and Culture in Indonesia." In *Love, Sex and Power: Women in Southeast Asia*, ed. Susan Blackburn, pp. 17–30. Monash: Monash Asia Institute.

Robison, Richard. 1982. "Culture, Politics and Economy in the Political History of the New Order." In *Interpreting Indonesian Politics: Thirteen Contributions to the De-*

bate, ed. Benedict Anderson and Audrey Kahin, pp. 131–148. Ithaca, NY: Cornell University.

———. 1990. "Problems of Analysing the Middle Class as a Political Force in Indonesia." In *The Politics of Middle Class Indonesia*, ed. Richard Tanter and Kenneth Young, pp. 127–137. Clayton, Victoria: Monash University.

———. 1996. "The Middle Class and the Bourgeoisie in Indonesia." In *The New Rich in Asia: Mobile Phones, McDonalds and Middle-class Revolution*, ed. Richard Robison and David S. G. Goodman, pp. 79–104. London: Routledge.

Rodgers, Susan. 1979. "Advice to the Newlyweds: Sipirok Batak Wedding Speeches— Adat or Art?" In *Art, Ritual and Society in Indonesia*, ed. Edward M. Bruner and Judith O. Becker, pp. 30–61. Center for International Studies Southeast Asia Series no. 53. Ohio University.

———, ed. and trans. 1995. *Telling Lives, Telling History: Autobiography and Historical Imagination in Modern Indonesia*. Berkeley: University of California Press.

Rofel, Lisa. 1999. "Qualities of Desire: Imagining Gay Identities in China." *GLQ: Journal of Lesbian and Gay Studies* 5 (4):451–474.

Rubin, Gayle. 1975. "The Traffic in Women: Notes on the 'Political Economy' of Sex." In *Towards an Anthropology of Women*, ed. Rayna R. Reiter, pp. 157–210. New York: Monthly Review Press.

———. 1992. "Of Catamites and Kings: Reflections on Butch, Gender and Boundaries." In *The Persistent Desire: A Femme-butch Reader*, ed. Joan Nestle, pp. 466–482. Boston: Alyson Publications.

Rutz, Werner. 1987. *Cities and Towns in Indonesia: Their Development, Current Positions and Functions with Regard to Administration and Regional Economy*. Berlin: Gebrüder Borntraeger.

Sadarjoen, Sawitri Supardi. 2005. "Konsultasi psikologi: Lesbi-kah?" (Psychological consultation: Lesbian?) *Kompas Cybermedia*, Feb. 6. Available at http://www.kompas.com/kesehatan/news/0502/06/162140.htm (accessed April 14, 2006).

Sanday, Peggy Reeves. 2002. *Women at the Center: Life in a Modern Matriarchy*. Ithaca, NY: Cornell University Press.

Sandoval, Chela. 2000. *Methodology of the Oppressed*. Minneapolis: University of Minnesota Press.

Sawicki, J. 1991. *Disciplining Foucault: Feminism, Power and the Body*. New York: Routledge.

Schein, Louise. 2000. *Minority Rules: The Miao and the Feminine in China's Cultural Politics*. Durham, NC: Duke University Press.

Sears, Laurie, ed. 1996. *Fantasizing the Feminine in Indonesia*. Durham, NC: Duke University Press.

Selasih. 1986. *Rantak si Gadih Ranti* (The tale of Si Gadih Ranti). Jakarta: Departemen Pendidikan dan Kebudayaan.

Sen, Krishna. 1994. *Indonesian Cinema: Framing the New Order*. London: Zed Books.

———. 1998. "Indonesian Women at Work: Reframing the Subject." In *Gender and*

Power in Affluent Asia, ed. Krishna Sen and Maila Stivens, pp. 35–62. London: Routledge.

Shihab, Quraish. 1994. "Women's *Kodrah* vs. Cultural Norms." Lily Munir, trans. In *Islam and the Advancement of Women*, ed. Lily Zakiyah Munir, Abdul Mun'im D.Z., and Nani Soraya, pp. 48–60. Jakarta: The Forum for Islam and the Advancement of Women.

Sinfield, Alan. 2000. "The Production of Gay and the Return of Power." In *De-centring Sexualities: Politics and Representations beyond the Metropolis*, ed. Richard Phillips, Diane Watt, and David Shuttleton, pp. 21–36. London: Routledge.

Sinnott, Megan. 2004. *Toms and Dees: Transgender Identity and Female Same-sex Relationships in Thailand*. Honolulu: University of Hawai'i Press.

———. 2007. "Gender Subjectivity: Dees and Toms in Thailand." In *Women's Sexualities and Masculinities in a Globalizing Asia*, ed. Saskia E. Wieringa, Evelyn Blackwood, and Abha Bhaiya, pp. 119–138. New York: Palgrave Macmillan.

———. 2009. "Public Sex: The Geography of Female Homoeroticism and the (In)visibility of Female Sexualities." In *Out in Public: Reinventing Lesbian/Gay Anthropology in a Globalizing World*, ed. Ellen Lewin and William Leap, pp. 225–239. New York: Blackwell Publishing.

Skinner, Debra. 1989. "The Socialization of Gender Identity." In *Child Development in Cultural Context*, ed. J. Valsiner, pp. 181–192. Toronto: Hogrefe and Huber Publishers.

Stack, Carol B. 1974. *All Our Kin: Strategies for Survival in a Black Community*. New York: Harper and Row.

Stanley, Julia P., and Susan J. Wolfe, eds. 1980. *The Coming Out Stories*. Watertown, MA: Persephone Press.

Steedly, Mary M. 1993. *Hanging Without a Rope: Narrative Experience in Colonial and Postcolonial Karoland*. Princeton, NJ: Princeton University Press.

Stein, Arlene. 1997. *Sex and Sensibility: Stories of a Lesbian Generation*. Berkeley: University of California Press.

Stevens, Alan M., and A. Ed. Schmidgall-Tellings. 2004. A Comprehensive Indonesian-English Dictionary. Athens: Ohio University Press.

Stoler, Ann. 1995. *Race and the Education of Desire: Foucault's History of Sexuality and the Colonial Order of Things*. Durham, NC: Duke University Press.

———. 1997. "Educating Desire in Colonial Southeast Asia: Foucault, Freud and Imperial Sexualities." In *Sites of Desire/Economies of Pleasure: Sexualities in Asia and the Pacific*, ed. Lenore Manderson and Margaret Jolly, pp. 27–47. Chicago: University of Chicago Press.

Stone, Sandy. 1993. "The 'Empire' Strikes Back: A Posttranssexual Manifesto." In *Body Guards: The Cultural Politics of Gender Ambiguity*, ed. Julia Epstein and Kristina Straub, pp. 280–304. New York: Routledge.

Stryker, Susan. 1994. "My Words to Victor Frankenstein above the Village of Chamounix: Performing Transgender Rage." *GLQ: Journal of Lesbian and Gay Studies* 1 (3):227–254.

Sullivan, Norma. 1994. *Masters and Managers: A Study of Gender Relations in Urban Java.* St. Leonards, NSW: Allen & Unwin.

Suryakusuma, Julia. 1996. "The State and Sexuality in New Order Indonesia." In *Fantasizing the Feminine in Indonesia*, ed. Laurie Sears, pp. 92–119. Durham, NC: Duke University Press.

Tambiah, Stanley. 1985. *Culture, Thought and Social Action: An Anthropological Perspective.* Cambridge, MA: Harvard University Press.

Tanter, Richard, and Kenneth Young, eds. 1990. *The Politics of Middle Class Indonesia.* Clayton, Victoria: Monash University.

Tempo. 1984a. "The Love Story of Aty and Nona." In *Gays in Indonesia: Selected Articles from Print Media*, ed. Translation Group, pp. 14–15. Fitzroy, Victoria: Sybylla Press [originally published in Indonesian in *Tempo*, May 23, 1981, pp. 26–27].

———. 1984b. "The story of Jossie and Bonnie." In *Gays in Indonesia: Selected Articles from Print Media*, ed. Translation Group, p. 5. Fitzroy, Victoria: Sybylla Press [originally published in Indonesian in *Tempo*, May 30, 1981, pp. 51–53].

Tiwon, Sylvia. 1996. "Models and Maniacs: Articulating the Female in Indonesia." In *Fantasizing the Feminine in Indonesia*, ed. Laurie Sears, pp. 47–70. Durham. NC: Duke University Press.

Towle, Evan B., and Lynn M. Morgan. 2002. "Romancing the Transgender Native: Rethinking the Use of the 'Third Gender' Concept." *GLQ: Journal of Lesbian and Gay Studies* 8 (4):469–497.

Translation Group. 1984. "I Was Cured of Homosexuality." In *Gays in Indonesia: Selected Articles from Print Media*, ed. Translation Group, pp. 16–17. Fitzroy, Victoria: Sybylla Press.

Tsing, Anna Lowenhaupt. 2004. "Global Connections." *Cultural Anthropology* 15 (3):327–360.

———. 2005. *Friction: An Ethnography of Global Connection.* Princeton, NJ: Princeton University Press.

Tyler, Carole-Anne. 1991. "Boys Will Be Girls: The Politics of Gay Drag." In *Inside/Out: Lesbian Theories, Gay Theories*, ed. Diana Fuss, pp. 32–70. New York: Routledge.

Umar, Nasaruddin. 1994. "Women's *Kodrah* in the Perspective of Al-Qur'an." Lily Munir, trans. In *Islam and the Advancement of Women*, ed. Lily Zakiyah Munir, Abdul Mun'im D.Z., and Nani Soraya, pp. 61–81. Jakarta: The Forum for Islam and the Advancement of Women.

van der Kroef, Justus M. 1954. "Transvestitism and the Religious Hermaphrodite in Indonesia." *Journal of East Asiatic Studies* 3 (3):257–265.

van der Meer, Theo. 1991. "Tribades on Trial: Female Same-sex Offenders in Late Eighteenth-century Amsterdam." *Journal of the History of Sexuality* 1 (3):424–445.

van Doorn-Harder, Pieternella. 2006. *Women Shaping Islam: Reading the Qur'an in Indonesia.* Urbana: University of Illinois Press.

Valentine, David. 2007. *Imagining Transgender: An Ethnography of a Category.* Durham, NC: Duke University Press.

Valentine, Gill. 2002. "Queer Bodies and the Production of Space." In *Handbook of Lesbian and Gay Studies*, ed. Diane Richardson and Steven Seidman, pp. 145–160. London: Sage Publications.

Vanita, Ruth. 2002. "Introduction." In *Queering India: Same-sex Love and Eroticism in Indian Culture and Society*, ed. Ruth Vanita, pp. 1–11. New York: Routledge.

Vicinus, Martha. 1993. "They Wonder to Which Sex I Belong: The Historical Roots of the Modern Lesbian Identity." In *The Lesbian and Gay Studies Reader*, ed. Henry Abelove, Michèle Aina Barale, and David M. Halperin, pp. 432–452. New York: Routledge.

Volcano, Del LaGrace, and Ulrika Dahl. 2008. *Femmes of Power: Exploding Queer Femininities*. London: Serpent's Tail.

Wadiantoro, Ninuk. 1984. "Three Factors of Lesbianism." In *Gays in Indonesia: Selected Articles from Print Media*, ed. Translation Group, p. 49. Fitzroy, Victoria: Sybylla Press.

Wahid, Abdurrahman. 1994. "Islam and Women's Rights." Lily Munir, trans. In *Islam and the Advancement of Women*, ed. Lily Zakiyah Munir, Abdul Mun'im D.Z., and Nani Soraya, pp. 32–47. Jakarta: The Forum for Islam and the Advancement of Women.

Wanita Indonesia. 2001. "Pasangan TKW lesbian ancam bunuh diri jika tak boleh menikah" (A lesbian couple working for TKW threaten suicide if they are not allowed to wed) and "Cinta sejenis dari Taman Victoria Hongkong" (Same-sex love in Victoria Park, Hong Kong), No. 622, Sept. 24–30, p. 9.

Watson, Rubie S. 1986. "The Named and the Nameless: Gender and Person in Chinese Society." *American Ethnologist* 13 (4):619–631.

Webster, Tracy Wright. 2005. "Negotiating Female Same-sex Relations and Identities in Yogyakarta, Indonesia." Senior thesis, Murdoch University.

———. 2008. "Re-articulations: Gender and Female Same-sex Subjectivities in Yogyakarta, Indonesia." *Intersections: Gender and Sexuality in Asia and the Pacific* 18. Available at http://intersections.anu.edu.au/issue18/wrightwebster.htm#n32 (accessed January 18, 2009).

Weismantel, Mary J. 2001. *Cholas and Pishtacos: Stories of Race and Sex in the Andes*. Chicago: University of Chicago Press.

Wekker, Gloria. 1998. "Of Sex and Silences: Methodological Considerations on Sex Research in Paramaribo, Suriname." *Thamyris* 5 (1):105–129.

———. 2006. *The Politics of Passion: Women's Sexual Culture in the Afro-Surinamese Diaspora*. New York: Columbia University Press.

Weston, Kath. 1991. *Families We Choose: Lesbians, Gays, Kinship*. New York: Columbia University Press.

———. 1993. "Lesbian/Gay Studies in the House of Anthropology." *Annual Review of Anthropology* 22:339–367.

Wiegman, Robyn. 2007. "The Desire for Gender." In *A Companion to Lesbian, Gay, Bi-*

sexual, Transgender, and Queer Studies, ed. George E. Haggerty and Molly McGarry, pp. 217–236. New York: Blackwell Publishers.

Wieringa, Edwin. 1997. "The Kaba Zamzami Jo Marlaini: Continuity, Adaptation, and Change in Minangkabau Oral Storytelling." *Indonesia and the Malay World* 73:235–251.

Wieringa, Saskia E. 1992. "Ibu or the Beast: Gender Interests, Ideology and Practice in Two Indonesian Women's Organizations." *Feminist Review* 41:98–114.

———. 1999. "Desiring Bodies or Defiant Cultures: Butch-femme Lesbians in Jakarta and Lima." In *Female Desires: Same-sex Relations and Transgender Practices across Cultures*, ed. Evelyn Blackwood and Saskia E. Wieringa, pp. 206–231. New York: Columbia University Press.

———. 2000. "Communism and Women's Same-sex Practises in post-Suharto Indonesia." *Culture, Health and Sexuality* 2 (4):441–457.

———. 2002. *Sexual Politics in Indonesia*. New York: Palgrave Macmillan.

———. 2007. " 'If There Is No Feeling ... ': The Dilemma between Silence and Coming Out in a Working-class Butch/Femme Community in Jakarta." In *Love and Globalization: Transformations of Intimacy in the Contemporary World*, ed. Mark Padilla, Jennifer S. Hirsch, Miguel Muñoz-Laboy, Robert E. Sember, and Richard G. Parker, pp. 70–90. Nashville, TN: Vanderbilt University Press.

———, and Evelyn Blackwood. 1999. "Introduction." In *Female Desires: Same-sex Relations and Transgender Practices across Cultures*, ed. Evelyn Blackwood and Saskia E. Wieringa, pp. 1–38. New York: Columbia University Press.

———, Evelyn Blackwood, and Abha Bhaiya, eds. 2007. *Women's Sexualities and Masculinities in a Globalizing Asia*. New York: Palgrave Macmillan.

Wilchins, Riki Anne. 1997. *Read My Lips: Sexual Subversion and the End of Gender*. Ithaca, NY: Firebrand Books.

Williams, Raymond. 1977. *Marxism and Literature*. Oxford: Oxford University Press.

Wilson, Ara. 2004. *The Intimate Economies of Bangkok: Tomboys, Tycoons, and Avon Ladies in the Global City*. Berkeley: University of California Press.

Wina. 2003. "Istilah/sebutan dalam dunia LGBT" (Terms/expressions of the LGBT world). *Lembar Swara* (Edisi Reformasi) 1:8–9.

World Gazetteer. 2006. "Indonesia: Largest Cities and Towns and Statistics of Their Population." Available at: http://www.world-gazetteer.com (accessed September 29, 2006).

Yafie, K. H. Ali. 1994. "Women's Status and Leadership." Lily Munir, trans. In *Islam and the Advancement of Women*, ed. Lily Zakiyah Munir, Abdul Mun'im D.Z., and Nani Soraya, pp. 95–109. Jakarta: The Forum for Islam and the Advancement of Women.

Yanagisako, Sylvia, and Jane F. Collier. 1987. "Toward a Unified Analysis of Gender and Kinship." In *Gender and Kinship: Toward a Unified Analysis*, ed. Jane Collier and Sylvia Yanagisako, pp. 14–50. Stanford, CA: Stanford University Press.

Yengoyan, Aram A. 1983. "Transvestitism and the Ideology of Gender: Southeast Asia and Beyond." In *Feminist Re-visions: What Has Been and Might Be*, ed. Vivian Patraka and Louise A. Tilly, pp. 135–148. Ann Arbor: Women's Studies Program, University of Michigan.

Young, Kenneth. 1990. "Middle Bureaucrats, Middle Peasants, Middle Class?: The Extra-urban Dimension." In *The Politics of Middle Class Indonesia*, ed. Richard Tanter and Kenneth Young, pp. 147–166. Clayton, Victoria: Monash University.

Zaini-LaJoubert, Monique. 1996. "Syair Cerita Siti Akbari Karya Lie Kim Hok (1884), Penjelmaan Syair Abdul Muluk (1846)" (A poem of the Story of Siti Akbari written by Lie Kim Hok, creator of the Story of Abdul Muluk). In *Sastra Peranakan Tionghoa Indonesia* (Chinese-Indonesian Literature), ed. Leo Suryadinata, pp. 277–321. Jakarta: Gramedia Widiasarana Indonesia.

Zimmerman, Bonnie, ed. 2000. *Lesbian Histories and Cultures: An Encyclopedia*. New York: Garland.

Index

About the Author

EVELYN BLACKWOOD is a professor in the Department of Anthropology, Purdue University. She has written extensively in areas of sexuality, gender, and kinship, including work on Native American female two-spirits, gender transgression in colonial and postcolonial Indonesia, gender and power, and matrilineal kinship. Her first monograph, entitled *Webs of Power: Women, Kin and Community in a Sumatran Village* (2000), examined the power of women in a matrilineal farming community in West Sumatra, Indonesia. Together with Dr. Saskia E. Wieringa, she published two award-winning anthologies on women's same-sex sexualities and female masculinities, *Female Desires: Same-sex Relations and Transgender Practices across Cultures* (1999) and *Women's Sexualities and Masculinities in a Globalizing Asia* (2007). In 2008 Dr. Blackwood was awarded the Martin Duberman Fellowship by the Center for Lesbian and Gay Studies at the City University of New York for her research on tombois and femmes in Indonesia and for her longstanding contribution to the study of LGBT issues.